Critical Incidents

Ethical Issues in Substance Abuse Prevention and Treatment

William L. White

A Lighthouse Training Institute Publication

Additional copies of this publication can be obtained by sending $17.95 plus
$3.00 shipping and handling to:

Lighthouse Training Institute
702 West Chestnut
Bloomington, Illinois 61701
(309) 827-6026

Other books by William White available from the Institute include:

Incest in the Organizational Family: The Ecology of Burnout in
Closed Systems (1986)

The Culture of Addiction, The Culture of Recovery (1990)

The Training Life: Living and Learning in the Substance Abuse Field
(with Bruce Joleaud, Felicia Dudek and Bob Carty) (1993)

Dedication

This book is dedicated to the legions of workers who have carried the message of prevention and recovery without a clear set of ethical standards to guide their journey, and to those who fell by the wayside because the hazards were so poorly marked.

Acknowledgements

This book would not have been possible without the help of numerous persons. LeClair Bissell and James Royce's *Ethics for Addiction Professionals* has been a widely read resource within the field and laid an important foundation for my own work. The addition of this text in no way diminishes the continued value of this contribution. The prevention and treatment professionals who have attended my workshops on ethics during the past six years have been an important source of inspiration and encouragement. There were many persons who reviewed particular chapters or who offered advice on some specialized areas of ethical concern. I am indebted to Dr. Alan Sodetz, Rita Chaney, Glenn Covert and Joleen Baum for their critical review of early drafts of the complete text. Thanks are due Roger Krohe and George Dirks for their thoughtful review of the chapter on ethical issues in staff-client relationships. Other experts who reviewed specific chapters or offered advice on technical issues were Russell Hagen (business), Mary Ann Anderson (business, lobbying, AIDS), Bella Selan (AIDS), Tom West (accounting practices), Don Davis and Nancy Speir (personnel practices), Alan Markwood (prevention), and Rita Chaney (employee assistance). Mark Godley, Michelle Pillen, Renée Hoewing-Roberson, Sandra Lott, and John Wallace provided helpful critiques of several key chapters. I am also deeply appreciative of Jeanette H. Milgrom of the Walk-In Counseling Center in Minneapolis for permission to adapt some of her work on boundary issues in psychotherapy for inclusion here.

Joyce Thomas and Robert G. Clayton, Jr. provided helpful assistance in the editing and formatting of the book.

Table of Contents

Chapter Six
Conduct in Client/Family Relationships

Chapter Seven
Conduct in Professional Peer Relationships

Internal Professional Relationships

External Professional Relationships

Chapter Eight
Conduct Related to Public Safety

Chapter Nine
Professional Standards Related to Special Roles
Prevention

Preface

This is a book written for people who work in the trenches of substance abuse prevention and treatment. The book contains almost 200 situations containing ethical dilemmas to enhance our ethical sensitivities and sharpen our ethical decision-making. Each situation is accompanied by a brief analysis and discussion. I don't expect readers to agree with all the points of view expressed in these analyses. The analyses are here only as beginning points for dialogue. This text is intended to stimulate discussion and help the reader clarify his or her own thinking about ethical issues within the field, not define standards for the field. I hope the book provides a structure for safe rehearsal—an experience of thinking through ethical dilemmas and ethical decisions outside the intense immediacy of crisis.

I believe the greatest threat to our field comes not from changing drug trends, external regulation, managed care, or cuts in public funding of treatment and prevention, but from our own lack of spiritual centeredness. Ideological splits, competition and a marked propensity for program isolation make it unlikely that the whole field will come together to create a consensus of ethical standards and values comparable to those of the American Psychological Association or the National Association of Social Workers. There is, however, a movement within local programs to more clearly define ethical standards and processes of ethical decision-making. This book is designed as an aid to speed the progress of this grassroots movement.

There are strong no-talk rules within the field on many issues contained within this book. Such rules spring not from any orchestrated conspiracy but from a sense of shame and a belief that ethical breaches are idiosyncratic rather than systemic—that open discussion of such issues and events would indelibly stain the agency identity. The stain we suffer is the stain of silence. It's as if an individual ethical breach shames us all into silence. These issues need sound and air and light. I hope the ethical vignettes and discussion formats set forth in this book can provide a safe vehicle for breaking silence.

There was some discussion at the training institute during the early design of this book whether legal annotations should be included since many of the situation involve legal as well as ethical issues. After some deliberation, it was decided not to include such annotations. The reasoning was that given the field's ethical passivity and obsession with legal and regulatory compliance, questions of "what is legal?" would overshadow questions of "what is ethical?" Our decision to exclude discussions of law does not mean we consider these structures unimportant. It does mean that we see a distinction between the ethical and the legal. To comply with the law in a particular situation does not in and of itself make one ethical; to disobey a law in a situation does not in and of itself make one unethical.

The creation of many of my books and monographs—the researching, thinking and writing processes—has given me great pleasure. That is not the case with this book. It was a difficult book to write because the situations contained in it are our most difficult. It was difficult to write because the words depict the pain of real people. The composite vignettes—though fictional as presented—represent real situations and real clients and real workers. They represent ethical violations from the subtle to the horrible. They represent exploitations and injuries to already injured souls. They represent injuries to careers. They represent injuries to agencies and to the profession. They represent injuries to third parties and whole communities. No, they were not easy to think about nor write about. It was my belief in the importance of the subject, not the pleasure of the process, that sustained work on this project.

As always, I welcome the opportunity to receive your comments, your criticisms, and your ideas. Correspondence can be sent to:

Bill White
Director of Training and Consultation
Lighthouse Training Institute
702 West Chestnut
Bloomington, Illinois 61701

Chapter
One

Introduction

Why a Book on Ethics

Ethical and professional practice dilemmas are occurring with increasing frequency within the substance abuse field. Workers in a broad spectrum of roles are frightened and overwhelmed by their lack of preparation in ethical decision-making. Our organizations have tended to define ethics as an individual rather than institutional issue. Ethical issues fester in the silence of denial until they detonate into humiliating exposés of our personal and institutional short-comings. Those of us on the sidelines of such explosions all too often react with self-righteous indignation, seeing ourselves and our institutions as immune from such a fall. And yet the explosions continue, setting up the climate through which outside institutions paternalistically promulgate regulations to legislate our moral and professional conduct. It has become painfully evident that the field has not developed a paradigm or process for ethical problem-solving nor has it developed a fully articulated set of ethical standards to guide professional practice. The field—as represented by the majority of its agencies—does not have an ethical framework that can consistently protect our service consumers, our workers, our organizations and the public. This book is a call to action and a battle plan to fill this developmental void.

The goals of this text are to outline a medium through which substance abuse workers can be sensitized to recognize ethical dilemmas and to introduce a framework of ethical problem-solving. The book is designed to provide a safe format—a rehearsal—for the exploration of ethical dilemmas *before* workers encounter such situations in the practice of their professional roles. The stories of ethical dilemmas that make up the bulk of this book are intended to provide workers an engaging medium through which to explore their own values and ethical decision-making abilities.

Another goal is to outline a process through which standards of ethical conduct can be developed as a component of a healthy, service-oriented organizational culture. The chapters which follow outline a process through which each organization can explicitly define the ethical and professional practice standards to which it and all of its members may be held accountable. The intent throughout the book will be to address ethics as both a personal-professional issue and as an organizational systems issue.

The reader will discover a work written not from the perspective of the ethicist but the perspective of a clinician and organizational consultant. This book is predicated on the belief that ethical sensitivity and service effectiveness are inseparable and that well-defined ethics and values can empower organizations and the people touched by them.

Ethical Issues in the Substance Abuse Field: Special Concerns

There are special concerns related to ethical and professional practice issues in the substance abuse field which are effecting this field far more intensely than other fields of health and human services. Such issues as the following demand a special recognition and perhaps add some note of urgency to this book's call to action.

The Composition of the Field: Few fields can boast a work force as heterogenous as the substance abuse field. Few fields have ever brought within a professional umbrella individuals so diverse in terms of their age, race, culture, religion, sex, sexual orientation, education, professional training, and life experience. Such diversity is a source of vulnerability as well as a source of enrichment. The vulnerability of such diversity springs from the lack of a shared system of values guiding personal/professional decision-making and conduct. No health care field has ever existed in which so many service recipients have evolved into professional roles of service providers. This phenomenon has raised new and more complex ethical issues for which there are no precedents to be gained from other helping professions.

The Short History and Transience of the Field: In the more traditional fields of psychiatry, psychology and social work, elaborate systems and rituals have evolved to define standards and values of professional practice and to internalize these values in new generations of professionals. The short history and rapid turnover of staff within the substance abuse field has resulted in an ambiguity of professional values and a regular bleeding out of the field's collective wisdom and expertise. While our short history has prevented the full evolution of formal systems of professional indoctrination, high staff turnover is a wound from which escapes our informal systems of technology transfer, e.g., the professional values imbedded within oral history, professional etiquette transmitted through story telling, and the collective wisdom channeled through mentor relationships.

The Industrialization of the Field: While the genesis of professionalization in the field can be pinpointed with the founding of the American Association for the Study and Cure of Inebriety in 1870, the full industrialization of the field has occurred only within the last two decades. Our most recent history has included the legitimization of addictive disorders via their inclusion in public and private health care reimbursement systems, the rapid proliferation of substance abuse treatment programs, the emergence of substance abuse services as popular and profitable business ventures, the intensification of competition within the field, and the explosion of legal and regulatory controls governing the delivery of substance abuse prevention and treatment services. For the first 100 years of our profession, ethical issues were addressed within the umbrella of our medical and clinical practices. Events of the past twenty years force us to extend the topic of ethics to cover our business practices.

The Changing Context of Substance Abuse: The dramatic increase in drug-related predatory crime, the increased violence within the culture of addiction, the emerging spread of HIV infection among drug consumers and the growing threat to public safety posed by drug impaired workers are among the many changes in the context of substance abuse in the United States that are raising infinitely complex legal and ethical issues for substance abuse prevention and treatment professionals.

Rethinking Our Assumptions about Personal and Professional Ethics

The failure to address ethical and professional practice standards rests on a foundation of unarticulated and unexamined assumptions that have governed the practice of substance abuse agency managers for decades. Listed and critiqued below are nine such assumptions.

1. *Workers bring with them personal standards of morality and ethical conduct that can be relied upon to assure the ethical conduct of the agency.*

Our culture is a turbulent ecosystem within which traditional values are in great flux, in part due to the turmoil and change within the major institutions which have historically transmitted these values—the family, the extended family, the neighborhood, the church, the school and the work place. Today, personal standards of morality of persons entering the field must be assessed rather than assumed. Where societal values are unclear and not well ingrained in the citizenry, organizations must take an active role in reinforcing values congruent with our mission of service.

2. *Workers have common sense.*

"Common" sense is that internalized wisdom that emerges from one's cumulative experience. It springs from the discovery that lessons learned in past situations are applicable to new situations. To assume that all workers have common sense and can thus think their way through ethical dilemmas without guidance from the organization assumes that staff bring a significant body of life experience and that what they have learned from these experiences is transferable to the situations they will encounter in their professional practice. The error of this assumption is that few , if any, staff will bring life experience so broad in its diversity as to produce a body of "common sense" applicable to the whole range of situations presented within this book. Even where historical experience is rich in its intensity and diversity, new ethical and clinical practice issues are arising for which there are no historical precedents within our collective experience. What is seemingly logical and common sense out of life experience can today be both clinically inappropriate and illegal. Professional common sense must be developed and nurtured rather than assumed.

3. *Workers have been trained in ethical issues and ethical standards as part of their academic and professional training.*

This assumption is particularly prevalent among persons whose own training in social work or psychology included a solid grounding in ethical standards and ethical decision-making. Scant attention is paid to ethical issues in the formal training of most substance abuse workers. The training that does exist is often narrow in its definition of ethical issues, is prescriptive (Thou Shall Not...) rather than methodological (ethical problem-solving processes), and rarely addresses both the subtlety and complexity of ethical issues currently encountered in professional practice. Persons not in clinical roles have quite likely had minimal orientation to ethical issues, and, in particular, an orientation to the kinds of ethical issues likely to be encountered in the substance abuse field.

4. *There is no need for the agency to concern itself with ethical standards development because workers are bound by ethical codes tied to their professional certification/licensure.*

There are numerous problems with this assumption. Not all workers at substance abuse agencies are certified or licensed or even hold positions or roles for which certification or licensure is available. Professional staff may be affiliated with numerous certification/licensure bodies, each of which has a separate code of ethical conduct. Many codes of ethics are abstract statements of values or principles for which workers—without significant training and experience—may have minimal abilities to operationalize in complex, real life situations.

5. *Ethical dilemmas are concerns for those staff in counseling roles.*

6. *Ethical dilemmas are personal/professional issues, not an institutional issue.*

Ethical conduct in the substance abuse field is defined as a clinical issue rather than as an organizational issue. Ethical standards embedded in personnel policies or codes of ethics focus upon and are written for application to clinical roles. They do not address ethical issues involving other roles (administrative, fiscal, clerical, prevention, education, consultation, research). Ethics must be extended beyond its application to a discipline or a role to the arena of organizational culture. Ethics must be broadened beyond the arena of the ethical values and demeanor of individual staff members. Ethics is an institutional issue.

7. *Workers who violate ethical principles are bad people. If we hire and retain good people, we will be assured of ethical conduct. Persons who violate ethical principles (since they are bad people) should be extruded from the agency/profession.*

This assumption is based on the belief that the etiology of all ethical breaches is a function of the moral character and personality of the staff member involved. There are bad people. There are predators who, in health and human service systems as with any system they are in, will systematically exploit the environment and the people with whom they come into contact. There are persons who lack the knowledge, judgement and personal integrity to effectively work in a professional helping role. It is our institutional responsibility—via promotion of quality care and protection of public safety—to keep such persons from working in our agencies and to exclude such individuals when they are identified. There are, however, numerous instances when ethical breaches are not made by bad people, but by good people who have historical patterns of both competence and personal integrity. Ethical breaches can reflect knowledge and skill deficiency, an ambiguity or conflict in agency policies, environmental stressors such as excessive overload, or the personal impairment of a worker. Where systemic issues compromise the ability of staff to act ethically, the extrusion of individual staff for ethical breaches constitutes a process of scapegoating that individualizes what is in essence an agency environmental problem.

8.   *A high calibre of professional and ethical conduct is assured because of the values and skills of our supervisors who place great emphasis in this area.*

The ability of supervisors to set (via role modeling) and monitor (via clinical and administrative supervision) high standards of ethical and professional conduct is a crucial aspect of assuring ethical conduct within a substance abuse treatment agency. The question is whether there are ingrained values and standards of conduct that transcend the presence of the unique individuals who hold supervisory roles within the agency. Are agency ethics merely a reflection of the personal/professional ethics of key supervisors? If a majority of our key supervisors left the agency in the next six months, would the nature of our professional ethics differ six months later? There must be organizational values to guide professional practice that transcend the unique characteristics of persons occupying key organizational roles.

9.   *If workers get in trouble (encounter a difficult ethical or professional practice issue), they'll ask for help. If we as managers don't hear about ethical conflicts, there must not be any.*

Workers may fail to bring ethical issues to supervision because they either fail to identify ethical dimensions of their work or they think that raising such issues would reflect negatively on their professional knowledge and competence. Unless there are both permissions and procedures to address ethical issues within the framework of supervision, agency supervisors are unaware of such issues until they detonate. What does it mean if no one is raising ethical issues within the day-to-day operation of the organization? No news is bad news.

Toward the Goal of Ethical Sensitivity

Ethics must be addressed as a personal-professional issue. This book calls for the development in the substance abuse field of what Biggs and Blocker (1987) have called ethical sensitivity. Ethical sensitivity is the ability to step outside oneself and perceive the complexities of a situation through the needs and experiences of the client, the agency, allied institutions and the public. It is the ability of the staff member to project the potential consequences of his or her action or inaction on these various constituency relationships. It is the ability of the staff member to recognize when he or she is in ethical terrain. It is the ability to identify and analyze the precise ethical issues involved in a particular situation and to isolate and articulate conflicting duties. It is the ability to weigh the advantages and disadvantages of various actions and to formulate ethically appropriate resolutions to complex situations.

Systemic Approaches to Professional Practice Issues

Ethics must be addressed as a systemic issue. A comprehensive approach to promoting high standards of ethical conduct within a substance abuse agency requires interventions at multiple levels of the organization. Such interventions and levels are reflected in the following checklist which may be used as an inventory of potential strategies to promote an ethical organizational culture.

Knowledge & Skills

Yes No
___ ___ Are education, experience and certification/licensure requirements for positions within the agency set at such a level

as to increase the likelihood that staff have prior knowledge and skills in ethical decision-making?

___ ___ Have ethical issues been addressed within the in-service training schedule, not just as a special topic, but integrated as a dimension within a broad spectrum of training topics?

___ ___ Are there opportunities for staff at all levels to explore ethical issues with other professionals within and outside of the agency?

___ ___ Does the agency have access to outside technical expertise for consultation on complex ethical-legal issues?

Ethical Standards

Yes No

___ ___ Does the agency have a code of professional ethics integrated within its personnel policies?

___ ___ Have agency staff had the opportunity to participate in the development or episodic review of the professional practice standards?

___ ___ Are the ethical standards and values written with sufficient clarity and have they been discussed sufficiently to allow their application in daily decision-making and problem-solving?

___ ___ Are violations of ethical conduct addressed immediately and consistently?

___ ___ Could staff, if asked, define the core values of the agency?

Organizational Culture

Yes No

___ ___ Are ethical issues raised within the context of employee hiring and new employee orientation?

____ ____ Do organizational leaders talk about ethical issues in their communications with staff?

____ ____ Is adherence to ethical and professional practice standards a component of the performance evaluations of all staff?

____ ____ Does ethical conduct constitute a core value of the organization as reflected in agency history and mythology, the designation of heroes and heroines, agency literature, storytelling, symbols and slogans?

____ ____ Are rituals built into the cycle of organizational life that help identify practices that undermine or deviate from our stated values and which provide opportunities to celebrate and recommit ourselves to those values, e.g., staff meetings, retreats, planning processes?

____ ____ Are there mechanisms in place through which agency leaders can identify and rectify environmental stressors (role overload, role conflict, etc.) that can contribute to impairment in ethical decision-making?

____ ____ Does the agency have an active, aggressive Employee Assistance Program to address areas of personal impairment that could affect the ethical judgement and conduct of staff?

Ethical Decision-making

Yes No

____ ____ Have staff have been oriented to the multiple parties whose interests must be reviewed in ethical decision-making?

____ ____ Are the forums clearly defined within which ethical issues can be explored, e.g., individual supervision, team meetings?

Ethical Violations

Yes No

___ ___ Are the potential consequences of breaches of ethical conduct clearly defined and communicated to staff?

___ ___ Are the procedures through which ethical violations are addressed at the agency clearly defined and communicated to staff?

How to use this Book

As an introductory text, this book has been written for many distinct audiences within the substance abuse field.

If you perform professional, technical or supportive roles in a substance abuse treatment program, you will find in Chapters Three through Eight a large menu of critical incidents which can serve as a medium for the self-exploration and study of ethical issues in the field.

If you perform a specialty role within the substance abuse field, you will find in Chapter Nine a selection of critical incidents that relate to such specialty areas as prevention, early intervention (employee assistance, student assistance), outreach, training, consultation and research.

If you are a substance abuse agency manager or supervisor, you will find in Chapter Two detailed instructions on how to develop and implement an agency Code of Professional Practice. Chapter Three also provides a discussion of ethical issue related to business practices within the field.

If you are a training specialist within the substance abuse field, you can utilize the critical incident format of this book as an extremely helpful aid in the design and conduct of workshops on ethical and professional practice issues within the field. The annotated comments following each critical incident are designed as learning aids for all of the above audiences.

A Review of Ethical Values

The judgement of an act to be ethical or unethical, good or bad, depends upon the values and principles utilized to judge the act. In the analysis of critical incidents in this book, there are a number of historical principles that will be referenced to help explore the nature of ethical issues in various situations. Some of the ethical principles and values that can be found scattered through discussions of ethics over the past centuries include the following:

Autonomy (Enhance freedom of personal destiny)
Obedience (Obey legal and ethically permissible directives)
Conscientious Refusal (Disobey illegal or unethical directives)
Beneficence (Help others)
Gratitude (Pass good along to others)
Competence (Be knowledgeable and skilled)
Justice (Be fair, distribute by merit)
Stewardship (Use resources judiciously)
Honesty and Candor (Tell the truth)
Fidelity (Don't break promises)
Loyalty (Don't abandon)
Diligence (Work hard)
Discretion (Respect confidentiality and privacy)
Self-improvement (Be the best that you can be)
Nonmaleficence (Don't hurt anyone)
Restitution (Make amends to persons injured)
Self-interest (Protect yourself)

The application of such principles and values will be explored through the discussion of critical incidents within the book with a particular focus on situations that bring principles into conflict, e.g., what to do when telling the truth may hurt someone.

A Note on the Relationship Between Ethics and Law

There are important distinctions between the question of whether a particular course of action is ethical and whether that same course of action is legal. Thompson (1990) has identified six different relationships between ethics and law. A course of action could be:

1. Ethical and legal.
2. Ethical and illegal, in the case of breaking an unjust law.
3. Ethical and alegal, in a case where no law applies.
4. Unethical and legal, in the case of complying with an unjust law.
5. Unethical and illegal, in the case of breaking a just law.
6. Unethical and alegal, in the case of committing an unethical act that is not legally prohibited.

The primary purpose of this text is the exploration of ethical issues and professional practice values in the substance abuse field. Legal issues will be referenced where appropriate but will not be a primary focus of the discussions.

Chapter
Two

The Code of Professional Practice

What is a Code of Professional Practice?

A Code of Professional Practice (CPP) is an explicitly defined set of beliefs, values and standards that guide organizational members in the conduct of activities related to the agency's mission. The Code articulates values to which organizational members should aspire in the performance of their duties. The Code defines boundaries of appropriate and inappropriate conduct. The Code sets forth guidelines to be used by staff to guide them through difficult and complex situations encountered in the performance of their respective activities. The Code provides a framework through which relationship boundaries can be defined and monitored. The Code is a framework for day-to-day decision-making within the organization.

What purposes are such codes designed to achieve?

1. The CPP serves to protect the health and safety of, and promote the quality of services provided to, clients receiving agency services.

2. The CPP serves to enhance public safety.

3. The CPP serves to protect the integrity and reputation of individual agency staff members.

4. The CPP serves to protect the integrity and reputation of the agency.

5. The CPP serves as a medium through which high standards of ethical and professional conduct can be imbedded within the culture of the agency.

Are all employees of the organization bound by the standards set forth in the Code?

This question marks an important distinction between a professional code of ethics and an agency's Code of Professional Practice. A professional code of ethics is a system of standards that dictate who, when, where, how and under what conditions one can claim adherence to and practice a profession. Such codes are usually tied to licensure or certification by independent organizations. Such codes transcend parochial concerns of a given agency and do not apply to any person outside the professional classification. In contrast, a Code of Professional Practice is a set of standards to which all members of an organizational unit are bound. The CPP explicitly defines standards to which all interdisciplinary team members will be held accountable, regardless of the individual codes of ethics to which staff may be accountable via their professional specialties. Codes of ethics shape standards of practice within professional specialties; Codes of Professional Practice shape values and standards of practice within organizations. All members of an organization are bound by a CPP regardless of their training or area of work activity. The CPP recognizes ethical dimensions in the institutional relationship between the client and the organization. Administrators, board members, clerical staff, maintenance staff, counseling staff, volunteers, and interns—all organizational members—are bound by the standards set forth in the CPP.

Why is there a need for the CPP? Shouldn't professional codes of ethics be sufficient in setting ethical standards of professional conduct?

Some of the conditions which have contributed to the desirability of Codes of Professional Practice include the following:

- The proliferation of undergraduate and graduate counseling programs—outside the traditional roles of social worker and psychologist—has resulted in a greater number of persons who lack training in ethical issues, who are not professionally licensed and/or who are not bound by a code of ethics as a condition of their vocational role.
- There are too many job functions in human service agencies that fall outside the realm of professional codes of ethics. What standards guide the conduct of administrators, planners,

- marketing and public relations staff, clerical staff, billing clerks, outreach workers, education and prevention staff, trainers, consultants, drivers, and maintenance personnel?
- Codes of ethics can guide the conduct of individual professionals but they contribute little to the development of a strong organizational culture through which *all* members *share* values related to standards of professional practice.
- Many human service organizations have found it beneficial to develop standards of professional practice that transcend the more narrow scope of issues addressed within professional codes of ethics.

How is the Code of Professional Practice Developed?

The author has experimented with a variety of processes through which organizations can develop a CPP. The following steps offer a systematic process of CPP development that has been refined through use with many organizations..

Step #1: Preliminary discussions related to the need for a Code of Professional Practice are discussed by the Executive Director with agency managers and supervisors and the Personnel Committee of the Board.

This step is to assure that support for the development of a CPP is initiated and sustained at the highest levels within the organizational hierarchy. It is recommended that agency managers and board members review the steps outlined in this chapter to explore what refinements may be required to fit the unique characteristics of their organization. Such refinement can continue to evolve as more staff are involved in the CPP development process. Other key questions to be addressed at this time include the following:

- Are there sufficient internal resources to facilitate the CPP development process or should the services of an outside consultant be acquired to assist with the process?
- Is there sufficient support for the benefits that can be derived from developing a CPP to warrant initiating the development and implementation process?

- Given other projects in various stages of development, when is the best time to initiate the CPP developmental process?
- What sources of resistance to the development of a CPP should be anticipated and how should such resistance be managed?

Step #2: All agency staff are oriented to the purpose of the Code and the steps that will be used to develop it.

This is an extremely important step in the CPP development process if staff involvement is to be maximized and staff paranoia is to be minimized. This can best be presented by the agency director at an all staff meeting (for smaller agencies) or at divisional meetings (for larger agencies). Most of the questions outlined in this chapter should be touched on during the orientation session.

Step #3: An ad hoc task force of organizational members is selected to guide the overall process of developing the Code.

It is essential that a Code of Professional Practice emerge out of the process of the team, and not be an instrument arbitrarily foisted upon staff by one or more managers or by the agency board. The creation of an ad hoc task force to help facilitate the development of the Code is one vehicle to assure continued staff involvement throughout the developmental process.

Task force members may be appointed by the Director or may be selected by agency staff using a preset format (e.g, one staff member selected by their peers from each program area). The most ideal task force size in my experience is 4 to 10 persons. Ideally, the task force should:

- include key representatives from the Board and the management team
- represent a cross-section of the professional disciplines that make up the staff of the agency
- represent a cross-section of the units that make up the structure of the agency
- represent a mix of persons with short and long tenure at the agency

- reflect the selection of persons who exemplify and can articulate standards of service quality and professionalism, and
- include members with skills in group facilitation and writing.

The major responsibilities of the task force are to:

- review and refine the steps involved in the development of the CPP
- solicit feedback from staff on issues and recommended standards that should be addressed or reflected in the CPP
- facilitate staff discussion groups about desired CPP standards
- write draft sections of the CPP
- play a leadership role in the review and redrafting process, and
- assist in the orientation of staff when the CPP is completed.

The responsibilities of the task force will vary depending on whether the agency utilizes an outside consultant to facilitate the CPP development. Where such a consultant is not utilized, those tasks normally performed by the consultant are performed by agency managers and/or task force members.

Step #4: Sample codes of ethics of various health and human service professions are circulated to staff for the purpose of identifying those standards staff feel should be incorporated into the agency Code of Professional Practice.

The Codes of ethics of those professional associations/disciplines to which agency staff are affiliated are circulated for review. Codes may also be included from professional associations whose standards address areas of service activity or job functions currently performed within the agency. One easy method of review is to have each staff person place their initials beside each standard which they feel should be incorporated into the agency CPP. There is a resource list included within the Appendix which lists professional organizations which may be contacted to obtain such codes of ethics.

Step #5: A series of small group meetings are held with organizational members in which critical incidents are presented to staff. Discussion of these vignettes of ethical dilemmas are used to elicit recommendations on standards to guide staff in responding to such situations.

The critical incidents presented in the remaining chapters of this book are designed to be used in conjunction with this step. Working with small groups of staff, the facilitator presents each small group with a critical incident and asks staff to: 1) identify the ethical/legal/clinical issues inherent within the incident, 2) identify how they would respond to the incident as presented, and 3) recommend a standard that could be included within the CPP that could guide staff who might find themselves in such a situation.

This step in the development of the CPP has an added benefit of sensitizing staff to a large range of ethical issues they are unlikely to have experienced or considered. Such critical incident training actually provides a safe and supportive environment through which staff can rehearse (or emotionally decompress from) their responses to very complex ethical/legal/clinical situations. Staff who complete this training often remark on their appreciation for the opportunity to explore such situations before being faced with them in real life.

The logistics of this training can best be handled by breaking staff into groups of 15-30 to participate in half to full day critical incident training. It is desirable to mix staff from different units and disciplines within each training group. The goal is that every organizational member will have an opportunity to participate in at least one training session in which they share in generating recommended standards for the CPP.

During each training session, staff should be divided into groups of 3-5 staff. The facilitator should assign each group a critical incident with all groups listening to all of the situations before they begin brainstorming. Each group should be given 20-30 minutes to address the three elements (issues, action, standards) with a recorder being selected from within each group to document the ideas and recommendations of the group. After the allotted time, each group reports the three elements of their critical incident. It is best to vary critical incidents with each training group. This assures the highest number of recommended standards coming from staff as a result of this step. It is also best if each training group gets a sampling of critical incidents that cross a variety of areas of professional practice (a cross-section of incidents is presented across the remaining chapters). Critical incidents within this book can be chosen by the task force to elicit recommendations on issues of greatest import to the agency. Critical incidents may also be supplemented with real incidents that have occurred in the life of the organization.

Task force members play important roles during this step. Where no consultant is utilized, they facilitate the small group discussions, and they have the very important role of recording the standards recommendations that emerge from the small groups reporting out their responses to the critical incidents.

Step #6: The task force uses the recommendations for standards generated in steps 4 and 5 to develop a draft Code of Professional Practice for the agency.

It is particularly important that the task force not edit standards recommendations coming from step 5. The job at this stage is to present the recommendations as they came from the small groups as accurately as possible within the draft CPP.

Step #7: Copies of the draft code are circulated for review and comment to all staff members of the organization.

Mechanisms of review which can be incorporated into step 6 include:

- written comments providing reactions/recommendations related to the draft CPP
- verbal comments solicited on a one-on-one basis by task force members from peers within their program area
- a review and discussion of the draft code at divisional or program meetings with recorded minutes submitted to the task force, and
- open task force meetings in which staff can drop in and provide feedback/recommendations related to the draft CPP.

Step #8: Copies of the draft code are circulated to the Personnel Committee of the Board, the Board as a whole, and the agency legal counsel for review and comment.

These reviews can occur concurrently with the staff reviews. The review by legal counsel is particularly important to assure that no standards inadvertently violate tenants of criminal or civil law or other regulatory standards governing the activities of the organization.

Step #9: The task force works with the Personnel Committee of the Board, the management team and the Executive Director to integrate recommendations from steps 7 and 8 into a final version of the CPP.

In this step the final decisions regarding standards and clarity of the language in which they are presented are made. Where consensus is not achieved, most organizations use the following procedure to achieve a decision on each standard in question. Recommendations for various options are set forth by the task force, discussed at the Board level, and voted on, with majority vote ruling the final selection process.

Step #10: The recommended code is integrated into existing personnel policies and disciplinary procedures.

This step entails 1) altering the personnel policies to acknowledge the existence of the CPP and to establish the CPP as the set of standards to which all staff members shall adhere, 2) clearly indicating that any member of the agency who fails to achieve such adherence shall be subject to disciplinary action, and 3) clarifying or creating appeal procedures regarding disciplinary action taken in response to violation of a CPP standard.

Step #11: The Code of Professional Practice is approved by the agency Board with an effective implementation date.

The effective date of the CPP should be set with sufficient lead time to assure that all staff orientations can be completed prior to the date. The lead time also provides the opportunity for staff to complete any required activity set forth in the Code. Several agencies in writing standards on staff representation of professional credentials have mandated in their CPP that all staff submit to the agency copies of all transcripts, diplomas, licenses, and certifications. The lead time of effective implementation provides staff an opportunity to complete such activity prior to the effective date.

Step #12:   All staff are oriented to the Board-approved Code of Professional Practice.

The use of the Executive Director, the Chairperson of the Personnel Committee of the Board, and staff representatives from the CPP task force to conduct the orientations symbolically placed the full resources of the agency behind the implementation of the CPP.

Step #13:   All staff sign a statement for inclusion in their personnel file affirming that they have read the Code, participated in an orientation session related to the Code, and understand the standards set forth in the Code.

This step reinforces the seriousness of the Code and the expectation placed upon staff for adherence to the standards and values set forth in the Code. The documentation eliminates the "Nobody ever told me about that" defense in response to serious breaches of the Code.

Step #14:   A mechanism is established by the Executive Director and the Board for future review and refinement of the Code.

An annual review of the Code by an ad hoc committee of Board-staff is suggested to allow for the continuing evolution of the CPP. Step 14 sets the time frame of when revisions of the Code will be entertained and the procedural steps that shall be used in such modification.

Step #15:   The Code of Professional Practice is included in all new staff orientations.

The use of the Executive Director, Board members and professional staff to assist with this orientation is highly recommended. The CPP should be an important tool of socialization for all new staff entering the organization. The orientation to the Code can include some of the same critical incident training that was utilized in the Code's development.

Step #16: Decisions related to dissemination of the Code beyond organizational members are discussed and finalized.

Some programs may choose to use the CPP in ways that transcend its use shaping the standards of quality and professional conduct to which staff will be held accountable. Two such uses are recommended for consideration. The first is the dissemination of the agency's CPP to its referral sources. This is a way of boldly communicating the essence of one's organizational culture to outsiders. As one director noted, "It's the best way we have of telling people who we are and how we are different from all the other agencies out there." A second use involves the distribution of a copy of the Code (or at least the section of standards governing client relationships) to each client at admission. This is a means of educating clients to the precise standards that will govern the nature of staff relationships and decision-making. Retrospective studies of clients who were sexually exploited by therapists, for example, reveal that a number of such clients were particularly vulnerable due to their lack of knowledge of what was appropriate and inappropriate in the therapy relationship. Distribution of an agency CPP to all clients clearly defines such boundaries of appropriateness and inappropriateness. Providing the CPP to clients is a way of saying:

> "This is who we are. These are the standards of practice by which you can judge us. If we fail to meet these standards, we expect and ask that you bring this discrepancy to our attention."

How long does it take to develop a Code of Professional Practice?

The development of an agency CPP should be done slowly and deliberately. This, after all, will result in the single most important document that communicates the professional values of the organization. A normal time span for completing the above steps can be anywhere from twelve months to eighteen months depending on how many other program and staff development activities are occurring simultaneously.

How is the Code of Professional Practice Updated?

One method of keeping track of new issues that may need to be addressed in the CPP is to refer all such issues for discussion and documentation to the agency's Quality Improvement Committee.   Since so many issues related to the CPP involve quality of care issues, this is a natural placement of responsibility.   The Quality Improvement Committee can make recommendations related to changes in the CPP that can be incorporated into the annual review of the CPP. Issues that cannot await such review can be handled by interim standards being issued by the Executive Director.   These issues that arise over the year can then be formally reviewed using the review and modification provisions set forth in Step #14.

An Introduction to the Critical Incidents

The next seven chapters of this book catalogue critical incidents that raise potential ethical and professional practice issues related to:
- our personal conduct outside the work environment
- the conduct of our business practices
- our adherence to professional values
- our relationships with clients/families
- our professional peer relationships
- our conduct in situations that pose a risk to public safety, and
- our performance of specialty roles within the substance abuse field.

The critical incidents in each chapter can be selected for use in the staff focus groups described earlier in step five of the CPP development process.

The critical incidents that make up the heart of this book were constructed using the following procedures.

1. Situations were drawn from the author's clinical and consulting experience and synthesized into representative composites with all names and identifying details altered.   The composites constructed from the author's experience are fictional as written, although the ethical issues were drawn from real events. The names of all persons and organizations contained in the critical incidents are fictitious.

2. Situations were solicited from professional colleagues. Similar situations were merged into a fictional composite incident. Names and insignificant details of all incidents were altered, maintaining an accurate representation of the ethical dilemma involved in the real situations.

3. Any uncanny similarity between a critical incident and a real situation is purely coincidental and simply reflects the tendency for such events to be episodically recapitulated in agencies and communities across the United States. The number of readers who will know of incidents similar to those presented in this book adds further evidence that these problems are widespread and systemic rather than idiosyncratic to person or place.

4. Where the author had no direct or indirect experience from which to illustrate a particular ethical issue, a fictional vignette was created which could be used to explore the issue.

The critical incidents in these chapters are followed by discussion questions and a brief discussion and analysis of ethical issues raised by the critical incident. These discussions are not intended as in-depth analyses of the full range of ethical issues in each situation, but rather are intended as starting points of discussion for the facilitator who will be leading the small group discussions of these incidents. Each analysis identifies real or potential breaches of ethical conduct where the recognition of the particular violation is universal within the substance abuse field and within the broader health and human service professions. For those critical incidents that lack such clarity of judgement, the analysis identifies and discusses various issues that must be weighed to plot an ethical course of action. The purpose of the analyses is to stimulate thinking about ethical complexity and ethical decision-making.

A Model for Ethical Decision-making

After experimenting with numerous models of ethical decision-making within workshops for substance abuse workers, the author has settled on the following framework for the analysis of ethical dilemmas. The framework involves the application of three questions.

1. Whose interests are involved and who can be harmed? Or put more simply: Who are the potential winners and losers?

    While the situations in this book span the interests and vulnerabilities of many parties, most boil down to the following: service recipients (clients / families), individual workers, the prevention or treatment agency, the substance abuse field, and the community. The analysis of interests and vulnerabilities is completed with the identification of areas of conflicting interest—where acting to benefit one party does harm to another party.

2. How could the application of various universal values shed light on the appropriate action to be taken in the situation?

    This second step explores how widely held ethical values (defined in Chapter One) could be applied to determine the right course of action in a particular situation. It is important in this discussion to not only isolate the values that apply to the situation but to also identify values that may be in conflict, e,g, the value of honesty conflicting with the value of loyalty. This opens the way to asking, "Which is the higher value in this situation?" The higher value is often determined by the degree of good to be achieved or the degree of harm to be avoided identified through the first question.

3. What standards of law or professional propriety apply to this situation?

    This third step looks at established standards of professional conduct that dictate or prohibit certain action relevant to the situation. These standards would include legal mandates, ethical standards of professional associations, Codes of Professional Practice, personnel policies, or employment contracts.

The worksheet on the following page provides a format through which staff can individually or in small groups apply this three step model of ethical decision-making to the critical incidents in the rest of the book.

Multiple copies should be made so that a worksheet can be used for each incident analyzed.

Worksheet For Critical Incident Discussion Groups

Critical Incident #_____

I.   Whose interests are involved; who can be harmed?

Interests and Vulnerabilities	Significant	Moderate	Minimal / None
Client / Family			
Staff Member			
Agency			
Professional Field			
Community / Public Safety			

Which interests, if any, are in conflict?

II. Application of Universal Values

_____   Autonomy (Freedom over one's own destiny)
_____   Obedience (Obey legal and ethically permissible directives)
_____   Conscientious Refusal (Disobey illegal or unethical directives)
_____   Beneficence (Do good; Help others)
_____   Gratitude (Pass good along to others)
_____   Competence (Be knowledgeable and skilled)
_____   Justice (Be fair, distribute by merit)
_____   Stewardship (Use resources wisely)
_____   Honesty and Candor (Tell the truth)
_____   Fidelity (Keep your promises)
_____   Loyalty (Don't abandon)
_____   Diligence (Work hard)
_____   Discretion (Respect confidence and privacy)
_____   Self-improvement (Be the best that you can be)
_____   Nonmaleficence (Don't hurt anyone)
_____   Restitution (Make amends to persons injured)
_____   Self-interest (Protect yourself)

III. Relevant Standards, Laws, Policies

IV. Discussion notes

Chapter Three

Conduct Related to the Practice of Business

The issue of ethics as traditionally framed in the substance abuse field has focused primarily upon complexities in the relationship between our direct services providers and our service recipients. The scope has been limited to clinical ethics. The ethical arena has been defined within the boundaries of the counseling relationship. A number of forces have emerged that force us to expand the ethical arena to encompass our business practices. The massive infusion of public dollars into community-based substance abuse programs, the legitimization of addiction as a treatable disease via insurance coverage, the proliferation of hospital-based and for-profit treatment programs, the competition-spawned marketing wars between service providers, and the rapid profusion of legal and regulatory standards governing substance abuse treatment have all intensified the need to explore ethical dimensions related to the business conduct of our organizations. There has clearly been the emergence of a "substance abuse industrial complex" in the United States over the past two decades. It is only proper that the exploration of ethical dimensions of business practices in the substance abuse treatment industry be as intense as the growing interest in ethics which is occurring in a broad spectrum of business and industry in the United States. This chapter will explore a broad range of critical incidents related to ethical issues involved in the business practices of substance abuse agencies.

Critical Incidents

Macro-Planning

Stewardship of Resources

A substance abuse prevention and treatment agency recently received a $500,000 donation from the estate of a local philanthropist with no strings as to how the money should be utilized by the agency. The management team of the agency has presented the following options for potential use of this new money for consideration to the Board:

1. Launch a desperately needed specialized service program for addicted women and their children (the new money could fund this program for two years).
2. Upgrade existing facilities and equipment.
3. Provide salary increases to all staff (the goal is to bring salaries up to par with other health and human service agencies and reduce problems related to staff recruitment and retention).
4. Add staff and material resources to do a better job (improve quality of care) with existing programming.
5. Create the beginnings of a capital fund for the eventual construction of new service facilities.
6. Maintain money as "rainy day fund" so agency would have ability to sustain services in the face of funding cuts or other financial crisis (interest made on money could be spent and the fund would reduce current interest paid by the agency on borrowed money used for operating expenses, due to delayed receipt of state reimbursements).

Discussion Questions

How might you ethically weigh the various choices above?

Which is more ethical: provide the highest quality of service to a small number of clients or provide an adequate level of quality of services to a larger number of clients?

What standards or values should guide our stewardship of agency and community resources?

Substance abuse policy makers and planners at federal, state, and local levels regularly confront the question of distributive justice—a kind of ethical arithmetic that determines how scarce resources are to be dispersed. Weighing alternative uses of resources from the above lists cannot be judged from an arbitrary designation of right or wrong choices. Given the particulars of a program's unique situation, each of the above options could arguably be the best or the worst option on the list. In real life, you would probably have staff and board members making precisely such arguments. What is important about considering ethical aspects of resource allocation is to assure that decisions related to the distribution of resources are filtered through and are congruent with the organization's stated mission and values. For a service organization to consistently utilize its resources in areas that do not enhance the accessibility and quality of services would represent a breach of honesty, fidelity and loyalty to the agency's clients and community constituents.

Planning

A community of 85,000 is served by two competing hospitals, one of which has operated a four bed medical detox and 20 bed residential rehabilitation unit for the past eight years. Since its initiation, the unit has gone from a 95% utilization rate to a 75% utilization rate, primarily due to the development of new substance abuse programs in other neighboring counties from which the unit once drew client referrals. The unit has maintained a good reputation and is clearly responding to a service need in the area. The competing hospital announces that it will be opening a 20 bed inpatient unit for the treatment of substance abuse. The internal planning data upon which hospital administrators based this decision suggested that the area could not fully utilize 40 beds for substance abuse treatment but that their hospital could pull 40-50% of the current substance abuse treatment admissions based on local physician admitting preferences. This hospital is opening a unit not in response to an unmet need, but to capture their market share of substance abuse treatment admissions from the other hospital. The internal rationale is that 50% utilization of a new substance abuse treatment unit is better than 0% utilization in the closed unit of the hospital in which the substance abuse unit will be located. Within 18 months of service initiation, the C.D. units of both are struggling with 25-30% utilization rates—rates that have further deteriorated due to the initiation of new substance abuse services and aggressive marketing from neighboring communities.

Discussion Questions

Are there ethical issues raised by this scenario?

Are there ethical principles that should guide the initiation of new services by an agency, particularly when such services are already being provided by other service agencies?

What are our values related to competition and collaboration?

What values can help us resolve potential conflicts between institutional self-interest and community need?

Vignettes like the above have not been uncommon in the past decade. There are a number of potential ethical dimensions involved in the planning and initiation of chemical dependency services in the above circumstances. The first issue is whether the short-term interests of the hospital violate the long-term interests of the community. The ethical command to "first, do no harm" can be applied to communities as well as individual clients. A hospital supported by a community—by personal and industrial benefactors and by its consumers—takes on certain ethical mandates related to its stewardship of resources. Part of that mandate is to expend resources in ways that can support rather than weaken the network of local health care services available to local citizens. This mandate comes from a contract implicit in the support the community provides the hospital. Private and corporate benefactors support the hospital in the understanding that the hospital will use those resources to the long-term benefit of the community. Maximizing short-term profits by moving into competition for a fixed number of clients already being served represents a misuse of the trust and the resources which the community endowed to the hospital. The plummeting occupancy rates on both units in the above vignette will inevitably lead to an erosion of resources—e.g., staff, consultants, training, etc.—and a potentially poorer quality of chemical dependency treatment services available within this community. Over time, the financial viability of both units may be threatened and could paradoxically result in both hospitals being forced out of the provision of chemical dependency services.

There may also be ethical issues involved in the planning processes through which new chemical dependency services are initiated. These issues can include the blatant disregard of planning bodies or planning documents; the misrepresentation, manipulation, or outright fabrication of planning data to support a certificate of need (CON) application; and the misrepresentation/exaggeration of the extent of the local substance abuse problem to garner support for the new unit.

Lobbying

Misrepresentation of Information

In a hearing regarding a request for funding of detoxification services by a local city council, Rex, the Executive Director of the local substance abuse agency was asked by a council member how many clients were turned away or faced arrest because of an inadequate number of beds in the detox unit. The unit this last year averaged three persons per week turned away in the winter months and one person per week turned away in the other months. Last week (time of a spring festival noted for its heavy drinking) there were an unusually high number of people (16 persons) turned away because of the detox unit being full. In response to the council member's question, the Director responded; "We have routinely turned people away all this past year because of lack of capacity. Only this week, we turned away 16 persons who were in desperate need of detoxification simply because our unit was already filled to its current legal capacity." This statement conveys the impression that the service demand is much higher than the actual service demand data would indicate.

Discussion Questions

Is it ever justified to over-estimate or misrepresent information related to service need, quantity of services delivered, or the frequency and degree of service success?

How could the misrepresentation in the above vignette backfire hurting the reputation of the director and the agency as well as damaging the future accessibility of client services?

The above action stretches, if not punctures, the ethical principle of honesty. The concern with this action is both the wrongfulness of misrepresenting the scope and intensity of a problem and the potential harm that could be created through such misrepresentation. If the misrepresentation was suspected or discovered by the city council members, it could destroy the reputation and credibility of the agency to such an extent that future funding of services to clients could be jeopardized. The misrepresentation could also lead to a misallocation of resources—committing resources to underutilized detox beds when other more critical needs are unmet due to limited resources. It is through this spiral of unforeseen consequences that stretching or misrepresenting the truth poses potential harm to the agency, to clients, and to the community. The potential for inadvertent misrepresentation can occur particularly under the pressure for condensation of verbal testimony at legislative hearings or hearings reviewing requests for funding. To avoid the dangers inherent in creating such time-induced oversimplifications and misconceptions, it is helpful to always take along or submit afterwards a more detailed presentation of information.

Exploitation of Clients

 ◇ ◇ **4** ◇ ◇

A program facing potential threats of having state funding cut for substance abuse services in their area, organizes community representatives and clients to go to the state capitol to lobby the legislature to stop the proposed cuts. Clients are actively recruited, transported to this event, provided with placards and T-shirts that clearly identify them as clients of the agency, are coached for interviews with the media, and are utilized to present testimony before a legislative committee considering the funding cuts.

Discussion Questions

Discuss the following issues and principles as they relate to the above vignette.
- discretion (protection of confidentiality and privacy)
- autonomy and freedom from coercion
- informed consent

Would the issues be different if the individuals in the above vignette were former clients not actively involved in services at the agency?

What standard should govern the involvement of clients in activities that transcend the service contract?

Would there be similar issues in soliciting parental (parents of active/former clients) involvement in such lobbying on behalf of funding for adolescent services?

The above experience may be exploitive of clients or it may provide a very positive experience of empowerment to clients. The judgement we place on this activity can be based on an analysis of the following contextual elements of the activity:

- *Were clients briefed on the potential positive and negative effects of the activity, e.g., their public identification as addicts / clients?*
- *Was the staff's solicitation of client involvement manipulative or coercive? Were there untoward consequences to any client who chose not to participate in the activity, e.g., the alternative to not participating for a residential client is an unpleasant work detail.*
- *Did the program avoid soliciting clients active in treatment whose autonomy of decision-making could be compromised by their dependence upon the program?*
- *Did the activity supplement rather than replace treatment services needed by the clients?*
- *Were there any aspects of staff-client relationships during the lobbying activity that would serve to undermine the capacity and quality of continued service to the client?*

Utilization of Staff Time for Political Lobbying

◇ ◇ **5** ◇ ◇

In the above vignette, staff members on paid work time accompanied clients and community representatives to participate in the lobbying effort.

Discussion Question

What ethical issues are raised by the use of paid staff time for lobbying particular issues or organizing support for or against particular political candidates?

The use of staff on paid time to participate in lobbying activities raises ethical issues and may also raise legal issues. Ethical issues raised by this practice include:

- *the involvement of staff in duties that far transcend the activities for which they were hired*
- *the potential use of coercion to involve staff in political activity*
- *the breach in the contractual commitment (with funding sources) to use staff only for specified service activities, and*
- *questionable to illegal billing practices in which third parties were billed for the staff time or bills for client services that encompass the time involved in lobbying.*

A more serious and enduring problem with political lobbying for some agencies would be the potential loss of their not-for-profit status (designation as a 501(c)(3) organization under Internal Revenue Service Code). The loss of this status as a result of political activity on paid staff time could threaten the future potential of the agency to sustain its role as a helping institution.

Advocacy: Interest of Field Versus Agency Self-Interest

◇ ◇ **6** ◇ ◇

Alisha is a local program director and the Third-party Payment Committee chairperson of a professional association of substance abuse agencies. She has just been called by a legislative committee staff member seeking her opinion on how criteria should be set for which agencies will be reimbursed through the state Medicaid program for the provision of substance abuse services to eligible clients. The legislative committee is considering using accreditation by the Council on Accreditation of Rehabilitation Facilities (CARF) as the primary eligibility criteria. The legislative committee is seeking Alisha's opinion based on her experience with the state association committee. Here is Alisha's dilemma: the CARF accreditation requirement would result in significant funding cuts to the large number of substance abuse agencies in the state who are not CARF accredited but who have been receiving Medicaid reimbursement for services. Alisha's own program is CARF accredited and would receive significant competitive advantage and a financial windfall if the legislature mandates the CARF requirement. The legislative committee staff person is asking for Alisha's off-the-record recommendation as to what action the legislative committee should take.

Discussion Questions

Identify the multiple constituents to whom Alisha is responsible in the above vignette.

What values might help Alisha sort out her conflicting role responsibilities in this situation?

If you were Alisha, how would you respond?

There is a clear role conflict depicted in this vignette in which the interests of Alisha as a program director are in conflict with her promise as professional association committee chairperson to represent the collective needs of substance abuse agencies throughout the state. To avoid exploiting the chairperson role for personal/agency gain, Alisha might consider one or more of the following actions:

1. *seeking consultation—perhaps from the director of the association—before she responds to the request*
2. *declaring her potential conflict of interests to the legislative staff member*
3. *articulating both the short- and long-term advantages and disadvantages of the course of action being considered by the legislature*
4. *declaring her personal preference while at the same time acknowledging an alternative approach that would better serve the needs of the majority of agencies*
5. *suggesting that the staff member solicit opinions from a broader range of persons who reflect different interests within the field, or*
6. *advocating for the development of criteria that would allow for the inclusion of a larger group of providers.*

Fund-raising

Use of Professional Fund-raisers

◇ ◇ **7** ◇ ◇

The Harambe Center—a local substance abuse treatment program—is considering entering into a contract with a professional fund-raising organization to raise funds for the construction of a new treatment facility.

Under terms of the contract, the fund-raising organization will receive 50% of all funds raised as their fee for running the capital fund drive. In short, only $350,000 of the $700,000 target of the fund drive will actually go toward construction of the new facility. All promotional material distributed as part of the fund drive would reference the need for $700,000 to build the new facility. Nowhere would there be public disclosure of the amount of funds that are covering the administration of the fund drive itself.

Discussion Questions

How could the choice to use the professional fund-raiser potentially help or hurt the profession, the agency, individual staff members, and current and potential agency clients?

What would be your position as a board member in response to this proposal?

Many substance abuse agencies have struggled with the most appropriate means of raising funds to support special needs and some have sought the help of professional fund-raisers. The ethical questions that emerge from the above vignette include the following:

1. *Are there alternatives to the above fund-raising strategy that will represent a better stewardship of agency and community resources? Is there a way in which the $350,000 going to support the administration of the fund campaign could be reduced so that these funds could be allocated to support needed community services?*
2. *Does the failure to disclose the portion of funds raised that will actually go toward building construction constitute a breach in the principle of honesty, candor, and fidelity implicit in the relationship between the agency and the community?*

Staff/Board Support

◇ ◇ **8** ◇ ◇

A fund drive by a local substance abuse agency has continually portrayed the importance of this drive to the continued access of critically needed treatment services to local citizens. The fund drive has been portrayed in crisis terms. A close examination of funds received to date would reveal almost no financial contributions by board members, staff, or volunteers of the agency.

Discussion Questions

Do the communications of the fund drive represent a breach of honesty if those most supportive of the agency's mission have not offered personal support of the fund drive?

If the funds are as critical as communicated, is it a violation of any ethical value for the Board, staff, and volunteers to not contribute to the fund drive?

This is an ethically grey area in which almost nothing has been written. The question raised in the above vignette is the following: if the persons most closely associated with the project to be funded do not feel strongly enough to commit even token support, do their repeated admonitions on the importance and criticalness of the project to the community represent a misrepresentation of their beliefs? The issue of the degree to which professional staff and board members participate in community solicitation for funds is a question that should be explored by professional certification bodies, professional associations and within agencies.

Solicitation of Funds from Clients/Families

An adolescent substance abuse treatment program launched its capital fund drive with a mass mailing to local businesses and private citizens appealing for contributions. Included within the many mailing lists used for this solicitation was a list of all clients/families who had received services through the agency, including those clients/families currently in treatment.

Discussion Questions

Comment on any ethical issues raised by agency solicitation of contributions from current or former clients and their families.

What standard could help define under what conditions, if any, such solicitation was ethically appropriate?

The concern raised by the above practice is the "targeting" of families in ways that manipulate and exploit their vulnerability as past or present service consumers. Such appeals may exploit the helping relationship to further the interests of the institution to the extent that they manipulate the gratitude, guilt or pain of family members and to the extent that the appeal is enhanced by the power obtained in the helping relationship. An important distinction may be the extent to which former or current clients are targeted to receive a solicitation for financial support. If, for example, a person received a fund drive mailing because he or she was the president of a local bank but also happened to be a parent of a child who went through treatment at the program, there was no targeting involved. In contrast, a solicitation sent from a mailing list of all former and current clients would in the view of many persons constitute exploitive targeting and could raise the risks of other ethical breaches, e.g., inadvertent violation of confidentiality. The critical issue in assessing the ethical appropriateness of soliciting clients may differ depending on the nature of the service relationship. The following two suggested principles may prove helpful:

1. *The greater the intimacy of the service relationship—power of the service provider/vulnerability of the service consumer—the greater the potential for exploitation.*
2. *The closer the solicitation is to the point in time of greatest service intensity, the greater the potential for exploitation (current clients are almost always more vulnerable for exploitation than former clients).*

(For a related discussion, see Chapter Six for a discussion of the ethical issues involved in the receipt of gifts from clients.)

Marketing

Misrepresentation of Scope or Intensity of Services

◇ ◇ **10** ◇ ◇

In an effort to increase admissions and rectify a chronically low utilization rate, an inpatient program announces two new specialized treatment tracks—one for cocaine users and one for chemically dependent women. The program promotional literature and media boldly proclaim the program's expertise and leadership in addressing the needs of these special populations of clients. In fact, the new tracks represent no substantive change in program design. The cocaine track consists of a cocaine lecture, recently purchased cocaine films and literature, and access to an exercise bike cast off from the hospital's cardiac rehab department. The women's track includes assurance of a woman counselor and a women's group held twice a week during a client's inpatient stay. There has been no new staff recruited with special expertise to direct these tracks. There has been no significant additional training of existing staff. Minor appendages have been added, but the basic treatment design has been neither reviewed nor revised for appropriateness to these new client populations.

Discussion Question

What ethical values are compromised through "overselling" that misrepresents or distorts the scope and intensity of services available from a program?

The marketing of specialty programs that represent exploitive experiments in superficial specialization to garner increased client admissions breaches a number of ethical principles. These practices first breach the principle of honesty through their failure to accurately represent the true scope and intensity of available services. Such practices also breach the principle of fidelity—the promises made to clients at admission that special services exist within the program to address their unique needs. Aggressive marketing of such specialty tracks of treatment that reflect only a superficial facelift of the existing program brings in clients whose needs will not only go unaddressed, but whose admission precludes their contact with more clinically appropriate treatment alternatives. Such superficial specialization also raises the danger of iatrogenic (treatment-caused) harm caused from such treatment.

Misrepresentation or Misallocation of Costs

The promotional materials emanating from a local substance abuse program highlight the fact that the program offers "free" assessments. The free assessment offer is, in fact, a marketing gimmick. The cost of assessment work is built into increased fees for all services provided by the agency.

Discussion Questions

Does the claim of "free" assessments constitute false advertising?

Does this arrangement bias an assessment process that technically can only be paid for if the person being assessed is determined to be in need of services?

If assessment fees are hidden within service fees, is it fair that persons requiring on-going services end up paying for the assessments of those clients deemed inappropriate for the agency's services?

While the marketing of "free assessments" or "free initial consultation" may help induce resistant clients to seek an initial discussion about treatment services, such marketing ploys do constitute a dishonest approach to soliciting client involvement. A more honest statement of fact would be that assessment charges are absorbed into fees for on-going services. While the client will not be billed for the initial consultation, costs for providing this service will be recouped through the fees paid by the client for any services that are provided after the assessment. Such an explanation places the service process on a more professional, contractual basis than on the stance of the client needing to be sold a bill of goods or otherwise manipulated into service involvement.

Exaggeration of Treatment Success

A substance abuse program carried out an independent follow-up study of clients who they had treated. Based on a five year follow-up of treated clients, 25% revealed continuous sobriety since discharge, 31% revealed patterns of sobriety interrupted by one or more episodes of relapse, 15% who continued drinking problematically but with less severity than prior to treatment, and 29% whose drinking became more severe following treatment. Program personnel looked at the first three groups as all showing a positive effect of their treatment exposure, meaning that the program had "successfully impacted" 71% of clients who entered the program. This study and its interpretation were the basis for the 71% "success rate" regularly cited in program promotional materials and by program staff.

Discussion Questions

What makes the accurate presentation of likely treatment outcome an ethical issue?

What potential harm is created by program marketing efforts that create the illusion that recovery is easy—all you have to do is call?

The claim of a 71% success rate in the above vignette constitutes a misrepresentation because the communications:

- *failed to define "success," conveying the impression to the public and to other professionals that the 71% figure represented continuous, uninterrupted sobriety from the point of discharge from service*
- *failed to identify that the drinking patterns of 29% of clients who went through treatment actually worsened following their treatment experience, and*
- *failed to offer copies of the study to any who were interested so that the research methodology and overall integrity of the study could be assessed.*

A more accurate representation of "success rate" in the above situation would be to actually provide persons with the number of clients who fell into each of the four subgroups used in the study. The ethical concerns with the accurate representation of likely treatment outcome include the avoidance of exaggerated or fabricated claims of success intended to enhance a program's professional reputation and financial success and the avoidance of communications that oversimplify or exaggerate the ease with which one can move from addiction to recovery. Exaggerated claims of success and statements conveying the image that recovery is easily obtainable misrepresent the lethality of addictive diseases—the number who will die or be severely disabled before they ever see a treatment program and those who will die or be disabled by their addiction following failed efforts at treatment.

Exploitation of Clients

The Get Well Drug Abuse Program is a community based substance abuse program which relies heavily upon donations from local civic organizations and grants from local branches of government to sustain its financial existence. The last several years the program has evolved a practice (internally referred to as "the dog and pony show") in which clients in treatment are recruited to present a highly emotional and well-rehearsed synopsis of their addictive histories and the role of Get Well in saving their lives. The presentation ends with a plea by the Get Well Director for additional dollars to save other lost souls who are "drowning in the ocean of drugs flooding our country." The presentations have been extremely effective as fund-raising and marketing devices.

Discussion Questions

Comment on any ethical issues involved in this practice.

What standards should guide decisions related to the use of current or former clients for marketing, fund-raising, or community education?

The imbalance of power between a client in active treatment and his or her counselor or the program director diminishes the capacity for free choice and raises the potential for coercive involvement of clients in such marketing and fund-raising activities. This is particular true where refusal would be framed pejoratively as an indication of their denial, resistance, or some related psychobabble intended to escalate pressure on the client for participation. Coercive involvement in such presentations violates client confidentiality and anonymity. It is very helpful for programs to articulate standards that will govern the conditions under which clients or former clients will, or will not, be used in marketing or fund-raising campaigns. The presentation of such programs is also a breach of honesty when they are represented to be educational programs but are in reality designed to generate referrals and contributions.

Exploitation of Family Members

The 30 second television spot for the newly opened substance abuse unit in the local hospital opens with a physician proclaiming that alcoholics and addicts are blinded by a disease of denial that makes it nearly impossible for them to initiate their recovery spontaneously. It is the family, the physician exhorts, not the addict that must initiate the change process. It is the family's responsibility. Panning through scenes of wrecked cars, then moving into a scene of a graveyard and finally a focused shot of one unnamed gravestone, the commercial ends with the words, "If you don't call us today, you may have no reason to tomorrow!"

Discussion Questions

Is this an effective tool to penetrate family denial or exploitive sensationalism?

Is this good advertising or poor taste?

Do such aggressive media campaigns unduly exploit and manipulate family guilt and emotional pain?

What standards should govern the design of such marketing devices?

A growing number of programs are attempting to define standards of good taste and standards of ethics that can be utilized to ethically critique potential marketing strategies. Some of the questions being used to evaluate and eliminate marketing pieces that breach standards of good taste and ethics include the following:

- *Does the spot manipulate and exploit the guilt and emotional pain of family members?*
- *Could the spot have unintended and harmful consequences to some viewers, e.g., a viewer of the above ad whose alcoholic family member recently died of disease, accident or suicide?*
- *Does the style (aggressiveness, inappropriate use of humor) of the spot demean the profession?*
- *Does the spot inadvertently contribute to stereotypes or myths about the nature of addiction or recovery?*
- *Do the images or words in the script of the spot contribute to demeaning ethnic or sexual stereotypes?*
- *Does the message of the spot oversimplify or create unrealistic expectations about the recovery process?*

(NOTE: Readers interested in exploring ethical issues in the marketing of treatment services may find the following resource helpful: "Advertising Code for Alcoholism Treatment Programs" in *Principles of Practice*. Irvine, CA: National Association of Addiction Treatment Programs, Inc., 1982.)

Resource Allocation

◇ ◇ **15** ◇ ◇

To "maximize its return on investment," a community hospital initiated a 16-bed substance abuse treatment unit using the following scheme. Unit direction was placed under the Director of Social Services of the hospital. All detoxification occurred on medical-surgical units of the hospital, necessitating only a skeleton crew of RNs and LPNs to provide 24 hour medical coverage of the unit. Two counselors were hired contractually who each worked four hours a day Monday through Friday providing individual and family counseling and education. Down time was filled with movies and reading or writing assignments. There were no active linkage with the self-help community. There was little individual contact with clients and families. No programming occurred on weekends. There was virtually no aftercare services. Daily rates for this unit were 40%

higher than medical surgical units because of the "special needs of alcoholics and addicts."

Discussion Questions

What ethical issues do you see in this allocation of resources?

At what point does the failure to allocate adequate resources become an ethical issue?

The description of the above program includes most of the elements of what this author (White, 1990) has referred to as an "institutional predator." The treatment design is itself exploitive, combining artificially inflated fees for a service design that falls far short of the state-of-the-art in both its scope and intensity. Ethical dimensions of resource allocation encompass such questions as the following:

- *Do the resources committed within the treatment design assure the physical and psychological safety of clients?*
- *Do the resources committed to support the treatment design provide services of sufficient intensity, quality, and duration that are likely to result in positive treatment outcomes?*
- *Are the fees charged for services fair? Do they represent an accurate account of the costs associated with providing the services?*

Financial Management

◇ ◇ **16** ◇ ◇

Ellen found herself increasingly frustrated in her role of Executive Director of a county-run substance abuse agency. Of particular note was the escalating layers of red tape it took to implement any decision, no matter how minuscule the issue. Lacking any petty cash mechanism that did not require weeks of time to successfully process, Ellen found herself taking money out of her own pocket to pay for minor needs rather than to confess to her staff that it would take three weeks to get the three dollars to buy felt tip markers for tomorrow's seminar. After months of frustration, Ellen found the following solution to her red tape nightmare. The agency was sponsoring quarterly workshops for human service professionals that were beginning to generate a substantial amount of income from registration fees. Ellen began to withhold the cash paid for workshop registrations to create a special "off the books" fund to deal with emergency needs and to make purchases unlikely to be approved by the county, e.g., food for an annual staff retreat.

Discussion Questions

What are your views on Ellen's solution to this problem?

What future problems might be anticipated with this secret fund?

While Ellen's intent in the above vignette may be benign, her actions have thrust her into an area of ethical and legal vulnerability. First, the practice of using her own money for agency expenditures could easily lead to a lack of clear boundary definition between Ellen's personal money and agency money. Secondly, her failure to turn over income through the normal agency procedure for the receipt of cash could leave Ellen open to charges of theft or embezzlement, particularly with no records as to how the cash was expended. This error in judgement and the eventual disclosure of this practice could damage Ellen's professional reputation and the reputation of the agency and lead to a crisis in confidence through which the county board decreases funds and community members decreases their contributions to support critically needed services.

◇ ◇ **17** ◇ ◇

A local not-for-profit substance abuse agency set up a sister corporation with overlapping Boards. The purpose of the new corporation was to hold capital assets for the agency and to initiate a new set of counseling, training, and consultation services on a fee for service basis. The long range idea was that the new corporation would generate profit that could be pumped back into the agency as a means to offset recent decreases in the levels of federal and state funding available to the agency.

Discussion Question

Are the following smart business practices or breaches in ethical business practice?

● Funds from the agency are used to seed the private corporation.

- The private corporation leases space from the agency at far below market value.
- The private corporation routinely utilizes equipment and supplies of the agency.
- Agency staff supported by public grants perform clerical, accounting, administrative functions/activities on behalf of the private corporation.
- Staff who work at the private corporation are able to be paid salaries considerably above the market because of the overhead costs absorbed by the agency.
- The Executive Director of the agency also draws a salary from the private corporation.

The development of linked corporate structures has proved very beneficial to some not-for-profit service agencies while for others such experiments have resulted in a disastrous drain on agency resources. While the structure of the relationship between the two organizational entities raises a host of potential legal issues and legal violations, the overriding ethical concern in these situations is the question of who benefits from the arrangement. Additional concerns relate to compromises in ethical standards in the evolving relationship between the two related organizations. The dangers in this experiment include:

- *The private corporation diminishes rather than enhances the agency's service capacity by exerting a drain on agency resources. The relationship progressively compromises the agency's stated mission and values.*
- *The agency-private corporation relationship is structured to the personal financial advantage of a single individual or a small group of individuals.*
- *The misappropriation of resources from the agency to the private corporation breaches the principles of honesty and fidelity governing the relationship between the agency and its funding sources.*
- *The agency-private corporation relationship is used for purposes of deception, eg., hiding the true extent of financial rewards being accrued by key individuals.*
- *The misappropriation of agency resources to the private corporation extends to the corporation an unfair advantage not available to its competitors.*

Fee Structure and Billing

◇ ◇ **18** ◇ ◇

A hospital differentially allocates administrative overhead across its departments. The chemical dependency unit which maintains a high occupancy rate and a low bad debt ratio bears an inordinate share of administrative overhead. In short, they are allocated overhead costs far beyond those resources they actually receive from the hospital. Other units that may be necessary for the hospital to maintain but which are money losers, e.g., pediatrics and maternity, are allocated lower levels of overhead. Client fees for services through the chemical dependency unit are substantially higher than those set for other units at the hospital, partially due to this overhead influence.

Discussion Question

Comment on this practice whereby high fees paid by addicts for services indirectly subsidizes the care being received by other patients at the hospital.

This practice of arbitrarily and artificially manipulating overhead costs raises an ethical issue to the extent that costs to patients for various services are unfairly calculated. To avoid clients being forced to absorb costs completely unrelated to the services which they were rendered, the formula or method used to allocate costs should be clearly related to the actual overhead required to operate that portion of the overall organization. The goal is to accurately and fairly assess and allocate the true costs to each organizational unit.

◇ ◇ **19** ◇ ◇

A substance abuse program, in an effort to improve its collection of unpaid service fees, contracted with a bill collection agency.

Discussion Questions

Does providing the names of clients with unpaid bills to a collection agency constitute a violation of client confidentiality?

What about providing the names of past clients with unpaid bills to whom no communication was made at the time of service entry that the failure to pay bills would result in the involvement of a collection agency?

What are the ethical concerns inherent within the issue of fee collection?

Helping professions differ from other businesses in the recourse available to collect unpaid bills in that the act of turning over the name of a client to a collection agency could itself constitute a breach of confidentiality. To avoid problems related to confidentiality, it is important that fee collection procedures be discussed with clients at the beginning of treatment and that the agency's fee collection policies be explained. If the treatment program utilizes a collection agency, clients should be so apprised and asked to sign a release of information giving the agency permission to forward their name to the collection agency in the event of nonpayment. The helping agency's methods of fee collection should, to the greatest extent possible, be congruent with its service mission and not place undue strain on the agency-client relationship. Talking openly and candidly about fee payment problems and maintaining an openness to arrange for extended payment plans usually results in the agency being paid for its services without so alienating the client that they would refuse to seek future services from the agency.

◇ ◇ **20** ◇ ◇

A family, following months of concern, has their son assessed at a local substance abuse treatment program. The assessment recommendation is that the youth participate in a 45-day program of inpatient treatment. The parents are told that the "daily rate" is $295 per day (or $13,275 for the 45 days) which with their 80% insurance coverage they estimate would leave them about $2,650 to pay out of pocket. Following their son's treatment, they are shocked to receive a total bill of more than $20,000. It appears that the physician's services are not covered in the "daily rate" and that numerous other billable services are provided daily which are also not included within this rate.

Discussion Questions

What ethical values were compromised in this situation?

What guidelines or standards should be used in discussing service fees, billing, and payment policies with clients?

If the same services a client was seeking are available from another community agency at half the price, is there an ethical duty to inform the client of this alternative to lower cost services?

Communication to the parents in the above situation constitutes a breach of the informed consent process by failing to adequately apprise the parents of the full financial burden they would have to assume related to their son's treatment. This breach involved the failure to inform the parents that there were fees for many services not included in the daily inpatient charge, the nature of those services and related fees, and a reasonable estimate of what the parents' portion of the total treatment costs was likely to be. While there is some variation from client to client based on the precise menu of services each receives, use of a regularly updated average of total treatment costs is a more honest representation of costs than the "daily rate" used in the above vignette. The ethical demand is that clients have as full and accurate a picture as possible of service costs with which they can make the decision to pursue or not pursue service involvement.

◇ ◇ **21** ◇ ◇

A substance abuse treatment program following several years of problems in collecting co-payments (that portion of client fees not reimbursable via private insurance or other third party) implemented the following procedure: Services fees were raised approximately 30%, insurance companies were billed for the 50-80% of the costs of client service, and client co-payments were routinely written off as uncollectible.

Discussion Questions

Comment on the potential ethical issues raised by this practice.

What is your response to a justification of this practice which says writing off co-payments increases client access to services and decreases the financial burden on the client?

Many health and human service organizations have utilized some variation of the above procedure and justified it as a service to its clients. For an agency to reduce the co-payment portion or waive the co-payment fee to be paid by the client in cases of extreme hardship would be beneficial. In such cases the agency absorbs the loss of all or a portion of the co-payment and there would be no problem of fraud or deception of the insurance company. In the above case, however, agency fees are artificially raised so that what the agency is alleging to be 80% of their fee to the insurance company is actually 100% of their fee. This practice would constitute a breach of honesty and fidelity in the relationship between the agency and the insurance company. This practice would leave the agency open to potential charges of deception or fraud.

◇ ◇ **22** ◇ ◇

A residential substance abuse program provides as part of its standard charges "free aftercare." Each client going through treatment at this program may attend the 16-week aftercare program which consists of weekly support groups. The cost of the sixteen weeks of aftercare participation is built into the daily rate of residential treatment—meaning that clients pay for aftercare services regardless of whether such services are utilized. Sixty percent of the program's clients, who come from out of the county, rarely if ever attend aftercare groups. Only about 20% of local clients fully utilize available aftercare services.

Discussion Questions

Who, if anyone, is being harmed by the above practice?

What alternative exists to assure client access to aftercare services and to assure that such services are reasonably reimbursed?

There exists in the above vignette the same misrepresentation issues related to "free" services as that discussed earlier in the vignette about "free assessments." In the above vignette, however, there exists an additional issue that involves the practice of routinely charging for services that clients do not receive. By building charges for 16 aftercare groups for each client into the daily inpatient rate, this program is charging for services that more than half of its clientele will not receive. The effect of this practice is that clients and their insurance companies are paying for services that were never delivered. An alternative would be for the program to use local sub-contractors to provide aftercare services (paid for by the fees built into client charges) or charge clients for aftercare services on a per unit of service attended basis.

A hospital recently integrated its psychiatric and substance abuse treatment services into a single unit, partially to bypass increasingly restrictive inpatient admission and length of stay criteria imposed by third party payers on alcohol-drug treatment admissions. No such restrictions currently apply to patients admitted with a psychiatric diagnosis. Under the new unit structure, those substance abuse clients who appear to need extended care are given a primary psychiatric diagnosis, e.g., depression, and a secondary substance abuse diagnosis. This use of a "billable diagnosis" is rationalized by the view that the practice opens up avenues of service for clients that would otherwise be unattainable. Some of these patients (due to their financial status) would be denied access to services if it were not for this "billable diagnosis" practice.

Discussion Questions

Who are the good guys and the bad guys in this story?

Discuss the short- and long-term effect of this practice on the profession, the agency, individual staff members and current or potential clients?

This practice of "billable diagnosis" or "administrative diagnosis" violates the ethical principles of honesty and fairness upon which the relationship between the service provider and the insurance company is based. In spite of the rejoinder that such misrepresentation is the only way to get clients needed services, such misrepresentation violates the integrity upon which diagnosis and treatment is based and opens the practitioner to charges of deception and fraud—charges that could damage the reputation of the individual practitioner, damage the reputation of the program, and threaten the future accessibility of client services. The diagnosis should reflect an objective and accurate assessment of the client's clinical condition, not the status of the client's income or scope of insurance coverage. When accurate client diagnosis falls outside the boundary of insurance coverage, efforts can be made to assure access to services by:

- *providing plans for long-term payment by the client/family*
- *soliciting public support to subsidize services to the uninsured or underinsured*
- *providing services on a pro-bono basis, or*
- *referring clients to lower cost or publicly funded treatment alternatives.*

Alliances

Over the past two years an informal arrangement has been made between a private practice therapist and your inpatient program. The private therapist refers a large number of clients to inpatient substance abuse treatment. The inpatient program refers a large number of its clients to the therapist for on-going outpatient counseling following inpatient treatment.

Discussion Questions

Does this practice simply reflect a good utilization of community resources both by the program and the private therapist?

What ethical issues or problems, if any, could arise from this arrangement?

If, in the vignette above, the inpatient program paid the therapist a fee of $250 for each inpatient referral, most persons would readily raise ethical concerns about this practice of what has come to be called "fee splitting." And yet there is a thin line between the exchange of dollars for referrals and the practice of referring other clients (in addition to those referred by the therapist) for outpatient counseling with the therapist. The concern is that the best interests of particular clients may be compromised by the institutional self-interests inherent within such informal arrangements. Exceptionally close scrutiny must be maintained to assure the clinical integrity of the referral process—an assurance that referrals are being made to a particular therapist because it is judged that the therapist will provide the best possible services for this particular client, not because of the financial self-interests of the institution.

Dual Relationships

Conflict of Interests

 25 ◇ ◇

Agency vehicles for the last four years have all been purchased from an auto dealership owned by the President of the Board of the agency. All of the cars have been bought at or below market value, but without competitive bidding.

Discussion Questions

What ethical issues could be raised about these transactions?

What standard or process could facilitate decision-making in situations where staff, volunteers or board members might have, or might be perceived to have, a conflict of interest?

The concern raised by the above vignette is the potential for someone to exploit their role within the agency to receive undue advantage and financial gain. Although a superficial investigation would lead to the view that the President is selling cars to the agency at cost as a personal favor, a closer analysis may be warranted. Since the wholesale price a dealer pays for his or her merchandise is often prorated according to volume, the President of the Board reaps an indirect benefit from these transactions even though the agency gets the cars at cost. By influencing the agency's choice of makes and models of cars desired, the President could also use this mechanism as a way to move cars he could not otherwise sell. Another concern is whether the local community's perception of potential impropriety in such transactions damages the professional integrity of the agency. Opening up the process for competitive bidding reduces both real and perceived problems.

 26 ◇ ◇

Horace and Mary have been close friends and professional colleagues for more than ten years. During these years, Mary served as Director of a large substance abuse agency and Horace served as Director of a statewide professional advocacy group, they shared many professional battles and through the years developed a close relationship between their respective families. Horace has just been appointed by the Governor to direct the state agency responsible for the licensing, funding, and monitoring of substance abuse services. More than 80% of the funding of Mary's agency comes from the agency Horace now directs.

Discussion Questions

What ethical issues might arise for both Horace and Mary given the nature of their past personal and professional relationship?

Will Mary inevitably have special access to Horace, not available to Directors from other agencies?

What would be examples of how Mary could try to take undue advantage of this relationship?

The challenge in the above situation is to assure that the pre-existing personal and professional relationships do not interfere with the judgement and actions of either Horace or Mary. Mary must be careful not to exploit the prior relationship for special favors, while Horace must guard against loss of objectivity through granting special favors due to the nature and duration of their relationship or withholding normal favor to Mary out of fear of perceived favoritism.

Management of Facilities, Property and Supplies

 ◇ ◇ **27** ◇ ◇

Your agency receives donations of a whole range of goods and services from individuals and businesses throughout the service catchment area. In recent months, donations of non-durable food items have far exceeded the quantities needed for your residential programs. The Director, rather than turning such donations down, has begun to disperse non-durable food items which are not needed to the staff. The thinking of the Director is that staff are underpaid and any extra perks such as the food items are well-deserved.

Discussion Questions

Do you agree or disagree with this practice? What unforeseen problems and issues could arise related to this practice?

What alternative solution might exist to such surpluses in non-durable food items?

The ethical principal of fidelity commits us quite simply to keep our promises. In the above situation, the agency made an implicit promise when it solicited food items that these goods would be used to help feed clients involved in residential substance abuse rehabilitation. The dispersal of these items to staff—no matter how underpaid and deserving they may be—constitutes a breach of this promise. The actions, furthermore, if revealed publicly could jeopardize the willingness of other local businesses to provide donated goods and services and could lead to an overall deterioration in community support for the program. The potential damage to the reputation of the program resulting from disclosure of such practices would also have to be measured in reduced willingness of clients, families and other agencies to seek out the program's services. Many agencies handle this situation by reciprocal agreements to share such expendable supplies with other helping organizations and inform their donors of this practice.

◇ ◇ **28** ◇ ◇

One of the largest budget items for your residential program is the contract for food services which for the past two years has been awarded to Food Services, Inc. The President of Food Services, Inc. stops by today to drop off a "token of appreciation" for your business. Knowing your passionate and masochistic support for the Chicago Cubs, the president provides you (and your spouse) with a packaged free trip, hotel, and box seat tickets for an upcoming series with the St. Louis Cardinals.

Discussion Questions

As the Director of your agency, would you accept this offer?

What ethical issues, if any, could be involved in accepting this "token?"

What standards should govern agency—contractor/supplier relationships?

There are a number of issues and problems raised by this vignette. The first is that acceptance of the gift may create a sense of obligation to continue contracting with Food Services, Inc., which may or may not be in the best interests of the agency. The concern is that social or financial relationships (including receipt of gifts) with contractors might unduly influence contracting decisions at the expense of the organization. Any gift or special benefit received as a result of the contract should accrue to the agency. It was agency resources through which the contract was executed and any secondary benefits derived from the contract should go to the agency, not the personal benefit of one or more of its staff persons. The other concern with accepting the gift is that such acceptance creates a special relationship that could alter the equity of access to contracts by other community vendors.

Management of Human Resources

See Chapter Seven: Conduct in Professional Peer Relationships

Chapter Four

Personal Conduct

Nearly every profession in the course of its birth and evolution must address the boundary line between personal and professional conduct, between the individual's right to privacy and autonomy and the ethical and moral conduct that constitutes an implicit duty of the profession. Where and how this line is drawn is likely to differ from agency to agency, differ across programs within agencies, and differ from professional to professional. The vignettes in this chapter will help the reader explore where that line should be drawn by the agency or by himself or herself. This chapter will focus on the nature of the personal and professional duties and obligations that accompany service roles within the substance abuse field. It will explore the tension between professional duty and right to privacy.

Critical Incidents

Use of Alcohol/Drugs

◇ ◇ **29** ◇ ◇

You are a supervisor at a community social service agency that provides mental health and substance abuse treatment services. Your emergency crisis calls are handled by alternating staff from the mental health and substance abuse units. You have just received a formal complaint from the Medical Director of a local hospital regarding the following situation: the hospital emergency room called your agency to assess an adolescent who had been brought to the hospital by his family in a state of alcohol and drug intoxication. When the emergency on-call staff person from the agency arrived, the ER charge nurse noted the strong smell of alcohol on the worker's breath. The non-drinking parents, also smelling alcohol on the worker's breath, took their child and left the hospital after voicing their strong condemnation of the hospital. When asked about the situation, the worker, who to the best of your knowledge has no history of substance abuse, responds that he had one beer before his beeper went off, and that he was neither intoxicated nor impaired.

Discussion Questions

How would you respond to this situation?

Identify the ethical or performance issues that would be of concern to you.

Is "on-call time" personal time or professional time? If you feel it is professional time, what is the implication for key supervisory staff who may technically always be "on-call?"

What standards would be appropriate to address the issues raised in the above situation?

Many agencies have found it necessary to define explicit standards of professional conduct related to on-call duty. These standards include such issues as accessibility, professional appearance in situations involving face-to-face contact with clients or allied professionals, and drinking/drug use. The primary concern is that smelling alcohol on the breath of a service provider assessing the needs of alcohol and drug dependent persons would immediately destroy the professional credibility of the helping person. Most of the agencies who explore this issue define on-call time as professional time and prohibit drinking. The application of professional standards to on-call time assumes that there is a clear schedule or other delineation of when these standards do and do not apply. It is best if such scheduling also applies to supervisory or administrative staff. This structuring of on-call assures that the issue of alcohol-impairment in the chain of staff-supervisory decision-making in an emergency situation should never have to arise. It also assures that the line between on and off call is clear enough that the private lives of staff members are not totally consumed by their professional responsibilities.

◇ ◇ **30** ◇ ◇

You are an employee of a local substance abuse prevention and treatment agency. You are at a social gathering of 15 persons and observe a stranger in a state of extreme intoxication leaving the party by himself to drive home.

Discussion Questions

What, if anything, would you do?

Would your action differ if you were hosting the party?

Is there any increased duty to act or increased liability in such situations given the nature of our profession? Would failure to act in the above situation be comparable to a physician, who while dining at a restaurant, failed to intervene and assist a fellow patron who was having a heart attack?

The question in this vignette is not what should anyone do in response to a person intending to drive in a state of extreme intoxication, but whether there is any special duty for action in such a situation that emanates directly from one's professional training and role within the substance abuse field. It is very helpful for agencies to explore staff responsibilities in such situations and articulate values or standards to guide staff who find themselves in such circumstances. Most such discussions conclude that substance abuse workers do have a special duty to model assertive intervention with the intoxicated person who poses a threat to public safety. This duty springs from multiple sources: the worker's training to recognize alcohol-drug impairment, the worker's advocacy of such intervention to the public through his or her professional role, the imminent harm posed by the impaired driver, and the damage to the reputation of the worker and the agency that could result from failure to intervene.

◇ ◇ **31** ◇ ◇

More and more substance abuse agencies are aggressively addressing the issue of smoking. The emergence of restrictive smoking policies, the growing number of smoke-free treatment facilities, and the definition of nicotine addiction as part of a client's total pattern of substance abuse reflect this current trend. Some substance abuse agencies are taking the position that only non-smokers will be hired to work at the agency.

Discussion Questions

Given the unique nature of substance abuse counseling, are there special standards of personal conduct to which staff can and should be held accountable?

If staff are to be held to a professional standard related to smoking, what about obesity, gambling, workaholism or other patterns of behavior that are viewed by some as excessive or addictive behaviors?

Are these important ethical and/or professional practice issues or signs of growing over-intrusiveness of organizations into the personal lives of their employees?

The abuse of drugs by a substance abuse counselor would be an ethical breach in no less measure than the immoral conduct of a minister. In the substance abuse field, one's relationship with drugs and beliefs about drugs are work-related issues. (Bissell and Royce, 1987). The only thing that has prevented the experience of this ethical duty related to smoking is the historical failure of the culture (and the professional field) to define nicotine as a drug and the continued use of nicotine as an addiction. As this changes, the issue of smoking will be posed as an ethical issue for substance abuse workers. This suggests that ethical sensitivities and ethical standards can evolve over time as knowledge and perspectives change. Private behavior is a professional issue to the extent that private behavior affects professional performance. What some might consider private behavior are issues of professional conduct to the extent that smoking or other excessive behaviors compromise the reputation and ability of a person to work with addicted persons or carry the prevention message—in short, to perform his or her job duties. Each organization must draw this line in a way that is consistent with and supportive of its mission and philosophy. Professional standards related to other excessive and compulsive behaviors are likely to evolve as the understanding of the etiology, prevention and treatment of these conditions evolves.

For a discussion of these issues as they relate more specifically to prevention workers, see Chapter Nine.

◇ ◇ **32** ◇ ◇

Ben, one of the staff members who conducts remedial education classes for DUI offenders at your agency was arrested last Saturday night for DUI. The arrest occurred at a time Ben was not on duty, and there was no agency vehicle involved in the incident. To the best of your knowledge, Ben has no prior history of substance abuse and did not self-identify himself as recovering when he was hired.

Discussion Questions

Could Ben be subject to disciplinary action to include firing for such behavior or does such behavior on non-work time constitute private behavior that is none of the agency's business?

Would the issue be different if Ben worked as a bookkeeper and had no direct client contact?

Discussion of this vignette with workers in the substance abuse field usually focuses on the following points:

- *The innocence of the worker should be assumed until the facts of the case prove otherwise. If facts confirm the act of driving while intoxicated by the worker, the following points would be relevant.*
- *Driving under the influence of alcohol violates the ethical mandate of honesty because the behavior so contradicts the most basic tenants of DUI education presented by the worker in his or her professional role.*
- *The worker's behavior violated the principle of nonmaleficence not only in threatening the safety of others but in harming, via damage to reputation, the capacity of the worker and the agency for continued service.*
- *The worker could be subject to disciplinary action on the grounds of a direct link between the private behavior and the ability to perform his or her professional role.*
- *Response to the DUI of a bookkeeper would depend on the personnel standards and ethical or professional practice codes which have been defined by the agency and communicated to its staff. Lacking any explicitly relevant standards, there may not be a link between the*

worker's private conduct and the performance of his or her bookkeeping functions.

Relapse

◇ ◇ **33** ◇ ◇

Ray is a recovering alcoholic working as a counselor in your agency. He is both a trusted friend and valued colleague. Ray has two years of substance abuse counseling experience and up until a month ago had seven years of uninterrupted sobriety. A month ago, Ray experienced a short relapse (two days) following the sudden death of his spouse. He immediately re-engaged himself in his recovery program and is receiving grief counseling. Your agency has a policy that recovering counselors must have two years of continuous sobriety to work in the counseling program. No one knows about Ray's relapse at the agency, and Ray fears that disclosure of this event will cause him to lose his job. Ray seeks your advice and counsel as a friend and trusted co-worker at the agency.

Discussion Questions

How would you respond to Ray's request for advice?

What standard could guide staff when presented with a situation or condition in their personal life that could potentially influence the quality of their clinical practice?

Would you be under any ethical obligation to report Ray's relapse to a supervisor at the agency?

There are ethical issues for you and for Ray in the above vignette. Ray feels his rapid return to an active recovery program and his current emotional stability will allow him to continue to be effective in a counselor role but many would question whether he can independently make this judgement. There are additional concerns that withholding the information about his relapse is a breach of honesty—a misrepresentation of his recovery status—in the relationship with his employer, his professional peers and his clients. There is concern of whether maintaining the secrecy of his relapse will not pose an obstacle to his continued recovery. For you, the trust and confidence of a good friend and colleague must be weighed against loyalty to the agency and the profession as well as against the potential threats to clients and public safety posed by a worker whose addiction recovery and mental status is of uncertain stability. The struggle to sort the conflicting interests in this vignette are eased if the agency has discussed and formulated its values related to such eventualities. Nearly all of the appropriate intervention strategies are contingent upon breaking the secrecy of the relapse either through Ray's self-revelation to his supervisor or through your judgement that such disclosure must be made to the agency. Strategies that address different interests and needs in the above vignette could include:

- *removing Ray from his active counseling duties*
- *offering support of agency EAP services to assist Ray in re-establishing his recovery program and dealing with the loss of his wife*
- *exploring Ray's need for a medical leave of absence*
- *developing with Ray a strategy of communication to other staff and to Ray's clients*
- *developing a structure of increased supervisory review and support of Ray's clinical work (if a decision was made to not remove Ray from his current role)*
- *developing an individualized process of client termination and transfer of clinical responsibilities*
- *exploring alternative professional role responsibilities for Ray within the agency, and*
- *providing continuing support for Ray and the re-activation of his recovery program.*

Moral and Legal Standards

◊ ◊ **34** ◊ ◊

A counselor you supervise at your agency was recently arrested for solicitation of prostitution in a highly publicized, local undercover sting.

Discussion Questions

What would your response, if any, be to this counselor?

Would the response differ if your agency was in a remote rural area compared to a large metropolitan area?

Would your response be any different if the charges involved theft, statutory rape, assault, or illegal possession or sale of drugs?

A review of the codes of ethics governing a wide spectrum of helping professionals reveals the consistent inclusion of an ethical duty for professional helpers to be sensitive to prevailing legal and moral standards in their communities and to the adverse effects the violation of such standards can have on their and the agency's professional reputation and their service relationships with client families. The ethical command in this area may be even more intense on the substance abuse worker given the nature of our clients. Given the high prevalence of alcohol- and drug-related criminal activity of substance abuse clients, the substance abuse counselor has an even greater duty than in other human service settings to exemplify and model appropriate legal and moral conduct. In a similar manner, personal involvement with prostitutes may have implications that are particularly important within the substance abuse field. The fact that a high percentage of male and female prostitutes are alcohol-drug dependent makes such persons likely candidates for agency services. Personal conduct with such vulnerable populations should enhance their receptiveness to treatment rather than posing obstacles to such treatment. It is doubtful that the addicted prostitute in crisis would feel comfortable with the discovery that the agency which he or she has chosen to get help is staffed with "tricks" known from his or her life in the culture of addiction.

Financial Investments

◇ ◇ **35** ◇ ◇

Shana, the business manager for a large substance abuse agency, owns stock in FutureTech, a company that specializes in computer sales and service. All of the computer hardware and almost all of the computer software purchased by the agency in the last five years have been purchased from FutureTech.

Discussion Questions

What ethical issues could arise in this convergence between Shana's personal interests and professional responsibilities?

What problems could this arrangement potentially create for Shana and the agency?

The personal financial affairs of an employee are none of the organization's business until their existence alters how the employee performs in his or her professional role. The fact that the agency has purchased equipment from the company in which Shana has investments may be a coincidence and may have involved decisions over which Shana had little input or control. The ethical concern of personal investments, like the above, is the extent to which personal investments can create conflicts of interests in professional decision-making. To the extent that Shana's personal financial interests influence her decision-making within the agency and at the expense of the agency, Shana's actions would represent a breach in her promise to serve the best interests of the organization. It is appropriate for a worker to declare any outside financial interests that might bias his or her objectivity in a particular situation.

(For a discussion of the ethical issues raised by substance abuse workers having financial interests in alcohol or tobacco industries, see Chapter Nine)

Discrimination

◇ ◇ **36** ◇ ◇

Miriam works in a small substance abuse agency in which she performs both administrative-supervisory responsibilities and provides some direct client services. Miriam is also a member of a local social organization which has never had any members who were men or non-white.

Discussion Question

> Under what conditions, if any, would Miriam's membership in this organization raise issues of inappropriate ethical and professional conduct?

Miriam's membership in the above organization would not necessarily mean that she has participated in any personal acts of discrimination. The fact that an organization has no men nor persons of color does not in and of itself prove the existence of discriminatory practices thus supporting an accusation that Miriam belongs to an organization that is blatantly sexist or racist in its orientation. But are these questions even appropriate to be raised? As long as Miriam does not commit overt acts of discrimination on the job, is her personal conduct away from work her own business even if that business might involve discriminatory behavior? Does Miriam stop representing the substance abuse profession and her agency when she leaves the work environment? As these questions have been raised within state associations of substance abuse counselors, a growing number of such organizations are saying that one's duty to the values implicit in the service profession do not stop when one leaves the job site each day. More and more of these agencies are stating that the professional must conduct his or her private life in a manner that does not compromise the reputation and integrity of the profession or otherwise decrease the willingness of clients to seek service within our organizations. Given the increased number of people of color, women and Gays and Lesbians receiving prevention and treatment services, sensitivity and competent responses to the needs of these persons is an absolutely essential ingredient for all workers. Discriminatory acts—even in one's private life—would reflect the lack of such sensitivity and competence and pose threats to the profession and the agency's capacity to serve these populations of clients.

Personal and Agency Reputation

◇ ◇ **37** ◇ ◇

You have just relocated to a new community and taken a position with a local substance abuse prevention and treatment agency. You have been invited to a party by a casual acquaintance and after your arrival find that illicit drugs are being openly used by many of the persons there.

Discussion Questions

How would you respond to this situation?

What situations or ethical dilemmas could arise from such a situation?

Is there any collective wisdom about how to handle incidents that could potentially damage our professional reputation as well as the agency's reputation?

One does not cease wearing the mantle of identification with the profession or with the agency simply because it is Saturday night. The ethical admonition to "first, do no harm" can be extended beyond our service procedures with clients to include managing our personal conduct in ways that avoid harm to our personal and institutional reputations. There are any number of unforeseen consequences potentially arising within the above vignette. Helping persons have been present and publicly identified in raids of such parties. Persistent and potentially damaging allegations or rumors about use of drugs have been traced to one's presence in such situations. Persons (potential clients) who know of your agency affiliation could, based on your presence at the party, eschew agency services on the assumption that staff are "dirty." Many workers have learned the painful lesson that it is best to avoid situations involving illegal or immoral activity in which one's physical presence could be interpreted as participation or approval.

◇ ◇ **38** ◇ ◇

Tim has worked as a therapist at your agency for the past four years, splitting his time between the adult and adolescent outpatient programs. Tim is gay, a fact that he has kept well-hidden from the community and the agency. Tim is considering "coming out of the closet." There is a forthcoming public hearing on the special needs of Gay and Lesbian clients in treatment at which he would like to speak. Tim feels that acknowledging his own homosexuality would add weight to his testimony. He has also felt himself moving closer to this decision for his own personal feelings of sanity and self-respect. Tim's one concern is the potential repercussions this decision could have on his job. He fears that his disclosure could trigger public reaction in this midwestern, rural community that could jeopardize his professional reputation and the reputation of the agency. Tim seeks your advice as a trusted friend and co-worker.

Discussion Questions

What advice might you offer Tim?

What ethical or professional practice issues are involved in this situation?

Is there any collective wisdom or standard that could guide staff facing such a situation?

If, in response to Tim's public disclosure of his homosexuality, a number of parents withdraw their children from treatment at the agency, the schools stop referrals to the adolescent program under community pressure, and a community group proposes that funds for the adolescent program be cut and transferred to another agency—an obvious effort to scapegoat Tim — how should the agency respond to these events?

Tim must explore how his personal needs can be reconciled with the needs of his agency and the needs of his clients. The decision to publicly disclose his homosexuality involves weighing the risks and benefits of such disclosure to himself and others along with the benefits and harm of continued secrecy. It involves exploring the potential short- and long-term effects such disclosure will have on the agency and the immediate effects such disclosure may have on the clients and families with whom he is working. It also involves weighing the harmful effect his silence has in perpetuating homophobic attitudes and discriminatory practices against Gays and Lesbians. While the decision of whether to disclose is a personal one, how such disclosure should be handled, if that is desired, would be very appropriate to bring into the process of supervision. This allows the agency some time to prepare for any potential public reactions and allows some structured time for Tim and his supervisor to talk about how the knowledge of this disclosure should be handled clinically with clients/families.

*A related issue that is likely to arise in the future involves the issues of "outing." The process of disclosing the homosexuality of public figures without their consent raises a number of ethical issues. The issue could arise where a gay substance abuse professional publicly identifies one or more other health or human service professionals as being gay without the consent of these persons. The question will be: is such disclosure a breach of **professional** ethics, particularly where the knowledge of the other person's sexual orientation was learned in the professional context.*

Personal Replenishment

◇ ◇ 39 ◇ ◇

Gary is by everyone's agreement one of the best workers at your agency. In some ways, he is too good. Gary works an excessive number of hours every week. He is clearly married to his job. Some staff have expressed personal concern about Gary's health, his excessive smoking, his weight, and his lack of exercise. Periodic admonitions about his excessive hours and poor habits of self-care have done little to effect Gary's pattern of work/living.

Discussion Questions

Is this a performance problem?

Are there any ethical issues related to care of oneself in the helping professions?

Is there a standard of personal care or replenishment to which staff should aspire?

Is there an organizational value related to this area that you would want reflected in an agency Code of Professional Practice?

Would these values only apply to staff in direct services roles with clients or in roles in which they represent the agency to the public? Would these values apply to clerical staff, maintenance staff, and administrative staff?

There are at least two values that could be raised in response to the above vignette—the value of self-replenishment and the value of self-care.

The value of self-replenishment is based on the supposition that sustained service to others is only possible if the helping person has and utilizes resources for personal replenishment outside the professional role. By participating in nourishing activities and relationships outside of the work setting, the helping professional is able to enter the service setting without his or her unmet needs contaminating the service relationship. In a similar manner, acts of self-care model the legitimacy of one's own needs and establish a foundation of health from which the service process is initiated. The failure of a helping professional to adequately mirror values of self-replenishment and self-care is an ethical issue to the extent that:

- *the individual models poor standards of physical and emotional health to his or her clients*

- *the unmet needs of the care-giver interfere with effective service delivery to clients or otherwise prevent the performance of one's professional duties, and*
- *the lifestyle of the worker contradicts and undermines the values the agency represents to its clients and to the community.*

As noted in our discussion of an earlier vignette, the line between personal and professional life should be drawn by the agency at the point one's personal behavior negatively effects work performance: (e.g., service relationships with clients, team relationships with professional peers, and service relationships within the community). Agencies can affirm this value of self-care by articulating it as an aspirational value within the Code of Professional Practice. One agency's standard reads as follows:

> "Working with individuals and families in emotional crisis can be both physically and emotionally depleting for staff. The health of both clients and staff hinge on the ability of each worker to seek physical and emotional replenishment outside the work setting. Center staff are encouraged to develop a network of replenishing relationships and activities that support their overall health and increase their ability to enter into nurturing relationships with clients."

Chapter
Five

Professional Conduct

There are many areas of professional conduct within the substance abuse field that do not involve issues related to our business practices or our relationships with service recipients. Issues of ethics, etiquette, and appropriate protocol can arise that fall outside these areas. One of the things that defines a profession is the articulation of standards to guide professional conduct within a broad spectrum of professional endeavors. This chapter will explore such issues as they relate to professional self-development, personal appearance, competence, representation of credentials, use of agency resources, use of information, secondary employment, and public statements. Clear standards of ethics and etiquette have not been defined in all of these areas within the substance abuse field. The critical incidents presented within this chapter can assist the individual worker or the substance abuse agency in defining values and standards applicable to these areas.

Critical Incidents

Self-development

◇ ◇ **40** ◇ ◇

Jeremy, a counselor at your agency, consistently resists exposure to in-service training and avoids participation in outside workshops and seminars. His rationale for this resistance ranges from being overwhelmed with seeing clients to a dislike of travel. As a result, Jeremy has not attended any significant training activity within the past two years.

Discussion Questions

Are there ethical issues inherent in the pursuit, or failure to pursue, new knowledge within one's profession?

What standard do you feel should guide staff conduct in this area?

The principle of self-development permeates nearly all defined professions. This principle establishes the professional duty to stay abreast of new knowledge and to acquire new skills throughout the development of one's career. While the idea of self-development is admirable and consistent with the ethical value of competence, an even greater ethical duty emanates from the potential harm that could be created through the lack of self-development. Substance abuse prevention and treatment professionals have a duty to incorporate the latest technology into their service interventions with individuals, institutions, and communities. The failure to pursue self-development denies service consumers the benefits that could accrue from new knowledge. Continued education and training are more than optional perks; they are professional and ethical mandates.

Personal Appearance

A very well-dressed client arrives at the agency at 7:30 A.M. and nervously announces that he has an 8:00 intake appointment. The receptionist greets him politely and offers him a seat in the reception room. The receptionist views this client fidgeting impatiently, his eyes darting to the door each time it opens, perhaps wondering if he might be recognized or possibly concerned about what other "clients" look like who come here. It is clear to the receptionist that sitting in the waiting area of a public service agency is quite a new and discomforting experience for this obviously well-to-do client. The entry door of the agency opens and a man walks in with jeans, a badly wrinkled shirt, cigarette hanging from his mouth with smoke curling up over bleary eyes and disheveled hair. The man walks to the reception desk, utters one word—"COFFEE!"—and leaves the reception area with a fresh cup of coffee provided by the receptionist. The impeccably dressed client who has watched this transaction wide-eyed, looks at the receptionist and says: "Some of the people who come here must be in pretty bad shape." The receptionist is speechless because the person who triggered this statement is the therapist scheduled to see this client in five minutes.

Discussion Questions

Provide any comments you might have on ethical or professional practice issues in this situation.

If you were the receptionist, how would you respond to this situation?

There are two issues raised in the above vignette: 1) the desired response of staff who observe any condition potentially compromising the quality of service or the safety or health of a client, and 2) the ethics and etiquette of professional appearance.

The receptionist could take the position that it was not her responsibility to get in the middle of this situation—the "it's not in my job description" position—or she could take some action to address the impending discomfort of the client. Which action she takes will depend not only on her personal characteristics and values but, to a great degree, the values and expectations of staff set by the organization. When the event portrayed above really happened, it occurred in an agency with a strongly instilled value that the care and comfort of clients was everyone's concern. The receptionist walked into the Clinical Director's office and briefly described the morning's events as portrayed above and expressed her concern about the likely discomfort of the client when he discovered that who he thought was a severely impaired client was to be his therapist. The supervisor proceeded to observe the therapist, informed the therapist that the supervisor would be seeing the therapist's 8:00 appointment, conducted the intake himself, and then met with the therapist to address the issue of professional appearance. This expectation for action to address client comfort and safety—which the receptionist acted upon in the above vignette—is an important component of a strong, service-oriented organizational culture.

There are many interests that influence appropriate professional dress of persons working in substance abuse agencies. The value of respect for clients (and professional peers) dictates standards of cleanliness. Disregard for appearance reflects a lack of respect or importance attributed to the client—a kind of "professional slumming." The service provider's professional appearance should signal to the client that the work they are to do together is important and serious. Respect dictates that dress not be sexually provocative. Other interests that influence how workers in the field present themselves is the reputation of the individual worker, the reputation of the agency and the reputation of the field. There is an implicit expectation that one's personal appearance will enhance and not detract from such reputations.

The issue of professional dress is difficult to define in many organizations due to the differences in program activities and roles for which different standards of comfort and appropriateness apply. The appropriate professional dress for an EAP counselor working with predominantly white collar companies would be different from a recreational therapist in an adolescent inpatient program or an outreach worker serving homeless alcoholics. Many agencies seeking to define professional standards of appearance do so by stating the expectation that workers will follow the standards of appearance that are appropriate for their program, their role, and the nature of their scheduled daily activities. This allows for standards to be set at the program or unit level and modified by the supervisor for appropriateness to daily activities.

Recognition of Limitations

◇ ◇ **42** ◇ ◇

Sarah administers the Minnesota Multiphasic Personality Inventory (MMPI) to all clients assigned to her within the inpatient program within which she works. Sarah is quite taken with the MMPI as an assessment instrument and has read everything she can get her hands on related to the MMPI and alcoholism. Although the MMPI's she is administering are not being placed in her clients' clinical records, indirect references to MMPI findings are being made in client progress notes and are frequently referenced by Sarah during clinical staffings of clients. The issue of concern is that Sarah has no formal training in psychological testing. She is a certified addictions counselor but there is nothing in her professional history that validates her ability to administer and interpret the MMPI.

Discussion Questions

What are your thoughts about this practice?

As a new supervisor assigned to Sarah's unit, how would you respond to this situation?

Haas and Malouf (1989) have defined three components of professional competence: 1) the knowledge to fully understand a particular issue, 2) the skill to effectively apply this knowledge, and 3) the judgement to know when, where and under what conditions to use, or not use, this skill. The ethical demand is to practice within the boundaries of one's own competence. That boundary is defined primarily by one's professional training and professional experience. In the case above, Sarah's administration, scoring and interpretation of the MMPI involve areas of professional practice for which she has not been trained, lacks supervised experience, and for which she possesses no external credential to validate her competence in this area. While she may have some technical knowledge of the MMPI, her lack of formal training exposes her to potential errors in technical skill and judgement that could result in potential harm to her clients. Sarah's use of information derived from the MMPI would constitute a breach of the ethical principle of competence.

Competence to perform may be defined by educational training, licensure or certification, or in some cases, through an actual demonstration of knowledge or skill. A growing number of substance abuse programs, particularly those involved in the JCAHO accreditation process, have implemented and have begun to refine a process of clinical privileging to address this ethical principle of competence. Like the hospital setting in which each doctor is granted privileges to perform certain medical procedures within the scope of his or her training and experience, the privileging process involves the delineation of the specific tasks each substance abuse worker may perform based on his or her academic and experiential preparation and his or her role in the agency. Within this system, workers may not perform activities for which they do not have clinical privileges. In the case above, Sarah would have been prohibited from administering or interpreting psychological tests because she would not have privileges to conduct this activity.

◇ ◇ **43** ◇ ◇

Bill, a therapist in an outpatient substance abuse agency, was raised in a family that took in numerous foster children who had been physically and/or sexually abused. Having seen the physical and emotional ravages of such abuse in his foster brothers and foster sisters, Bill has always viewed the perpetrators of such abuse with great hostility. In his few years in the counseling field, he has not been involved in assessing or treating any child abusers. Today, Bill recognizes the name of a court referred intake assessment as a person who has appeared prominently in the local newspapers due to his arrest for a particularly brutal beating of his five year old son. Bill's evaluation could have a significant influence on whether this client gets probation and treatment or incarceration.

Discussion Questions

What should Bill do regarding this evaluation?

What should any staff member do in response to any unique match between themselves and a particular client that would potentially contaminate their objectivity and clinical effectiveness?

How does one handle a situation like the above when one works alone or is in a similar situation in which there are no options for transferring a client to another worker?

The vignette above illustrates a situation in which an otherwise competent worker could have that competence compromised because of the unique characteristics or circumstances of a particular client. All helping professionals experience problems of countertransference with some clients that can impede the relationship-building and service delivery process. Many of these problems can be resolved through self-awareness of potential bias and supervisory consultation. There may, however, be areas of bias so strong as to make such resolution impossible. Under such circumstances the worker has a responsibility to identify this problem with his or her supervisor and seek a reassignment of the client to a person who can more objectively and more adequately assess and respond to their needs. While many workers may hesitate to acknowledge such a problem to their supervisor for fear it will reflect on their competence or motivation, such notification reflects a high level of ethical sensitivity and professionalism.

◇ ◇ **44** ◇ ◇

Counselors and other non-medical interdisciplinary team members in substance abuse programs can often be heard giving advice to clients about the dangers of mood-altering medications. Such dialogue inevitably triggers a give-and-take about specific medications—which are "safe" and which are "risky" for the alcoholic or addict in recovery. These questions usually elicit a professional opinion or recommendation.

Discussion Questions

Are substance abuse professionals ethically bound to address issues of secondary drug use with their clients, or does this role for nonmedically trained members of the team constitute a gross breach of ethical conduct—practicing beyond one's training and competence?

How would you draw the boundary between appropriate and inappropriate professional conduct in this area?

What are the responsibilities of the substance abuse counselor who works in an area where no medical expertise is available for consultation with clients?

The line defining the boundaries of knowledge and appropriate role behavior has not been clearly defined for the above vignette within the substance abuse field. It may be possible, however, to define at least the ends of the continuum from appropriate to inappropriate conduct. It is within the province of the substance abuse counselor to speak of the abuse potential of prescribed psychoactive drugs and the potential risks such drugs may pose to the recovering alcoholic or addict. It is not within the boundaries of competence of most substance abuse counselors, unless they are also trained in medicine or psychopharmacology, to speak authoritatively about:

- *the appropriateness or inappropriateness of a particular medication for a particular client or for a particular condition*
- *drug dosages that would be safe or unsafe for a particular client, or*
- *the contraindications or potential side-effects of various prescribed medications.*

While the substance abuse counselor may have acquired considerable knowledge over the years about various prescribed drugs, he or she lacks the specific training to pronounce judgement about the risks/benefits of a particular drug on a particular client. The counselor should defer to his or her medical consultants when queried about such issues. Medical consultants who have expertise in treating persons with addictive disorders can answer such questions based on both their knowledge of the drugs and the unique medical and addiction history of the particular client. Where such medical expertise is not available for consultation with clients, the counselor can refer the client to a growing number of books written by physicians who address the issues related to prescribed medications for persons in addiction recovery. The danger is that the counselor, by overstepping the boundaries of competence will, through oversimplification or misinformation, threaten the health or safety of the client. The counselor making pronouncements about prescribed medications should be very explicit about the basis and limits of knowledge from which he or she speaks.

◇ ◇ **45** ◇ ◇

Maribeth, a substance abuse counselor in a remote rural area, has a client that needs special counseling related to childhood sexual abuse. There are no local mental health services and no geographically accessible persons who have been trained or have prior experience counseling client's around sexual abuse issues.

Discussion Questions

Given the client's current emotional pain, would it be unethical for Maribeth to fail to counsel the client regarding these experiences?

Given Maribeth's lack of training and experience in this area, would it be unethical for her to attempt such counseling outside the boundaries of her current expertise? If you were Maribeth, what would you do?

While the ethical command to practice within the boundaries of one's own competence is a noble one, there are numerous instances, like the one above, where this command conflicts with the desire and duty to address a client's immediate needs. In an ideal world, Maribeth would have alternative resources who were trained and experienced in addressing sexual abuse issues. But in the real world, she is in an area where no such services exist that are both geographically accessible and affordable to her client. Under such circumstances, Maribeth might seek a solution that represents the best effort to address the client's needs while minimizing the potential for harm resulting from Maribeth's lack of prior training and experience. She might agree to counsel her client on these issues while seeking technical support through:

- *reading books and journal articles on the counseling of persons sexually abused as children*
- *finding and attending one or more workshops that would increase her knowledge of how best to assist this client, and*

- *identifying and seeking an outside clinical consultant to help supervise (even by phone if such expertise was not geographically accessible) her work with the client.*

Representation of Credentials

◇ ◇ **46** ◇ ◇

Your agency just received a contract to provide managed mental health care for a local hospital. You have agreed to provide this care through three of the senior therapists at the agency. Following signing of the contract, the hospital requests that verification of the credentials of the therapists be provided. Two of the therapists immediately comply, while the third begins what will be a long string of delays and excuses as to why the educational credentials cannot be supplied, e.g., diplomas were lost, there are delays getting transcripts sent. Getting somewhat concerned, you review the employee's personnel file and discover that the employee came with glowing recommendations from former employers but that no verification was made of the employee's education and training. Before you investigate further, the employee in question resigns, reporting that he has taken a position at another agency with a substantial raise in salary.

Discussion Questions

As a supervisor in this situation, what, if anything, would you do?

Is the verification of employee credentials an ethical issue and should such verification be maintained on all employees?

Should the supervisor in the above situation contact the director of the agency to which the staff person is going to express his or her suspicions about the worker's credentials?

Is there an ethical mandate for the supervisor to continue some action related to documentation of the worker's credentials as a protection of public safety or would such action constitute an invasion of privacy of the staff person who has now left the agency?

The protection of the health and safety of clients and the protection of the reputation of the agency demand that the credentials of all staff be verified and accurately represented to clients and the community. In the historical development of many substance abuse organizations, there were periods in which credentials of staff were never verified. Emerging fields, due to their lack of such rigorous scrutiny, are vulnerable for deception by persons who bring great exploitive proclivities along with their fabricated educational and/or work histories. Verification of credentials should be submitted and validated BEFORE a worker begins the performance of his or her professional duties with clients.

◇ ◇ **47** ◇ ◇

It has come to your attention that a new detox counselor who you supervise is grossly misrepresenting his length of time working in the substance abuse field in his self-introduction to other professionals within the community. This counselor has apparently divided his "experience in the field" into three phases—the number of years he drank, the number of years in early recovery, and the number of years he has actually worked as a counselor—and decided to simply report the total number of years represented in all the phases. According to this formula, he has "16 years experience in the field" versus the one year he has worked as a detox counselor.

Discussion Questions

How would you respond to this situation?

What ethical issues are involved in the representation of work experience?

The misrepresentation of the length of work experience is no different than the misrepresentation of an academic credential—particularly in the substance abuse field which has often valued depth of experience on an equal par with academic preparation. The counselor should be confronted and told that no matter how benign his intentions, his current references to "16 years experience in the field" constitute a misrepresentation of his professional credentials and that such references should stop immediately.

Use of Agency Resources

◇ ◇ **48** ◇ ◇

Ginny frequently takes pens and legal pads from the office home with her in case she decides to work on a particular project in the evening. The problem is that these office supplies never seem to find their way back to the office.

Discussion Question

What ethical issues are involved in the use or misuse of agency resources?

The ethical principles of honesty, fidelity and stewardship are potentially all involved in the above vignette. There is a breach of fidelity when resources are given and received with the understanding that they will be utilized for agency business but are subsequently taken for personal use outside the work environment. When agency resources are diverted to personal use, additional resources that could have gone to support service delivery must now be re-allocated to make up the deficit. This often represents an area more characterized by "moral drift" than malicious intent. The homes of staff for whom the thought of stealing from the agency would be reprehensible can be filled with an assortment of supplies from the agency without the staff having any awareness that the continued presence of these items in their homes constitutes, by consequence if not intent, a theft of agency resources. There are similar ethical concerns related to the use of other agency resources: misuse of staff time, use of phones for personal calls, misrepresentation of travel expenses, use of agency vehicles for personal activity. The appropriate stewardship of agency resources must be a value raised to a high level of professional consciousness to avoid the problems of "moral drift" described above.

Use of Information for Personal Gain

◇ ◇ **49** ◇ ◇

You are seeing the vice-president of a local company in outpatient counseling. In today's session the client is extremely disturbed about news he has just received. The financial reports for the company have just been completed and quarterly sales have dropped so precipitously that he fears the public announcement in two weeks will trigger a dramatic fall in stock price for the company and trigger a call for a shakeup in company leadership. The client communicates this information within the context of the counseling relationship, unaware that you recently inherited more than 400 shares of stock in the company. If the stock drops as far as your client projects, your stock will drop more than $4,000 in value.

Discussion Question

Do you sell your stock prior to the public announcement?

The use of information obtained in the therapeutic setting outside that setting for the financial gain of the therapist is not only unethical, but sometimes, as in the case above, illegal. The use of special knowledge gained from the counseling relationship—not available to the general public—to make decisions on the sale or purchase of stock would fall within the parameters of what is referred to as "insider trading." The use of this information for the personal gain of the therapist would be a breach of ethical conduct and a potential violation of law. If such misuse of information were discovered by the client, it could seriously undermine the integrity of the counseling relationship. Any public exposure of this use could damage the reputation of the counselor and the agency—compromising the capacity for continued service due to the loss of public confidence.

Secondary Employment

◇ ◇ **50** ◇ ◇

Lana, a full time counselor at your agency, is also involved in providing counseling services through a private practice in the same community served by the agency.

Discussion Questions

Which of the following behaviors would be of concern to the agency as professional conduct issues and which behaviors would you want addressed in that portion of the Code of Professional Practice that addresses ethical and conflict of interest issues in secondary employment?

1. Lana is providing the same services through the private practice that she is providing through the agency. In short, she is both an employee and a competitor of the agency.
2. Lana visibly identifies her affiliation with the agency in the promotional materials for her private practice.
3. Lana responds to crisis calls from private practice clients during working hours at the agency.
4. Lana receives calls to schedule, cancel and change private practice appointments at the agency.
5. Lana refers/channels agency clients into her private practice.
6. There are some clients that Lana sees both at the agency and at her private practice.
7. Lana uses agency time, e.g., attendance at inter-agency meetings, to market her private practice.
8. Lana uses her agency office to see private practice clients on a routine or emergency basis.
9. Lana uses proprietary products or information from the agency for her financial benefit in the private practice.
10. Lana consistently requests attendance at workshops (to be paid for by the agency) which include knowledge and skills more applicable to her private practice work than her agency role.

What potential problems could arise if the secondary employment involved working part-time for a competitor of the agency or a primary funding source of the agency in which the staff person is employed full-time?

The potential range and complexity of ethical issues that can arise from secondary employment are illustrated in the above list. The dual roles of employee and competitor raise potential conflicts of interests and conflicts of loyalties. The use of the agency name in the promotion of the employee's private practice exploits the name and reputation of the center and may deceptively imply agency involvement or endorsement of the services provided through the private practice. The use of agency time and resources (telephones, office) to support one's private practice without formal negotiation with the agency constitutes a misuse of such resources. Channeling agency clients into one's private practice, by diverting paying clients, reduces the total resources available to the agency for service delivery. This practice may inject financial self-interest as a source of bias in the client assessment and service delivery process. Seeing clients both at the agency and in private practice creates a dual relationship with the client that can result in both role confusion and role conflict.

The nature and conduct of secondary employment, particularly the conduct of similar services on a private basis, can, in addition to the issues raised above, damage the reputation of the individual practitioners involved, damage the reputation of the agency and provide a source for disruption of team relationships within the agency. Due to the scope of such effects, each agency should establish clear guidelines governing the ethical and professional conduct related to secondary employment.

Publishing

◇ ◇ **51** ◇ ◇

Robert, a supervisor at a community substance abuse treatment agency, assigned several staff to research and write papers on various issues related to the assessment and treatment of clients who presented concurrent patterns of substance abuse and psychiatric illness. When these assignments were completed, Robert wrote an introductory chapter, edited the staff materials, and published the manual through the agency. Robert listed himself as the sole author of the manual, with other staff who contributed neither listed as co-authors nor acknowledged for their contributing role.

Discussion Questions

Discuss the ethical issues in this situation.

What suggested guidelines or standards might be considered to prevent this kind of situation?

The principles of honesty demands that authorship of documents presented to the public be accurately represented. The principle of justice demands that credit for work should be proportionate to one's contribution. Both ethical principles were violated in the above case. Many hard feelings and misunderstandings can be avoided if agencies clearly delineate policies governing authorship of professional products prepared at the agency. Recommended etiquette for the appropriate acknowledgement of contributions for a written product would be the following:

the principal author (name listed first) should be that person who had the most direct responsibility for the design, conduct of the research, interpretation and writing of the material in the manual. Co-authorship should be shared by all persons who shared leadership in these same functions. Persons who provided significant supporting roles should be acknowledged in a preface or in a footnote to the manual. Institutional contributors to the work—whether through funding of the project or support of staff time—should also be acknowledged.

◇ ◇ **52** ◇ ◇

You have written a program manual which is being published by your agency for sale to other agencies. In preparing a direct mail flyer on the manual, you have solicited reviews from four nationally known persons in the field whose words you would like to appear on the brochure supporting the quality of the material. One of these personages who has known you for quite some time suggests that she has no time to review the manuscript or prepare comments but that you are welcome to write your own suitable comments and attribute them to her when they appear on the brochure.

Discussion Question

What do you do?

The misrepresentation of your own words as those of the recognized expert constitutes a breach of honesty even if the expert has given you permission for such action. While the inclusion of the fourth expert's name on the brochure would be attractive from a marketing perspective, an ethical response would be to decline the offer and use the three remaining reviews in the promotion of the manual.

Respect for Proprietary Products

◇ ◇ **53** ◇ ◇

Randy was the lead therapist for four years in an innovative project designed to work with chemically dependent men who presented with histories of physical violence toward family members. During this period, the team developed a number of assessment instruments, program designs, roughly drafted descriptions of the intervention and treatment process and client educational materials. At the end of four years, Randy left the agency and spent a considerable amount of time updating and expanding the above materials which he then was able to get published. Although the agency and other team members were acknowledged in the introduction to the book, the materials were published without consultation with the agency, and copyrighted under Randy's name, with all potential royalties being paid to Randy.

Discussion Questions

Comment on any ethical issues inherent within this situation.

Who do you think "owns" these materials?

What if these were materials that Randy had himself brought to the agency and it was the agency who had copyrighted and published the materials?

Many hard feelings and misunderstandings can spring from the failure to clarify issues of ownership in situations like the above. The general rule is that products developed on work time belong to the agency. In the case above, the original materials—instruments, written treatment designs, and all other written products—clearly represent proprietary products owned by the agency. It would have been advisable for Randy to approach the agency and request formal permission to use and expand the original materials. Arrangements for co-authorship or acknowledgement of the agency's contribution in the original work upon which the book was based could have been negotiated at this time. Discussion of any portion of the royalties due to the agency from sale of the book could also have been discussed at this early point in the process. If Randy had brought much of the original material with him to the agency and the agency had asked him to continue development of the material for use by the agency, Randy should have clarified the status of ownership of the materials before proceeding with the development work.

◇ ◇ **54** ◇ ◇

In a highly competitive substance abuse treatment environment, Troy left one program to take a position with its primary competitor. In the earliest weeks at the new program, he is asked many questions about the program which he just left. The questions solicit details of his former program's financial and clinical operations that Troy would not have disclosed to outsiders while he worked for the program.

Discussion Questions

Does Troy's ethical responsibility for confidentiality of proprietary information stop with his exit from the program?

Should Troy, out of loyalty to his new employer, disclose information that would help strengthen the program position in the market and improve the quality of their clinical operations?

If you were Troy, how would you respond to such questions?

Troy is being asked information, not with the intent of improving the quality of services to clients, but to improve the competitive positioning of his new agency in the substance abuse treatment marketplace. As an employee at his former agency, there was an implicit agreement that confidential program information would not be disclosed to persons outside the program. Just as the ethical demand for client confidentiality does not end with the termination of counseling services, the demand to hold confidential proprietary program information does not end with one's termination of employment unless there are other overriding commands, e.g., imminent threat to health and safety of clients, threats to public safety, etc. Troy is free to share his knowledge and skill but the disclosure of propriety information that could harm the competitive position of his old employer would be a breach of his promises of loyalty and discretion.

Use of Name and Professional Judgement

◇ ◇ **55** ◇ ◇

Rory, a counselor that you once worked with, is calling to request that you write a letter of reference in support of his application to work in an adolescent treatment center. During the time you worked with Rory, you had serious concerns about both his clinical competence and his ethical judgement.

Discussion Question

What do you say in response to his request?

This is a difficult situation in which the potential to hurt the feelings of an acquaintance must be weighed against the potential harm this person could do if misplaced in a helping role. The ethical command is to avoid becoming an accomplice in the placement of someone in a caretaking role who could through breaches of competence or judgement harm clients, a substance abuse agency, the professional field, or the public. In practice, managing this command differs widely from person to person, to include the following responses:

- *telling the individual quite candidly that you would not feel comfortable writing such a letter of recommendation because of concerns you have about his or her knowledge or skills*
- *telling the individual you would be uncomfortable writing the letter of recommendation because of the length of time since you had worked with him or her*
- *telling the individual you are overwhelmed with work and will not have time to prepare such a letter*
- *agreeing to write the letter but never getting around to it, or*
- *writing a letter that is so lukewarm in its praise that any potential employer would be able to intuit your reservations about the person.*

Public Statements

◇ ◇ **56** ◇ ◇

You have become active in supporting a political issue that is very unpopular in your local community. To date, there has been no conflict between your role as a supervisor in a local substance abuse program and your outside political activities. You have now been asked to serve as spokesperson for the grassroots political organization which will involve frequent interaction with the public and the press.

Discussion Questions

What ethical issues might arise in these dual roles?

What standards could assure the separation of these roles?

The challenge in this vignette is to avoid harming your professional reputation and the reputation of the agency without compromising your rights of free speech and political participation. Perhaps the most important strategy in this situation is to rigorously separate one's professional role from one's personal/political role. This separation would entail the following actions:

- *not utilizing your agency affiliation to add support or credibility to your political position*
- *avoiding the conduct of political activity, — e.g., phone interviews, on professional work time, and*
- *making explicit that you are speaking in your role as a private citizen and not in your professional role as a substance abuse counselor or as a representative of your agency.*

◇ ◇ **57** ◇ ◇

A local television station has approached your agency with the following idea. The station would like to begin a local talk show in which callers could call the station and seek information and personal advice regarding substance abuse problems. The format will be a ten minute opening between the television host and your agency "expert" followed by 20 minutes of calls from the public. Calls will be screened by the station for appropriateness and public interest and each call-response will be limited to two to five minutes to maximize the number and variety of calls.

Discussion Questions

How would you respond to their proposal?

What ethical issues and problems can arise from the many formats in which substance abuse professionals are called upon to make public statements through the major entertainment media?

Ethical issues raised in one's involvement with the information media have increased dramatically for the helping professions as the press, radio and television vehicles have explored, and at times exploited, the information and entertainment value of human problems. Ethical concerns raised simply by the structure of the media format in the above vignette, for example, would include the following:

- *Will potential callers be screened out by the station if their problems lack audience appeal and, if so, what would be the effect of such refusal?*
- *What happens to the calls—persons waiting on the line to seek the advice of the expert—for which there is not time within the structure of the 20 minute call-in period to handle?*
- *What potential to do harm is inherent in the program's time limitations of two to five minutes per call, e.g., misunderstandings due to time-induced oversimplifications, misinterpretations?*
- *How could the problems posed by lack of continuity of contact and lack of follow-up be overcome?*

Haas and Malouf (1989), after discussing the way in which ethical principles could be positively served through media appearances, define and discuss the following five prescriptions to guide the human service practitioner involved in media appearances:

1) *Take full and personal responsibility for public statements.*
2) *Speak within, and only within, the limits of your competence.*
3) *Recognize and actively manage potential conflicts of interests, e.g., needs of caller versus entertainment concerns of the show's host.*
4) *Do not demean or otherwise exploit callers for purposes of entertainment.*
5) *Seek consultation from the growing body of knowledge on media psychology.*

(Substance abuse prevention and treatment professionals concerned about ethical issues in media work are encouraged to investigate the growing body of literature being produced by members of the media psychology division of the American Psychological Association.)

◇ ◇ **58** ◇ ◇

In conducting an interview with a client (in early recovery) and his wife, it is clear that there are serious long-standing problems in the couple's sexual relationship that are presented as a central issue within their relationship. Since the treatment of such disorders is beyond your area of expertise, you make an appointment for the couple later in the week at a nationally-recognized center that specializes in treatment of sexual disorders that is only a few hours from your community. You re-schedule the couple for another appointment to continue to focus on substance abuse recovery in the family. You receive a message a week later that the couple has canceled this appointment and on the following Sunday morning awake to the following: your client's spouse has written a letter to the editor in your local paper stating that two dear friends of hers who were having marital problems sought services at your agency (mentions you as the counselor by name) and that you recommended that the husband seek the services of a prostitute. The letter charges the agency and you with gross immorality, demands that the county stop funding the agency, and suggests that an investigation of the agency would reveal practices that would shock everyone in the county. The letter is signed by the client's spouse. The second you walk into the agency on Monday morning, a reporter is on the phone wanting to do a follow-up story on the letter to the editor.

Discussion Questions

Identify the multiple clinical and ethical issues inherent within this situation.

How would you respond to the overall situation?

What, if anything, would you say to the reporter?

What standards should guide staff interactions with the news media? Who can speak for the agency?

May a client's affiliation with the agency and comments on his or her problems or progress be discussed with the media if the client has signed a release of information for such disclosure?

Could disclosure under certain circumstances be fully legal but still represent a breach of ethical conduct?

Unbeknownst to the counselor, what actually occurred in the above story is the following: the couple kept their appointment at the clinic but while waiting in the reception room to be called into an office for their initial interview, the wife looked through a variety of informational brochures on the clinic and picked out a brochure on sexual surrogates. Having read little more than a paragraph, she grabbed her husband and demanded that they leave immediately. Her outrage that her husband might have sex with another woman in the name of therapy propelled the letter to the editor about her "two dear friends" which she composed in the car on the way home from the clinic.

There are any number of clinical and ethical issues raised in the above vignette. Questions to be reviewed in clinical and administrative supervision would include the following:

- *Was it an appropriate time to make sexuality a focal issue in the counseling process or to refer the couple to a specialty clinic that focused on problems of sexual dysfunction?*
- *Was the couple adequately prepared for the referral?*
- *Within the agency procedures established to maximize client rights, the couple has the right to file a formal complaint with the agency. Who should contact the couple to express the concern about the letter and inform them of their grievance rights?*
- *What continuing responsibility does the agency have to serve the couple and who would be the best person to contact the family to re-initiate the service relationship or refer them to alternative resources?*

The letter to the editor poses threats to the reputation of the individual worker and to the reputation of the agency. The agency's response to the media must address these threats without violating the rights of, or otherwise harming, the couple involved as clients at the agency. Ethical responses to media inquiries involve two fundamental questions: 1) who within the agency can speak on behalf of the agency? and 2) what are the scope and limits of what may be shared with the media?

Defining who may speak for the agency is critically important. It serves as protection for both the agency and individual staff persons. It also protects clients from inadvertent breaches of confidentiality that could be made by the direct service provider who might be defensive over what he or she did or did not do in a particular situation.

The spokesperson for the agency must represent the interests of the worker and the agency without harming the client. In the case above, the spokesperson can and should talk about any number of agency policies relevant to the inquiry. The spokesperson can respond to and solicit questions related to:

- *the agency's client grievance procedures*
- *the agency's use of outside referral sources*
- *the relationship between the agency and the clinic identified in the letter to the editor, and*
- *the agency's policies governing client confidentiality.*

Under no circumstances can the author of the letter be identified as an agency client or the details of the couple's particular case be disclosed to the media. Questions can be answered in terms of agency policy, not in terms of detailed transactions involving individual clients.

Chapter
Six

Conduct in Client/Family Relationships

The exploration of ethical and professional conduct governing relationships between health and human service workers and their service recipients (clients) is predicated upon an understanding of the special nature of these relationships. It is the special legal (fiduciary) and moral obligation to care for the welfare of the client in contractually prescribed ways that distinguishes professional helping relationships from all other human relationships. This fiduciary and moral duty to the client connotates an inordinately high commitment of the professional helper by way of loyalty, personal advocacy, objectivity, fairness, integrity and honesty. Ethical concerns encompass the broad range of conditions under which this duty and commitment to protect and serve the interests of the client can be compromised or abdicated.

The boundaries of appropriate and inappropriate behavior within professional helping relationships can be portrayed across a continuum of intimacy and involvement. (See Figure 6-A)

Figure 6-A

The Intimacy Continuum

A professional relationship on the extreme far left of this continuum would reflect physical and emotional disengagement of the professional helper from the helping relationship. Ethical breaches at this end of the continuum reflect abandonment of the client and a failure to fulfill one's commitment to loyalty and service. They include: inappropriate exclusion from services, a disregard of informed consent, breaches in confidentiality, depersonalization of the client, demeaning and disrespectful communications, neglectful and abusive behavior, and precipitous termination of services. A professional relationship on the extreme right end of the continuum would reflect a violation of intimacy barriers through over involvement with the client. Ethical breaches at this end of the continuum includes: cultivation of client dependency, paternalistic decision-making, violations of privacy, unnecessary invasive service interventions, and the social, financial and sexual exploitation of the client. The task for each agency and each worker is to define the zone of effectiveness that represents a level of appropriate and effective involvement based on the nature of the helper-helpee service contract.

If the intimacy and involvement continuum is bent (Figure 6-B), a more complex portrayal of ethical dimensions in the helper-helpee relationship emerges. This figure shows that both ends of the continuum represent zones of abuse and exploitation, suggesting that the extremes of disengagement and over involvement may be more dynamically related than would be superficially apparent. In both cases, the primary force shaping the helper-helpee relationship is something other than the needs of the person seeking help. The zone of effectiveness is marked with dotted rather than firm lines, suggesting greater relativity based on the unique synergy between worker, client, service contract, stage of service delivery, agency, and ecosystem mandates. A new zone—the zone of marginality—has been added that marks an area of increased vulnerability for the client and/or the professional helper. The zone of marginality represents areas of professional and "moral drift" that often precede the more blatant and visible violation of ethical and professional conduct in our relationships with service consumers.

Figure 6-B

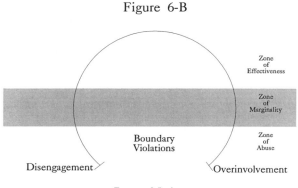

Zones of Intimacy

It is the belief of this author that many extreme breaches of ethical conduct in professional helping relationships are not isolated incidents but are, in fact, the consequence of a progressive disengagement or progressive over involvement in the helper-helpee relationship. To see such breaches as processes rather than events has important implications for the elimination or minimization of breaches in ethical conduct within the helping professions. If sexual exploitation of clients, for example, is an event that happens without context or history, little prevention or early intervention measures would be accessible to stop such incidents before they occur. If, on the other hand, sexual exploitation often reveals itself through a progressive violation of intimacy barriers in the helper-helpee relationship, then a broad range of educational and supervisory strategies become available to abort this progressive over-involvement prior to sexual exploitation. The zone of marginality represents behaviors to which increased supervisory surveillance and education must be directed. This zone represents a territory of increased vulnerability for the client and the worker. If it is clinically appropriate for workers to move into this zone of increased involvement or disengagement, then they should not be there alone, but rather should be there strategically under the guidance and support of peers, supervisors, and clinical consultants.

The critical incidents described below will help each worker and each agency clarify and define the boundaries of the zones of effectiveness, marginality and abuse. Such boundaries will differ based on the organizational setting, staff characteristics (style and professional training), client characteristics, service provider role, and stage of service delivery. While such boundaries may vary across agencies, they should be clearly defined and articulated *within* each agency. While such boundaries may vary across persons and roles within a service agency, it is crucial for each worker to define their own zone of effectiveness and for each agency to define those boundaries of effectiveness to which *all* organizational members will be held accountable. While such boundaries may vary somewhat from client to client, it is essential that they be defined *within* each staff client relationship.

Critical Incidents

Definition of Client

All expectations and standards shaping the relationships between professional helpers and clients are based on an assumed definition of "client." The critical incidents below will help the reader explore the following three dimensions of this definition.

1. Of the large number of persons the agency interacts with, e.g., individuals, family members, friends, employers, and personnel from other agencies; which are encompassed within the term "client?"
2. How and when does one achieve the status of client?
3. Once attained, when, if ever, does one lose the status of client? Does a client stay a client forever even if service delivery has ceased?

◇ ◇ **59** ◇ ◇

You (supervisor) receive a formal complaint from the family member of a client alleging that a therapist at your agency is sexually involved with this client. Although your agency has a personnel code which explicitly defines sexual activity with a client as unethical, the therapist, in response to your questioning, makes the following points:

1. The therapist says that he was not sexually involved with the client when she was receiving services from the agency.
2. Treatment has been terminated and the woman is no longer a client at the agency.
3. Since the woman is no longer a client, what she and the therapist do is a private matter and none of the agency's business.

Discussion Questions

How would you respond to this situation?

What ethical issues are involved?

Does a client ever lose the status of client as it relates to references to "client" in standards of ethical conduct?

While the ethical prohibition against sexual activity with clients is consistent across the human service disciplines, there is an avoidance of and variance on the issue of sexual activity with former clients and a lack of consistent definition of when, if ever, a client ceases to be a client. The following are representative.

"Sexual activity with a patient is unethical. Sexual involvement with one's former patients generally exploits emotions deriving from treatment and therefore almost always is unethical." The Principles of Medical Ethics with Annotations Especially Applicable to Psychiatry, American Psychiatric Association, 1986

"Sexual intimacies with clients are unethical" Ethical Principles of Psychologists, American Psychological Association, 1981. A proposed 1986 expansion of this statement to include former clients raised such complex issues and triggered such intense debate that a decision was made to continue study and discussion before any modifications could be made.

"The social worker should under no circumstances engage in sexual activities with clients." Code of Ethics, National Association of Social Workers, 1979 A 1985 revision of this code added the following: "Clinical social workers do not initiate, and should avoid when possible, personal relationships or dual roles with current clients, or with any former clients whose feelings toward them may still be derived from or influenced by the former professional relationship."

While the National Association of Alcoholism and Drug Abuse Counselors Code of Ethics does not explicitly define post-termination sexual relationships between counselors and clients as unethical, a number of state alcohol and drug counselor associations have begun to address this issue. The Minnesota Chemical Dependency Association, for example, prohibits sexual relationships with former clients during the first year following termination of services.

Minnesota has taken the lead in defining criminal and civil penalties for sexual exploitation of a client by a psychotherapist. The Minnesota Criminal Sexual Conduct Code (609.341-609.351) was revised in 1985 to make psychotherapist sexual exploitation of a client a felony. This revision included as a violation, sexual activity with former clients under two circumstances:

1. *The former client is emotionally dependent upon the psychotherapist.*
2. *The sexual contact occurred as a result of therapeutic deception.*

Minnesota created avenues for civil redress of sexual exploitation by professional helpers through Chapter 372 Minnesota Statues. This statute allows suits to be filed if the sexual contact between the client and professional helper occurred within two years of the provision of psychotherapy.

Each helping agency must define the status and tenure of the designation of "client" based on the nature of vulnerability of their service recipients and the degree of power (potential for exploitation) implicit within the service delivery process.

(Schoener (1989) has prepared an excellent review of the clinical/ethical/legal issues involved in the debate over post-termination sexual relationships).

◇ ◇ **60** ◇ ◇

It has come to your attention that a therapist you supervise is involved in an intimate relationship with a family member of a client being served within the program in which the therapist works. The relationship was initiated by the therapist following the family member's participation in a "family night" educational meeting at the agency. While the agency personnel policies explicitly prohibit sexual relationships with clients, the issue of whether family members of "identified patients" are included within this prohibition has never come up.

Discussion Questions

What ethical issues are involved in this situation?

Should family members be included within the definition of "client?"

How would you respond to the therapist in this situation?

Are family members involved collaterally in agency services included within the definition of "client?" Would a sexual relationship with a sister of a client whom the involved staff member met while the sister was attending family week be prohibited? Would the degree of the family member's involvement in the service process make a difference in our judgement of the appropriateness or inappropriateness of the therapist's actions?

If family members are included in the dual relationship prohibition, does this include a non-traditional definition of family, e.g., paramours, and other persons of significance, involved in the identified client's treatment?

How should prohibitions related to dual relationships differ, if at all, for agency staff who were not directly involved in the provision of services?

Is a client's vulnerability lessened and the staff member's power decreased if the staff member is the executive director rather than the primary counselor of the client? What if the staff member involved is the accountant or a receptionist?

Here is one view; what is yours?

> *If we are to articulate ethical and professional standards governing the relationships between agency personnel and clients, then we must first explicitly define who is and is not included within the parameters of "client." A growing number of human service agencies are developing family centered models of treatment, education and support, yet our thinking about ethics continues to be tied to the relationship between a professional helper and an individual person with a presenting problem. The concern in this situation is that a therapist could use his or her position of power to exploit the vulnerability of a family member in the same manner that the vulnerability of the individual client could be manipulated. Two issues appear critical. First, we must expand our definition of "client" in our ethical discussion to include the family network in which the individual client is nested. Secondly, we must stretch our definition of "family" to include those individuals whose involvement in the service process and whose importance to the client warrant the designation, "family of choice." Family of choice*

would include those significant others in the client's life who with or without benefit of blood or law perform the functions of family. Family of choice would include everyone from domestic partners and paramours to intimate social networks that serve as a surrogate family structure for the client. It is imperative in our organizational communications that professional helpers understand that ethical mandates referring to "client" encompass family by both blood and function.

Joan has been a therapist at your agency for the past three years. Three months ago she began dating a man—Mark—whom she had met through mutual friends. This past weekend Mark mentioned in passing that he was in counseling with his ex-wife at the agency before they decided to divorce. This morning Joan enters your office to discuss this situation in light of the agency policy that prohibits social and intimate relationships between staff and clients (and former clients). Joan was not involved in a primary counseling relationship with Dan nor was she employed by the agency when Dan was a client. She was completely unaware of Dan's status of "former client" until this past weekend.

Discussion Questions

What ethical or professional practice issues do you see, if any, in this situation?

Should the ban on social/intimate relationships apply to this situation?

What is your response to Joan?

Many professional helpers would cite a case like Joan's to suggest that there are exceptions to the "once a client-always a client" policy, particularly when applied to:

- *staff who weren't directly involved in the service delivery to the client*
- *staff whose relationship with the client originated from a context outside the agency, and*

- *clients who no longer receive services and who are unlikely to need services in the future.*

Joan clearly did not initiate a relationship with Mark with knowledge of his status as a former client nor did she possess special power based on Mark's pre-existing service history.   While there is no exploitive intent and minimal exploitive potential in this situation, it would be appropriate to raise this situation as an issue in supervision.   What would you do as a supervisor if such a situation was brought to you?   One ethics workshop participant, when given this critical incident, took the following stance:

> "I would contact the former client to make sure he understood that a relationship with a staff person could preclude his future access to services at the agency due to our policy governing dual relationships. If the former client, understanding this policy, gave up this access to services, I would wish him well and tell him that from this point forward the relationship was none of the agency's business."

What would you do?

◇ ◇ **62** ◇ ◇

Jerry, who was once a client at your agency, has been hired as a detox technician.

Discussion Questions

Does Jerry lose his status of "client" now that he is a staff member of the agency?

Would socializing outside the agency or a sexual relationship between another staff member and Jerry be ethical or unethical?

What ethical issues might come up as part of Jerry's role transition?

Should there be any change in the disposition of Jerry's clinical service record?

If there is a recurring need for service, can Jerry be seen at the agency now that he is on staff?

There are a number of potential ethical issues in the transition from client to staff member within a service agency. The first issue is whether Jerry's status as a client was prematurely terminated to meet the staffing needs of the program. The concern is that critical short-term staffing needs can contaminate the integrity of the clinical decision-making process resulting in a precipitous termination of a client's access to service and placement of a client in a situation that could undermine his or her health and long-term recovery. Some programs who employ former clients address this danger of exploitation by utilizing external consultants to review the client-to-staff decision-making process and/or by building in a required period of time that must pass following service termination before a former client becomes eligible for consideration in a staff position.

A second issue involves whether the process of Jerry's transition from client to staff was managed honestly and with sensitivity to the potential strain involved in such transitions. Active management of this process would include such questions as:

- *Was there full disclosure related to the potential consequences inherent in the role transition? Was Jerry told that his taking on the role of staff member could jeopardize his access to future agency services? Was Jerry informed of the stress inherent within the role transition and the staff role he would be assuming?*
- *Was there a formal structure and process signaling Jerry's role transition to himself, his treatment peers and to all agency staff?*

A third issue involves the protection of Jerry's right to privacy as a staff member. The disposition of Jerry's permanent service record is an important dimension of what is now an issue of a staff member's right to confidentiality. Access to Jerry's prior service record by other staff members could violate Jerry's right to privacy by inappropriately revealing to his peers details of his personal and service history. Some agencies address this situation by removing the former client's record and placing it under the control of the Executive Director. Other agencies, where regulatory law would permit, make arrangements for the destruction of the client's record at the time the person moves into a staff position.

What standards now govern relationships between Jerry and other staff members? Most agency's take the position that if Jerry is no longer a client, he and other staff are bound by whatever values and ethical standards govern social and sexual relationships between staff. This position is not without its ethical vulnerabilities. Though widespread, this stance leaves open the potential of a supervisor to prematurely terminate services to a client, move the client into a staff position, and then use the power derived from both the clinical and supervisory relationship for the purpose of sexual exploitation.

See Chapter Nine for a discussion of the definition of "client" as it relates to prevention workers, trainers, and employee assistance counselors.

◇ ◇ **63** ◇ ◇

Rene has been court mandated into residential treatment at your facility under an agreement you have with the county court system. Rene's referral is part of a contractual arrangement whereby your agency is paid by the county to provide assessment and treatment services to addicted offenders. The court has mandated Rene's treatment, selected your program as the site for such treatment and will be paying your program for the costs associated with Rene's treatment.

Discussion Question

Who is the "client?"

The question of who is the client in this vignette is not a rhetorical question but an important avenue through which the problem of "double-agentry" may be examined. There exists in this case both an individual client and an institutional client, raising such important questions as: to which client is ultimate loyalty owed? Do the duties and obligations to the individual client conflict with those of the institutional client? How are conflicts of best interests of the respective parties decided? Where the financial interests of the individual therapist and the agency are dependent upon continued referrals from the institutional client, how can therapist objectivity be assured? It is important that professional helpers recognize situations that pose problems of "double-agentry," communicate the potential of such conflicts to their individual and institutional clients and have access to supervision to minimize the contamination of professional judgement via personal or organizational self-interest. The sensitivity of staff to problems with "double-agentry" is enhanced where organizations have identified via training and supervision the most common conflicts unique to their setting and have created procedures and processes to follow when potential conflicts of loyalty arise.

Informed Consent

◇ ◇ **64** ◇ ◇

Implicit within the concept of informed consent is the notion that an autonomous, competent client, having been informed of the potential risks and benefits of a prescribed treatment regimen, freely and voluntarily enters into an agreement to participate in the recommended treatment.

Discussion Questions

How do we apply the concept of informed consent to Rene whose status would preclude the definition of an autonomous agent and whose court-mandated treatment clearly surpasses the bounds of voluntary choice?

What ethical issues can arise when external coercion contaminates the normal meaning of informed consent?

Discuss potential ethical issues related to the following practices:

A.   Accepting parental placement of adolescents in a locked substance abuse unit who do not desire treatment and would run from an unlocked unit
B.   Seeking legal guardianship/payeeship of an alcoholic or addict
C.   Working with individuals entering treatment via court mandate
D.   Working with clients entering treatment to save their jobs
E.   Application of state mental health commitment laws to alcoholics and addicts via interpretation of "in danger to self or others" and
F.   Testifying on behalf of the prosecution in a probation revocation hearing initiated as a result of a client leaving court-mandated treatment against staff advice.

Is the informed consent process violated if the treatment center is in control of the external agent and is dictating to the family or court the threats and consequences which they should apply to the client if he or she fails to enter or complete treatment?

Some authors (Szasz, 1974) have posited and vigorously defended the right of an individual to be addicted, suggesting that our society has medicalized and pathologized certain forms of drug use as a form of social control. Rarely do substance abuse workers have the opportunity to distance themselves from their day-to-day activities to consider the validity or utility of such perspectives and yet issues related to the appropriateness of control and coercion frequently arise as issues in client treatment.

Informed consent is the linchpin in the contractual relationship between the professional helper and the helpee and yet situations like the above raise difficult issues in assessing the elements of competence and freedom from coercion so important to the concept of informed consent.

Where the competence of the client is compromised through acute intoxication, drug-induced neurological deficits, or severe psychiatric impairment, a treatment site may have to rely on what Haas and Malouf (1989) call "substituted consent." Where competence to weigh risks and benefits of, and alternatives to, treatment is clearly lacking, the treatment site may have to rely on an independent party, e.g., parents, family member, advocate, or the court, to act on the client's behalf.

The question of autonomy versus coercion in the informed consent process can be a difficult one, particularly with the growing number of individuals mandated into human service settings via the criminal justice system. To what extent do such clients have free choice in the informed consent process when refusal may mean violation of probation or parole and their potential incarceration? Is an informed consent valid under such circumstances? Most human service agencies who have wrestled with this question would answer that the consent is valid. They would posit that the informed consent does not imply that there may not be coercive forces pushing the client toward treatment nor will there not be painful externally imposed consequences resulting from the client's refusal to participate in treatment. The critical factor is that the treatment agency is not coercing the client into treatment nor does it have control over the external coercive agent, e.g., family, court, employer.

◇ ◇ **65** ◇ ◇

Jan, a fourteen-year-old adolescent, has contacted your agency requesting counseling services for problems that include her alcohol and drug use. She is adamant, however, in her refusal to allow you to contact her parents. Jan states that she will seek counseling only under the condition her parents know nothing about it. From the brief information you have collected so far, she is clearly in need of services.

Discussion Questions

How would you respond to this situation?

Does this client have a legal right at age fourteen to consent to treatment services?

Do you have any ethical or legal responsibilities to the parents in this situation?

Jan's story raises legal and ethical issues involving two separate issues:
1) Can minors provide consent for their own treatment or must such consent come from parents or legal guardians?
2) Can minors access services without the knowledge of their parents?

The age at which minors are legally competent to enter into financial contracts (i.e., loans), relationship contracts (i.e., marriage) or service contracts (i.e. medical treatment, counseling) varies from state to state. The legal mandates may also vary according to the type of services youth are seeking, e.g., recent trends toward increased ability to self-initiate substance abuse counseling without parental consent or decreased ability to initiate abortion counseling and abortion procedures without parental consent. Each agency must assure that it is working within the legal framework of state and federal statutes and regulations governing the consent process for minors.

Answering whether minors can legally consent to treatment does not in and of itself address the question of whether such consent is ethical. The ethical prerequisites of informed consent or refusal demand that: 1) the minor client be fully appraised of the risks, likely benefits, and alternatives to proposed service procedures; 2) coercion is not utilized to achieve consent; and 3) the client is mentally competent to make the consent or refuse decision (GAP, 1990). It is the third of these prerequisites that poses difficult ethical dilemmas with minors.

Grisso and Vierling (1978) suggest that the issue of competence must be addressed in three distinct situations:

1. *Does the minor have the right to consent to treatment without knowledge of or with disregard of his or her parent's wishes?*
2. *Does the minor have the independent right to refuse treatment which his or her parents wish to proceed?*
3. *Does the minor have a right to active participation in discussions related to his or her treatment needs, but no right to consent or refuse treatment?*

The ethical dimension, as opposed to the clinical and legal dimensions, of these questions hinge on the question of competence of the minor to provide informed consent or refusal to treatment. Competence, at a minimum, must encompass sufficient autonomy of the minor client from parental influence and coercion to assure autonomous decision-making, the maturity of the minor client to project out of past life experience a realistic assessment of the risks and benefits of proposed services, and the cognitive ability of the minor client to analyze alternative forms of treatment in relationship to his or her future well-being. The clear presence of maturity, cognitive development and autonomous decision-making is so rare among minor clients that a substantial body of ethical literature from the human service professions has taken the position that parents or legal guardians should always be involved in the informed consent process except under circumstances where such consent would threaten the safety of the minor, e.g, child abuse. This stance may be even more justified for minors whose patterns of substance abuse and/or psychiatric impairment compromise the judgement required for informed consent. Most counseling organizations have taken the position that they will not see a minor child without first communicating with the parent and receiving the parent's informed consent for services to proceed. In many states, counselors may legally see a minor for a certain number of sessions without parental consent if the minor is seeking assistance for certain problem areas, e.g., drug abuse, sexually transmitted diseases. Even in these states, most agencies require a supervisory review mechanism to assure that counseling minors without parental consent is the exception rather than the rule. Agencies serving children and adolescents should formulate a clear philosophy and guidelines regarding the informed consent process for minors, the situations under which these normal guidelines may be excepted, and the situations that require a mandatory supervisory review.

"Informed" consent implies that a potential client is fully appraised of the potential risks and unexpected or undesirable effects that could result from a particular course of treatment as well as other available treatment alternatives prior to agreeing to initiate the recommended course of treatment.

Discussion Question

What potential risks or unexpected or undesirable consequences should clients be appraised of as part of the routine informed consent process within your program?

The exact nature of potential risks varies widely across human service settings based on the types of service rendered. Communication regarding potential risks to assure informed consent to treatment could include:

- *pain, discomfort or disability resulting directly or indirectly from a service procedure, e.g., potential medication side-effects*
- *inconvenience resulting from the service commitment, or*
- *inadvertent effects, e.g., stigma related to service affiliation.*

A client seeking outpatient counseling, for example, might be told the following as part of an informed consent process.

- *"Your decision to involve yourself in counseling will require the commitment of time and expense which we have just gone over."*
- *"You are likely during the counseling process to experience discomfort related to the exploration of painful events in your life."*
- *"You are likely to experience periods of stress related to the changes in how you see yourself and how you see the world that result from the counseling process."*

Communication of potential risks is balanced by communicating at the same time what the client can reasonably expect to gain from the counseling process. An additional critical step includes a brief and objective summary of alternative approaches to problem resolution that may be available to the client. With this step, for example, a client presenting herself at a methadone clinic would be informed of alternatives to methadone as part of the informed consent process. The counselor does not need to be competent to deliver all modalities of treatment but they must be knowledgeable enough to objectively represent these alternatives to the client. Once potential risks, benefits, and alternatives have been clearly summarized, the client is then able to decline participation in the proposed service procedures or provide informed consent to proceed.

Labeling: The Ethics of Diagnosis

An adolescent inpatient substance abuse treatment program has aggressively marketed its services in your community and has achieved a very positive public image in its first two years of operation. The unit is becoming a "catch-all" for affluent kids with problems in your area. While the patterns, intensity and duration of substance abuse vary widely, all youth admitted to this unit are given a primary substance use diagnosis at admission and discharge. If the records were carefully scrutinized, they would reveal that adolescents are being regularly admitted and labeled as having an addictive disorder in spite of the lack of sufficient data in the record to justify such a diagnosis (or the rote listing of symptoms that match admission and/or diagnostic criteria). When asked about this practice, one is told that these kids need help regardless of the diagnosis and that such a diagnosis is required for the insurance company to cover the adolescent's treatment costs.

Discussion Questions

What ethical issues, if any, do you see in this practice?

To what extent does the dimension of informed consent include the exploration of the potential effect of the label "alcoholic" or "addict" on the developmental trajectory of such an adolescent?

How can the legitimate counseling needs of adolescents and their families be addressed without the misapplication and potential iatrogenic effects of a diagnostic label?

The vignette above raises a number of ethical issues. The vignette hints at the possibility that the program may be inappropriately admitting and diagnosing adolescents for the financial gain of the institution. The indiscriminate admission of troubled adolescents into a substance abuse unit leaves the institution open to charges of financial exploitation. Even in the absence of malicious intent—where there is a true desire to assist the adolescent and the family—the placement of a chemical dependency diagnosis on the adolescent for purposes of third party reimbursement raises two concerns. The first is the potential iatrogenic effect of labeling. Placement of a diagnostic label—without the clinical data to justify such a diagnosis—ignores the potential impact of such labeling on the client. The admission to a chemical dependency unit and the accompanying diagnosis could have potentially harmful effects via social stigma, future occupational restrictions, or reduced insurability. A second concern involves the potential breach of contract with the reimbursing agent. To misrepresent a diagnosis breaches the expectation of professional integrity and honesty in the relationship between the service agency and the reimbursing agent. Where financial gain is involved, such misrepresentation leaves the program open to charges of fraud. Programs must guard against charges that they practice "checkbook diagnosis" or "administrative diagnosis"—the misapplication of a diagnosis to achieve some programmatic or financial goal.

Substance abuse programs, particularly those serving adolescents, have responded to this potential for client exploitation and financial fraud by establishing more rigorous criteria and standards for admission and by implementing both internal and external systems of utilization review to assure that the client's history and symptoms have been documented and warrant primary and secondary diagnoses and the intensity and duration of prescribed treatment.

Right to Treatment

Refusal to Treat

◇ ◇ **68** ◇ ◇

Your agency can accommodate 25 residential clients at a time. You are currently operating at capacity, but have another 35 persons who are seeking (and have been prescreened as appropriate for) residential admission. These 35 persons present a diversity of demographic characteristics, a wide range of problem acuity and chronicity, financial resources ranging from the wealthy to the indigent, good and poor treatment prognosis, and varying referral sources. Their service requests are scattered over the past six weeks.

Discussion Questions

Who do you admit next?

What standards govern access to treatment at your agency?

What ethical issues can arise in the management of waiting lists?

When service demands outstrip resources, the management of the waiting list for services become the point of crisis through which conflicting needs and interests meet. Perhaps most critical in such situations is that there exists a clear set of standards that govern the decisions of who will be served, that such decisions are clearly communicated to all relevant constituencies, and that the standards are adhered to on a consistent basis. To create standards for waiting list management, the agency must identify how it will differentially apply the following principles:

1. *Principle of fairness: first come, first served.*
2. *Principle of greatest good: spreading resources to reach the greatest number of people.*
3. *Principle of greatest need: allocating intense resources to those few clients with the greatest number and intensity of problems.*
4. *Principle of client mix: selecting clients to enhance the best therapeutic chemistry within the treatment milieu.*
5. *Principle of payee mix: allocating access across a formula of the best % mix between paying and non-paying and public pay and private pay clients.*
6. *Principle of influence: allocating or bypassing normal access to accommodate favored persons or institutions.*

7. *Principle of least needs: creating mix of client characteristics that minimize excessive time or emotional demands on staff.*

◇ ◇ **69** ◇ ◇

A social setting detoxification program has refused admission to a chronic public inebriate on the following grounds:

1. The client has had dozens of admissions without exhibiting any sincere desire to stop drinking.
2. The client uses detox for free food and to sober up until his next check comes.
3. Based on the above, the staff believe that continuing to admit this client for services is a form of "professional enabling" and should be stopped.

Discussion Questions

What ethical issues do you feel are involved in this situation?

How do you view a client's right to treatment?

Under what circumstances or through what procedures could such rights be revoked?

Is this an appropriate or inappropriate application of the concept of enabling?

If this client dies shortly after refusal of assessment or admission services at the detox unit, do you feel the unit would be morally or legally responsible? Is this type of blanket denial of services a form of "abandonment?"

What principles should govern clients' access to services?

See next vignette for analysis.

◇ ◇ **70** ◇ ◇

Marvin, a late stage alcoholic, was court mandated into residential substance abuse treatment following his third DUI. Within 48 hours of his admission, it is discovered that Marvin brought alcohol into the treatment facility and has been sneaking drinks since his admission. The program administratively discharges Marvin for failure to follow program rules. Marvin's family challenges this decision using the following logic: If Marvin has the disease of alcoholism, which is characterized by an inability to abstain from and/or loss of control over alcohol use, and if he was admitted to treatment because he lacked such control, then why should Marvin be excluded from treatment for exhibiting the primary symptom (drinking) of the disease for which he was being admitted?

Discussion Questions

If Marvin, in the hours or days following his administrative discharge, were to kill himself or others in some alcohol-related incident, would the program bear any moral responsibility?

What ethical issues can arise in the administrative discharge of clients from treatment?

When is the application of a clinical concept an ethical issue? Consider this view:

Refusal to admit previously served clients or the precipitous termination of clients, without objective clinical criteria, can leave a program or worker vulnerable to charges of failure to provide equitable access to treatment or charges of abandonment. The concept of professional enabling—actions that inadvertently support continued pathology by protecting the client from the consequences of his or her behavior—has been proven to have great utility in the substance abuse field. Great care must be taken, however, that the concept not be misapplied to justify the exclusion or extrusion of undesirable clients from treatment. The concept of enabling presupposes that if those human and situational buffers that prevent the alcoholic from experiencing the consequences of his or her alcohol use are removed, a crisis of pain will result with the potential of igniting a change process. It assumes that there are still losses that can compete with the power of the drug relationship and that the alcoholic has the capacity to initiate action as a result of a crisis of pain. Great care must be taken in applying this concept to clients whose organicity or imbedded characteristics of dependency, passivity, helplessness and hopelessness leave them incapable of utilizing the experience of pain to spontaneously initiate a recovery process. To misapply the concept of enabling to such clients with the admonition that they must "hit bottom" is a form of abandonment that creates preconditions for treatment access of which these clients are constitutionally incapable of demonstrating, thus condemning them to continued addiction and high risk of death. While "enabling" has been an important concept to confront dysfunctional patterns of over-involvement with alcohol and drug dependent clients, it should not be used to justify the physical or emotional abandonment of these clients.

That is one view. What is your view?

It is very important that poor-prognosis or chronically-relapsing clients not be denied access to services through elaborate philosophical justifications that may serve to mask problems of counter-transference or counter-resistance (negative feelings experienced by staff about the client). Many programs address this problem by building in peer review, supervisory review and external consultation related to refusal to admit decisions, as well as decisions related to administrative discharge or premature termination decisions.

◇ ◇ **71** ◇ ◇

Sally, a client who has been seen for the past nine months at your agency will exhaust her lifetime benefit for chemical dependency treatment within the next month. Sally is facing severe financial problems related to her addiction history and does not have the financial resources to purchase continued services at their full cost.

Discussion Questions

How would you respond to this situation?

If agency policy dictates that clients cannot be seen if they are unable to pay for their services, what ethical issues and clinical standards should guide the process of termination?

The delivery of most human services involves a reciprocal contract of loyalty and continuity. The client commits himself or herself to the emotional effort and sustained time necessary to stabilize or resolve the dilemma for which they sought help. The agency/worker, in turn, pledges itself to remain accessible to the client for the time required to address the identified problems. If the client's financial resources change in a way that jeopardizes this relationship, it is appropriate for the agency to assess whether an ethical duty exists to sustain client services. Many agencies/workers have built in administrative/supervisory mechanisms to review the clinical, ethical and financial issues at stake in such situations. Many agencies sustain what they believe to be their ethical duty of loyalty and continuity by:

- *exploring alternative sources of private and public funds to support the current or most critical level of client services*
- *providing continued services on a pro bono basis*
- *providing the services at reduced fees*
- *arranging extended payment plans for the client, or*
- *providing a structured period of termination through which services to the client may be transferred to an affordable treatment alternative.*

Confidentiality

◇ ◇ **72** ◇ ◇

Jim, a good friend and a counselor who recently resigned from your agency to take another position, returns for a visit and, in casual conversation, asks you how Joe is getting along. Joe is a well-known and long-term client that Jim had transferred to you when he left the agency. Jim had worked with Joe for a long time and was quite concerned as he approached his exit date about how Joe would handle his transfer to a new counselor.

Discussion Question

How do you respond to Jim's question?

This vignette illustrates a common breach of confidentiality. While one tends to see Jim as having rights to information about Joe because of his long history of delivering services to Joe and his clear continued concern, Jim's right to access of this information ended the moment his employment with the agency ceased. Without a signed release of information specifying Joe's consent to release information to Jim, as well as specifications as to the scope of what may be communicated, no information about Joe can be ethically communicated to include the acknowledgement that Joe is or has been a client of the agency.

◇ ◇ **73** ◇ ◇

You are at a mall shopping with your spouse and children when a former client appears, gives you a hug and tells you how glad he is to see you.

Discussion Question

How do you respond a few moments later to the strange looks and inevitable "who was that?" from your family?

Persons who work in any community for a sustained period of time are likely to encounter situations like the above. The concern related to confidentiality is that agency staff members do not inadvertently identify to others that persons they encounter are clients of the agency. On a practical level, it is probably important that workers orient their family members to the mandates of confidentiality to which the worker is bound and request that family members respect this confidentiality through their silence in situations in which the family members could reasonable guess that someone was a client.

◇ ◇ **74** ◇ ◇

You work in a clerical position at a substance abuse treatment agency and part of your routine responsibilities involve typing dictations of client assessments. Today, in the midst of typing such dictation, you are shocked to begin hearing a dictation of an assessment of a young man your daughter just began dating. You had no idea this young man was an agency client and have not faced the dilemma of typing dictation or otherwise encountering information about someone you know in your personal life.

Discussion Questions

What do you do in this situation?

You have been worried about your daughter's choice of friends. Do you listen to the dictation?

If so, let's assume you hear information that alarms you to the extent that you want to confront your daughter and/or prohibit her from seeing this client.

What would you do?

The above vignette illustrates both why it is so crucial to orient clerical staff to issues of client confidentiality and why it is important to protect both the client and the staff person within such situations. With no clear orientation or standard to guide his or her response to this situation, the clerical staff person would in all probability listen to the dictation and, in spite of declarations to the contrary, use the information gained to influence judgements related to the daughter's continued contact with the client. If the information gained led to a demand that the daughter terminate the relationship, the client would be quite justified in protesting that confidential information disclosed within the agency found its way outside the agency and resulted in harm to the client. To prevent intrusive or inadvertent breaches of confidentiality, staff access to information about persons with whom they are closely involved can be precluded or severely restricted. By creating a standard or policy whereupon clerical staff shall signal to their supervisor their involvement with a client, the above dictation could be transferred to another worker and the potential breach in confidentiality avoided. Some exposure to confidential information of neighbors, acquaintances, or associates may be inevitable within the small agency, where there are no backup roles through which such exposure could be limited, or within the rural catchment area where "everybody knows everybody." Regular orientation on the ethical imperative to guard such information is a crucial preventative measure.

◇ ◇ **75** ◇ ◇

Jerry, a client you have seen in counseling for the last month, reports that something horrible has bothered him for a long time that he's never been able to talk about with anyone. He wants to talk to you about it but says he will only do so if you swear never to repeat it to anyone.

Discussion Questions

How do you respond?

What situations could arise in which you might feel compelled to break this promise?

Many of us would experience a desire to provide Jerry an open invitation to talk with our assurances of confidentiality and silence. To fully protect Jerry's rights as a service consumer, however, we must communicate to Jerry the limits of such confidentiality and the specific circumstances under which the vow of silence would be broken, such as in clinical supervision, in response to subpoena, and for legally mandated reporting of child abuse. All written and verbal communications about confidentiality must encompass both the scope (inclusions) and limits (exclusions) of confidentiality. Failure to communicate the latter can lead to an unintended, and often much more serious, breach of client confidentiality. It is also important to note that the contract of confidentiality is between the agency and the client. The counselor working for the agency is not an independent agent and may not on their own power and authority grant exclusions to agency policies governing confidentiality.

◇ ◇ **76** ◇ ◇

In an informal conversation between two outpatient counselors at your agency, Rodney shares with another counselor a very "interesting case" he is currently seeing. The disclosure identifies the client by name along with the details of the client's personal history, as well as the client's special difficulties in treatment.

Discussion Questions

Is such disclosure within the agency—outside the boundary of clinical supervision or formal clinical consultations—a violation of client confidentiality?

Is the informal discussion of case material with co-workers a breach of client confidentiality?

What standards should govern internal disclosure of client information?

What information is provided, verbally or in writing, to clients of your agency informing them of the types of internal disclosures that could occur with information they share with their primary caregiver(s)?

The above vignette illustrates an ethical quagmire rarely addressed in codes of professional ethics. Most legal interpretations of confidentiality address disclosure of information to agents or institutions outside the service agency. The ethical, as opposed to the legal, issues of confidentiality raised by this incident involve both the client's right to privacy and the nature and scope of confidentiality that were communicated verbally and in writing as part of the agency-client contract. If the clients orientation to confidentiality identified the exclusions to secrecy to include only clinical supervision, legal subpoena, legally mandated reporting of child abuse or imminent threat of risk to others, and emergencies in which failure to disclose would jeopardize the safety or health of the client; THEN the casual discussion noted above would constitute a breach of confidentiality because it extended the boundaries of disclosure beyond those agreed upon with the client. If the discussion above could be broadly encompassed within the rubric of "peer supervision," such potential disclosures should be communicated to the client at the beginning of the service relationship. Perhaps more importantly, there seems to be no justification for utilizing the client's name in such discussion unless it is part of an interdisciplinary staffing with other persons who will be involved in the care of the client. Identification of client name or identifying data constitutes gossip where such disclosure is not strategically designed to benefit the client. There seems to be increased recognition among human service professionals that confidentiality must be protected as rigorously within the agency as one would protect external disclosure. In a survey of counselors (Wagner, 1981), 80% of those surveyed felt that informal discussion of case material with coworkers not directly involved with the client constituted a violation of confidentiality.

◇ ◇ **78** ◇ ◇

A client that you saw briefly in counseling discontinued therapy and some months later committed suicide. The parents of this adult client approach you with a request for any information that would help them understand why their son killed himself. They are in great pain and are each experiencing guilt over real and imagined sins of commission and omission in their respective relationships with their son. You possess information gained from the therapy relationship with their son which could absolve them of this guilt.

Discussion Questions

How would you respond to this request?

Is sharing information about the deceased client to his parents a breach of confidentiality?

Could similar information be shared with legal authorities investigating the client's death?

Does the moral imperative to not share confidentially disclosed information continue even after the death of the client?

Stein (1990), in his treatise on counselor ethics, states unequivocally that "the moral imperative not to share confided information remains viable even after the death of the client." This position has evolved in the clear belief that any compromise to this moral imperative would fundamentally diminish the safety and effectiveness of the counseling relationship. Clients who feared subsequent counselor disclosure to the client's significant others after death might very well withhold, alter and fabricate material, compromising the power of the therapist by casting him or her in the role of biographer.

A query of substance abuse treatment supervisors regarding their response to the above vignette revealed markedly different responses. Most felt that a fundamentalist interpretation of confidentiality would prohibit any disclosure to the parents without a signed consent. Others felt that full disclosure should be made on the grounds that the positive effect (emotional healing of the parents) outweighed the potential harm that could be done by disclosure. A third group felt the therapist could assure the parents that the suicide was not a response to their actions or inactions without divulging the true nature of the issues contributing to the client's suicidal intent.

◇ ◇ **78** ◇ ◇

A residential treatment facility routinely holds its business and board meetings at this facility. To get to the meeting rooms, persons must walk through the day room and living areas of the facility. Tours are also routinely provided through the facility to persons visiting the program.

Discussion Questions

Do such practices violate the confidentiality of clients in treatment?

How might these situations be managed to avoid inadvertent violations of confidentiality?

Hosting community meetings within human service facilities and the routine touring of service facilities to include client activity areas and residential dorms constitute potential areas of non-malicious, inadvertent violation of client confidentiality. The unannounced introduction of outsiders into the treatment facility exposes clients to individuals, who based on prior contact with the client, may identify the client as a service recipient of the agency. Such inadvertent breaches of confidentiality can be avoided by:

- *holding meetings outside of, or away from, client living and traffic areas*
- *conducting facility tours during days or hours clients are not at the facility or are in group activities in areas not visible to visitors, and*
- *announcing the presence of outsiders within the facility and providing clients with the opportunity to remove themselves from common areas during visits or tours.*

◇ ◇ **79** ◇ ◇

Jeff, a client that Dan has been seeing for a short time in counseling, has not confided with his spouse about his involvement in treatment, partially because he is trying to sort out whether as a sober person he wants to invest energy in salvaging his marital relationship. Jeff has resisted Dan's efforts to involve his spouse and has made it very clear that he does not wish her to know about his counseling activities. An emergency arises which requires Dan to contact Jeff to change their weekly appointment time. When Dan calls, Jeff is not at home, so Dan leaves his name and a phone number and requests that Jeff call upon his return. Jeff's wife, who takes the call, calls the phone number and discovers that it is a well-known, local counseling agency. Upon Jeff's return, she confronts him about his involvement with the agency.

Discussion Questions

Did Dan violate this client's confidentiality?

How should such situations be handled?

To leave a phone message for Jeff in a manner that would allow those who took the message to directly or indirectly identify Jeff as a client of the agency is an inadvertent breach of confidentiality unless the agency has a signed release to communicate with the person with whom the message was left. While reasonable effort should be expended to contact Jeff regarding Dan's emergency, any message which linked Jeff to the agency should be avoided.

◇ ◇ 80 ◇ ◇

A client walks out of a treatment center after telling you that he has no intention of quitting his cocaine use, that he's been using cocaine every day in treatment and that he only came into treatment because of the threat of jail. Saying he'd rather do the time, he leaves the facility without saying anything to the other residents. An hour later in group, residents want to know what happened to this client.

Discussion Question

What do you say in response to their questions?

The area of staff-to-client communication about other clients represents ambiguous and ethically vulnerable territory in milieu-oriented treatment environments. The fact that the client is no longer involved in treatment is a fact that must be communicated to those clients whose treatment brought them into significant interaction with the client who left. The reactions of other clients to the client's absence can and should be explored. The reasons and circumstances under which the client left which were communicated to you alone are confidential and not proper to share within the broader treatment community. At a practical level, it is very appropriate to ask the exiting client what he or she would like communicated to other clients about their disengagement from services. This can often open the door to appropriate and approved explanations to other clients as to the client in questions status.

Lee works as a nurse in a residential substance abuse treatment program. A client admitted this morning reports that he is HIV positive but has had no AIDS-related illnesses.

Discussion Questions

What factors should Lee consider in determining which other staff persons need access to this client's HIV status?

Should other residents within the program be informed of the client's HIV status?

Ethical duties to protect confidentiality and to prevent harm to other parties must be carefully weighed in the care of clients who are HIV positive or who have AIDS. Most programs have infection control policies that have been updated to accommodate the new service complexities posed by the spread of HIV that will guide persons like Lee in the discharge of their duties. Both legal and ethical discussions of confidentiality of a client's HIV status in the health care setting focus on the phrase, "need to know." Need to know policies basically contend that only those staff persons who need to know a client's HIV status for purposes of more effectively serving the client or for protecting themselves (e.g., during invasive procedures or medical emergencies) should be provided this information. Some substance abuse agencies interpret this policy "medically," with only physicians and nurses informed of a client's HIV status, with no communications made to other staff and no seropositive documentation in the client's chart. The exception to this rule would be disclosure in the event of a life-threatening medical crisis. Even in this situation, a client may be encouraged to share his HIV status with other staff or the treatment community for purposes of support. In other agencies, the definition of "need to know" is expanded "clinically" to include the clinical supervisor and the primary counselor who will be working with the client. The use of rigorous infection control procedures for all clients obviates the need to identify a client that needs special precautions. Given the risk of HIV infection among all substance abusers, special precautions are warranted with all clients seeking treatment.

Agencies also have a duty to reasonably protect other clients from exposure to contagious illness. This duty can generally be met without disclosing a client's HIV status. Agencies can reduce the risk of client-to-client sexual contact or needle sharing through one-on-one and group educational formats that clearly communicate the sources of transmission and methods of risk reduction. Many programs utilize peer educators to conduct such orientations for all clients entering treatment. The Illinois Alcoholism and Drug Dependence Association has a curriculum entitled, "Addicts Helping Addicts Prevent AIDS" which is designed specifically for such peer education processes. Many agencies also are developing treatment policies that prohibit sexual interaction between clients.

Where all clients are being educated about HIV/AIDS and where the HIV positive client is cooperative (i.e., avoiding unprotected sexual activity), no disclosure of the client's medical status is warranted or legally permitted. Such disclosure is only permissible with the client's written consent or when the client voluntarily shares the information. An exception to this general rule could apply where risks of HIV transmission to another client was imminent, e.g., a sexually aggressive client with compromised mental status (use of restraint or precautions would be unlikely). Some programs feel that dealing with HIV/AIDS is such an important clinical and public safety issue, they will admit a seropositive client only if the client agrees to disclose this status to the treatment community. One approach to HIV/AIDS education in situations where clients may find it difficult to talk to one another about HIV/AIDS is to indoctrinate all clients to act as if they and all persons they interact with were HIV-infected.

See Chapter Eight for a discussion of the conditions under which client confidentiality can be suspended to warn third parties of their HIV exposure.

◇ ◇ **82** ◇ ◇

A long-term adolescent treatment program utilizes their residents to make anti-drug presentations to local school and community groups. These presentations are built in as a component of every adolescent's treatment experiences and may not be refused.

Discussion Questions

Does this practice constitute a forced violation of confidentiality and anonymity?

What issues are involved in such situations?

What guidelines would you suggest related to such activities?

While the treatment program may posit that such presentations are an effective tool to break down adolescent denial and a means to construct an anti-script congruent with addiction recovery, the ethical question is whether the role of coercion robs the adolescent and his or her family of their right to anonymity and confidentiality. To the degree that coercion (real or threatened untoward consequences of client refusal to participate) restricts or removes the client's freedom of choice to participate in such programs, the practice is unethical. To use clients within such programs on a voluntary, non-punitive basis would not violate the client's right to confidentiality. Many programs have moved to the use of former clients who serve in a volunteer capacity to conduct such programs. This practice minimizes the potential compromise of anonymity and confidentiality through positive or negative coercion.

◇ ◇ **83** ◇ ◇

An extremely famous sports figure has checked into your facility (based on its proximity to his family members) under conditions of duress following his most recent failed drug test. Within hours the sports media is aggressively trying to penetrate the veneer of secrecy surrounding this client's treatment. Numerous reports are already appearing in print quoting "reliable sources" about the client's drug choices, drug history, treatment duration and treatment prognosis. As days progress, the program administrator is being pressured from above to set up a public statement by the client regarding his treatment and future plans in order "to take the media pressure off the hospital." At the unit level, the client experiences verbal coercion to make a public statement as a "positive step out of denial." There are rumors within the hospital that the Public Relations Director has been feeding tidbits to the press and orchestrating the pressure for a public statement by the client from the hospital—all for the PR benefits of the hospital and the chemical dependency unit.

Discussion Question

What are your reactions to this situation?

There are at least two critical questions raised by the above vignette. The first is whether confidential information about the client has been released without the client's permission. The exploitation of the client's fame for institutional gain via the breach in confidentiality is clearly an ethical violation. Such disclosure by an employee is grounds for immediate termination in nearly all hospitals. A second issue is whether the integrity of this client's treatment has been compromised for the potential benefit of the institution. The pressure from counseling staff for a public statement from the client as a "positive step out of denial" may be more aimed at enhancing the unit's occupancy rate than the client's recovery process. The furor and general excitement that inevitably surrounds the treatment of a famous person can often lead to a suspension of normal professional and ethical conduct. Rigorous supervisory review and the use of external clinical consultants in such cases can help assure the ethical and clinical integrity of the service delivery process.

◇ ◇ **84** ◇ ◇

Bernie, a client you are seeing in outpatient counseling, reports today during his counseling session that he needs you to write a summary of your substance abuse assessment and a progress in treatment summary for his upcoming court date. To comply with this request, you prepare a letter to the probation officer briefly summarizing the material upon which you based Bernie's need for substance abuse treatment and a brief synopsis of the course of treatment. Prior to sending the letter, you review its contents with Bernie and ask him to sign a written consent for release of the information to his probation officer. After reviewing the content of the letter, Bernie says he will sign a release for all information except the reference to one episode of relapse which he experienced during the early stage of his treatment. He is concerned that the mention of the relapse episode may result in a revocation of his probation rather than his release from probation.

Discussion Questions

How do you respond? Can a client selectively delete portions of clinical information to be disclosed to an outside source?

How would you respond if the deletion of the material which the client refused to have released substantively altered the overall content and meaning of the communication?

Would it be an ethical breach for the counselor to forward the report to the probation department with the relapse episode deleted?

While Bernie is free to withhold his consent to release information to outside sources, the counselor is free to assess when the selective withdrawal of that consent alters the nature and integrity of professional communication. Bernie may choose to permit or not permit his counselor to provide a synopsis of his response to treatment to the local probation office. If Bernie says he will provide permission for such communication but will not permit the mention of his relapse, then the counselor is in a position of either refusing to provide such edited communication or making the communication with all of its consummate risks.

Respect

 ◇ ◇ **85** ◇ ◇

Your agency director has received a call from the mother of an adolescent client. The mother is registering a formal complaint related to the following incident. The mother confronted her son about swearing and demanded to know where he had heard that kind of language. The son defended himself by telling his mother that there was nothing wrong with his language because his counselor, who the mother forced him to see, uses that kind of language all of the time. The mother informed the director that she was a born-again Christian and would not tolerate her son being in a situation where such language was used. She announced that her son would no longer be allowed to come to the agency and that she was writing a formal complaint to the agency board.

Discussion Questions

What ethical and professional practice issues are involved in this situation?

How would the issue vary in different geographical and cultural environments?

The use of profanity or argot from deviant subcultures involves both clinical (is it effective?) and ethical (is it right?) dimensions. While some clinicians proclaim the need to get down and talk at the client's level in language their client can understand, others (White, 1990) attack the frequent use of profanity and argot by professional helpers on the grounds that it reinforces the client's involvement within pathology-enhancing subcultures. Others contend that the use of profanity in some settings reflects an insensitivity to prevailing community values and that such insensitivity threatens the reputation of the agency and, as in the above case, the access of clients to the agency's services. The most central question is: is there any language used by agency staff that weakens the client/family-agency relationship or staff member-agency relationship. There must be concern with any language that is offensive, demeaning or depersonalizing. The shaping of standards related to language is an important element in building a healthy, and ethical, organizational culture. What explicit or implicit standards exist within your organizational culture that are related to profanity or argot? Are there standards or values governing the use of derogatory language that reflect racism, sexism, or homophobia?

Respect for Personal/Political/Religious Beliefs

◇ ◇ **86** ◇ ◇

Roger, shortly after entering treatment, refuses to go to AA meetings, because he feels that it is a religious program. As an atheist, Roger believes that forced attendance at such meetings is both offensive and counterproductive. He is adamant in his desire to address his alcoholism but demands that such treatment not involve religion.

Discussion Questions

How would you respond to this situation?

Would forced AA attendance or denial of treatment under these circumstances constitute a form of religious discrimination?

Where does one draw the line between respect for religious and political beliefs of clients and the responsibility to confront a defense structure or gambit that allows the client to escape the experience of treatment? The ethical issue is the mandate to respect a client's beliefs about religion, to include the right to refrain from religious belief. Several options might be considered in this case. If the program's philosophy and approaches are broad enough to encompass highly individualized approaches to treatment, then it may be quite possible to address the client's need for treatment while exploring alternatives to twelve step or religious frameworks for long-term support for abstinence. If the program philosophy and design of treatment activities are not broad enough to explore alternatives to AA meetings and its related step work, it may be appropriate to explore alternative treatment approaches and sites through which the client could explore a recovery pathway congruent with his atheism. There is legal support for this position. Courts are consistently ruling that Alcoholics Anonymous meets the descriptive criteria of a religion and that court mandated (state coerced) participation in AA violates the First Amendment separation of church and state. In the wake of court rulings that clients who profess atheism must be provided non-religious treatment alternatives, a number of self-help structures are springing up around the United States. The more well known of these include Women for Sobriety, Secular Organization for Sobriety/Save Our Selves, and Rational Recovery. The literature describing these alternatives include works by Kirkpatrick (1986, 1986), Christopher (1988) and Trimpey (1989).

◇ ◇ **87** ◇ ◇

Jeremy has requested a formal evaluation from your agency to assist in getting his drivers license reinstated. Jeremy openly acknowledges his past addiction and is equally candid about his two prior DUI offenses that occurred more than five years ago, resulting in the loss of his license. Jeremy reports that he was "born again" in 1985 and hasn't had a drink since he turned his life over to Jesus. Jeremy has received no treatment and has no involvement in Alcoholics Anonymous or other formal addiction recovery support group. His sustained sobriety and church activities are fully corroborated through collateral interviews.

Discussion Question

How do you view such persons with Jeremy's history?

Respect for a client's religious and political beliefs also includes a recognition of the legitimacy of religious and political pathways to change. Many treatment programs and many administrative systems set up to assess the stability and durability of a client's pattern of sobriety and to assess a client's potential risk to public safety via future drinking and driving have a great deal of difficulty responding to cases like Jeremy's because the substance abuse field has provided them little if any understanding of non-traditional pathways of recovery. As the field matures, respect for religious and political beliefs will increasingly come to encompass the recognition of the role of religious and political beliefs as a medium of personal transformation.

If we are to recognize the legitimacy of religious pathways of recovery and respect the client's choice to explore this alternative, then we must resist attacking or undermining the client's beliefs and explore how to work within rather than compete with this belief system.

There are exceptions to the general mandate of respect for religious beliefs of clients. What should a clinician do when a client's affiliation with a particular religious or political institution escalates pathology rather than promotes health? (See Howard Clinebell's (1956) discussion of the distinction between salugenic [health-enhancing] religion and pathogenic (pathology-enhancing) religion in alcoholics.) While the confrontation of such influences may be clinically warranted, ethical mandates require that the clinician take great care in assuring that his or her own religious or political beliefs are not biasing clinical judgement in such cases. Serious introspection and self-analysis as well as clinical supervision or consultation should precede such a confrontation process.

◇ ◇ **88** ◇ ◇

Bud, a late-stage alcoholic and recent admission to your residential treatment program, is the most racist, sexist, homophobic man you have ever met in your life.

Discussion Questions

To what extent, if any, are each of these dimensions of character an issue of addiction treatment?

If Bud becomes a sober racist-sexist-homophobe, is this successful treatment?

Bud's black-white thinking, rigidity, intolerance, excessive and unreasonable resentments may be treatment issues. His use of a racist, sexist or homophobic mask for purposes of defensive posturing could be a treatment issue. His verbalization of racist, sexist or homophobic remarks in violation of treatment norms or his commitment of acts that demean or injure others in the treatment environment would be treatment issues. If you are Bud's assigned counselor and your views are so conflicted with his views as to preclude the possibility of effective clinical work, then YOUR problem with counter-transference is an issue in Bud's treatment. Bud's beliefs are not a treatment issue unless they surface as a concrete obstacle to his continued recovery or unless it is Bud's choice to explore these beliefs as part of a broader treatment issue that he has self-identified. It is crucial that staff maintain a clarity of purpose in their service interactions and not get manipulated out of their service effectiveness by either the client's or staff's religious and political beliefs. While we may find a client's political views repugnant, the nature of the client's political beliefs are not a criteria for access or denial of services nor should they become a focus of, or an obstacle to, addiction treatment services.

Honesty

◇ ◇ **89** ◇ ◇

A counselor and a physician are both concerned about a particular client with a pattern of chronic relapse. Both are convinced that if something does not get his attention, this client is going to drink himself to death. In spite of a chronic drinking history and a broad array of high risk activities (e.g., repeated drinking and driving), this client does not exhibit any significant alcohol-related medical diseases. As a last resort the physician grossly exaggerates the severity of the client's medical condition—suggesting advanced liver pathology in somewhat vague but ominous terms and talking about the threat of death to the client.

Discussion Questions

Is such a fabrication or exaggeration ethical if designed to benefit the client?

Would it still be unethical if this communication proved to be the turning point in this client's recovery?

See analysis after following vignette.

◇ ◇ **90** ◇ ◇

A counselor and a physician are both concerned about a client who has just been readmitted for treatment. The client's liver profiles reveal late stage liver-disease. The client is responding better to treatment this time than during any previous contact and the physician and the counselor are both concerned that an honest presentation of the client's medical condition will disrupt his fragile sobriety and lead the client to—in hopelessness—drink himself to death.

Discussion Questions

Is it ethical or unethical for the physician and the counselor to withhold information from this client about his medical condition?

What would you do in this situation?

Both of the above vignettes test the general rule of honesty as a value upon which helping relationships are based. Candor and truthfulness make up the foundation of the helping relationship. The helping relationship would seem so impossible without this bond of honesty that most helping professions have made the value of honesty a cornerstone in their respective standards of professional ethics. The question raised by the above critical incidents is whether lying or deception can ever be ethically justified within a helping relationship. Most texts on ethical issues involved in health and human services do not contend that there are never any circumstances in which it might be appropriate for a counselor to lie. They do, however, consistently contend that a lie should be a last choice and chosen only after considerable deliberation. Bok (1978) recommends two tests in such a situation: 1) is there a truthful alternative to lying? (If so, choose the truthful alternative.) and 2) What moral arguments can be made for and against lying in this particular situation? The concerns about the effect of lying are many. It threatens, and if detected, could lead to a severing of the helping relationship and damage the credibility of the profession in the eyes of the client. This could damage, not only the current relationship, but the client's willingness to seek assistance in the future. Lying disempowers the client—and places that power in the hands of the therapist—by depriving the client of all the knowledge available to influence his or her life decisions. How can a client begin a program of recovery based on honesty when the foundation of that recovery is a lie? Lying reflects poor role modeling by the professional helper,—who holds up deception as a viable method of problem-solving.

Right of Privacy

◇ ◇ **91** ◇ ◇

You are seeing a 13-year-old in counseling who constantly seeks reassurance about the confidentiality of what she discusses with you. Her parents, who initiated her contact with the agency, are quite intrusive in their efforts to know the nature of the problems their daughter is discussing and the direction in which the counseling is proceeding.

Discussion Question

In working with children and adolescents, what legal and ethical guidelines help you balance the child's right to privacy and confidentiality versus the parent's traditionally defined right to know about and approve of the nature of care being received by their children?

Children and adolescents have been afforded few legal rights to confidentiality. With the exception of some states that allow some time-limited counseling for specified problems without parental consent, parents have a legal right to know what is transpiring in a counseling process with their child. In spite of this situation, many substance abuse counselors have found that their effectiveness with adolescents hinges on the adolescent's ethical, if not legal, rights to confidentiality. To avoid conflict and crises later in the counseling process, the scope and limits of confidentiality and an explicit agreement of what will and will not be shared with parents is best completed at the beginning of counseling as part of the informed consent process.

◇ ◇ **92** ◇ ◇

A client signed a release of information allowing her counselor to disclose information to her probation officer related to her attendance in treatment and the results of random urine testing which had been performed at the program site. In responding to this request for information, the counselor forwarded a report that in addition to the information requested included disclosures of the client related to her sexual abuse as a child and confusion related to her present sexual orientation.

Discussion Question

Was this client's rights to privacy violated even though she had signed a release of information for disclosure of treatment information?

Professional helpers may ethically disclose only that specific information prescribed within the client's signed release of information and should take great care to avoid violating the client's right to privacy via professional gossiping. Clinical reports, whether presented in writing or orally, should include only data relevant to the role of the requesting party and only data that has been specifically sanctioned for release by the client. Release of the client's history of sexual abuse and current struggle with sexual orientation issues goes beyond the report of attendance and urinalysis results and as such constitutes a breach of client confidentiality and a violation of privacy.

Empowerment Versus Paternalism

Cultivating Dependency Versus Autonomy

◇ ◇ **93** ◇ ◇

Rolanda, a client admitted for residential treatment a week ago, has just approached you (her primary counselor) and reported that she wants to look through her record and see what has been written about her. In this same record are notes from interviews with Rolanda's parents who reported that Rolanda was adopted—a fact they have not discussed with Rolanda — and a psychiatric assessment that catalogues an unending list of pathologies under the diagnosis of Borderline Personality and notes that she has an extremely poor prognosis for treatment.

Discussion Questions

Do you feel clients should have full access to their clinical records?

Under what conditions could client access to records do harm?

Whose interests, other than the client's, must be taken into consideration in the decision to give a client access to his or her complete record?

There are innumerable legal issues governing clients' access to their records in the substance abuse treatment setting. Although individual clinicians and agencies have been given wide discretion on their client access to records policies, the trend has clearly been toward increased legal access to a client's own record, particularly in agencies that receive federal funding. The ethical issues involved in client access to their records hinge to a great extent on differing views of autonomy and paternalism. Autonomy dictates full client access to records; paternalism dictates no client access to records. The growing exploration of ethical issues within the substance abuse field has led to decreased paternalism in many areas including a significant increase in client access to records within treatment programs. More and more programs are opening records to clients as part of increased client autonomy and client rights. Programs may still confront situations in which an overriding reason exists to deny or limit client access to information from their clinical record. The most frequent example would is full disclosure of information in the record to the client could harm the client or a third party. Particular care must be taken to avoid disclosing information to the client from other care-givers whose records were forwarded without the knowledge that they could be potentially shown to the client.

◇ ◇ **94** ◇ ◇

You have taken a position as clinical supervisor at a local substance abuse treatment agency. John, one of your most popular counselors, has a style of relationships with clients that alarms you the more you come to understand it. There seems to be a high level of dependency cultivated between John and his clients. John seems to be the primary focus of long-term support for clients with whom he works. Former clients are constantly calling in emotional crisis. Couples (clients and their spouses) frequently request and receive marriage counseling from John in spite of his lack of formal training in this area. John's clients seem to be incapable of making decisions without first consulting him.

Discussion Questions

Although no clients are expressing harm resulting from John's approach (they, in fact, proclaim he has saved their lives), what ethical issues are raised by this vignette?

How would you respond to John as his supervisor?

The ethical value of autonomy posits that the helping professional should maximize the client's experience of personal freedom. Counselor interventions that inadvertently undermine a client's personal efficacy by cultivating dependency upon the therapist violate this value. As such relationships proceed, clients feel better and better about the therapist but worse about themselves. Cultivated dependence is a process of clinical disempowerment. As a supervisor, it would be very appropriate to monitor John's clinical work and begin a supervisory process aimed at supporting a restructuring of John's relationships with his clients. While many variations in counselor-client relationships can be attributed to nuances of personal style, dimensions of counselor style that undermine the freedom and autonomy of clients must be brought into the process of clinical supervision.

Restrictiveness of Treatment Environment

◇ ◇ **95** ◇ ◇

Psychiatric treatment programs have attempted in recent years to operationalize the principle that clients have a right to treatment in the least restrictive environment that is capable of addressing their current needs. In contrast, the substance abuse field has until recently been dominated by a strong bias toward the "28 day residential model" of treatment. In short, the fields first choice has tended to be the most rather than the least restrictive environment.

Discussion Question

What value on this issue should guide decision-making of staff as they make recommendations and decisions regarding the choice of treatment modality for each client?

The ethical value set forth in most human service disciplines is a command to address the problems of a client with the least possible infringement on the freedom and autonomy of the client. Because the substance abuse field relied for years on residential treatment models, the restriction of client freedom became automatic rather than a matter of clinical utility based on the assessment of an individual client's needs. Such modality biases result in unduly restricting the freedom and autonomy of many clients whose problems could be addressed without removing them from their home and work place. Such undue limits on client freedom can be minimized by:

- *developing a continuum of care that provides less restrictive modality options, (e.g., outpatient or intensive outpatient) for problem resolution*
- *developing and adhering to clear admission procedures that define clinical criteria by which clients are placed in more or less restrictive treatment environments*
- *developing rigorous programs of admission review via clinical supervision or formal utilization review programs, and*
- *imparting information to clients about less restrictive treatment alternatives as part of the informed consent process.*

 ◇ ◇ **96** ◇ ◇

As an intake worker in a residential substance abuse program, you encounter a situation today that is becoming all to frequent in an age of managed care and increasing restrictions on substance abuse treatment benefits. A client presents himself to treatment dependent upon cocaine and alcohol—a pattern of great chronicity and intensity which has severely affected nearly every sphere of this client's life. The client has prior histories of failure in outpatient treatment, has acute medical problems that need to be assessed and treated, and comes from a drug-saturated social milieu. The managed care firm controlling this client's access to treatment informs you that they will grant four days of inpatient treatment and will then pay 80% of up to ten outpatient sessions.

Discussion Questions

What ethical issues are raised by this vignette?

How does one maintain clinical integrity at a personal and programmatic level in an age where the modality and intensity of services available to a client are dictated by external agents based on criteria of cost containment rather than client needs?

Counselor patience can be stretched to the breaking point in a system where days of service or number of counseling sessions are being doled out by benefits managers with minimal regard for the history and needs of the client. To maintain personal and professional sanity in situations like the above, the counselor is left with several options. The first is to become an advocate seeking to broker the largest amount of resources required to address the clients needs. This requires not only assertiveness, but a gift for the details of documentation involved in appeals and extended stay requests. Beyond the scope of these resources, the counselor can work with the client to select the best possible services that are commensurate with the client's resources. The counselor can also respond to this situation at a broader level by speaking out in his or her professional associations and adding support to counter the current trend toward erosion of substance abuse benefits.

Stewardship of Clients Resources

◇ ◇ **97** ◇ ◇

A client presents himself for admission to a 14 day inpatient substance abuse treatment program via a court ordered mandate for treatment. The client presents a fourteen year history of opiate addiction, extensive involvement in predatory crime, and deep and long-term enmeshment in the illicit drug culture. The program that is assessing this client is a traditional short-term, step program whose program design has been very successful in treating high functioning alcoholics and polydrug users who are at early to middle stages of addiction and who retain strong social supports that can be enlisted in the treatment process.

Discussion Questions

What should be the response to this client's request for admission ?

Are there ethical issues involved in accepting clients into a treatment modality that has neither the intensity nor duration of contact that is likely to address their problems?

Looking at the above critical incidents, what do you feel are the ethical issues related to the "over-treatment" or "under-treatment" of clients?

The above vignette raises the question of whether it is unethical to admit a client into a treatment modality with a structure and intensity that is unsuited to address the chronicity and severity of the client's problems. Acceptance of the client into the above program communicates to the client and the court that the client has a reasonable chance of addressing his or her problems within the structure of the program's treatment activities. If the client fails to respond to the program via initiation of a sobriety-based lifestyle, the client may be penalized by both the program (denial of re-admission) and the court (probation revocation) for failing to respond to a treatment structure that had little likelihood of success. The misplacement of clients with severe and chronic addiction problems in low intensity modalities—whether out of naiveté or financial exploitation—constitutes a type of shame-based treatment system. Clients not only fail to respond to such systems—they exit such programs with their original problems intact—but have their potential for future recovery diminished by the experience of treatment failure. The experience of failure by misplaced clients breeds passivity, dependence, helplessness and hopelessness and enhances the likelihood that the client will enter the pool of chronically relapsing clients within the substance abuse treatment system. To the extent that clients are inappropriately accepted into modalities within which there is a high probability of failure, under-treatment is indeed an ethical issue. There may be circumstances under which the admission of chronic clients into low intensity treatment regimes may be appropriate, but the potential and probable benefits must be ethically weighed against the potential iatrogenic effects of treatment failure.

Experimental Counseling Techniques

Special Treatment Procedures

◇ ◇ **98** ◇ ◇

Bill, an outpatient therapist at your agency, recently attended a two day seminar in which he was exposed to a new technique of rage reduction. In this technique the client is physically held by the therapist and goaded into rage reactions related to key areas of developmental trauma. Bill began using this technique immediately following the seminar. Other therapists are complaining to you that the approach is highly experimental and that there is no body of literature documenting the efficacy of the technique. Parents of two clients have called the agency to express concern that their children have been emotionally upset and volatile following their most recent appointments.

Discussion Questions

How would you respond to this situation?

What standards should guide the use of new and experimental counseling techniques with agency clients?

Should there be some supervisory or peer review process before a therapist uses strategies or techniques that fall outside standard clinical practice in the field?

To protect the health and safety of clients and the reputation of the agency, many organizations have established mechanisms of clinical privileging which are designed to assure: 1) that clinical practices (procedures, interventions, techniques) performed by staff are within the boundaries of the agency's mission and scope of services and 2) that the staff person performing such procedures is practicing within the boundaries of his or her education, training and expertise. Other agencies have set up special procedures of supervisory review, or staff committee review, related to the implementation of new or experimental methods or techniques within the agency. To protect clients from potential harm, the establishment of mechanisms for prior approval and on-going monitoring of experimental techniques is essential.

◇ ◇ **99** ◇ ◇

Pops is a late stage alcoholic with numerous alcohol-related health problems and a well-documented failure to sustain voluntary abstinence. The only history of any sustained sobriety was several Antabuse-aided experiments at sobriety several years ago. Pops' medical problems would normally contraindicate the use of Antabuse—both his age and medical history could make drinking on Antabuse life-threatening. On the other hand, Pops' medical problems have reached a point where his death is imminent if nothing intervenes to disrupt his cycles of prolonged intoxication. Both the medical and counseling staff are split on the potential risks and benefits of Antabuse in this situation.

Discussion Questions

What is the best procedure through which this risk-benefit analysis could be conducted at your agency?

Are there special procedures or guidelines to be followed in reviewing special treatment procedures that pose potential risks to the client?

Our discussion here will focus, not on the pros and cons of Antabuse, but the process utilized within a treatment program to evaluate the potential use of treatment procedures that may pose substantial risks to the comfort and health of the client. The adage, "first, do no harm" is operationalized within many treatment centers by procedures that require a justification, review and approval process prior to implementation. Such processes include preparation of a detailed procedure justification noting likely benefits and potential risks, review of the proposed procedure by the medical and clinical directors, review by a special committee of the clinical staff, assurance of voluntary informed consent of the client prior to procedure implementation, and a definition of monitoring procedures and indicators that would call for cancellation of further use of the procedure.

Freedom from Exploitation

◇ ◇ **100** ◇ ◇

Many substance abuse programs have incorporated "work therapy" into their daily regimen of treatment activities. In many cases the work involved is work that, if not done by clients in treatment, would require the hiring of additional staff or the completion of such work through contracted labor.

Discussion Questions

When is work "therapy" and when is work exploitation of a client?

What guidelines do you think should exist to prevent the potential exploitation of client labor?

Work assigned to clients can be therapeutic and it can be exploitive. Programmatic review of the following questions can help separate appropriate and inappropriate use of work within a treatment milieu.

- *Is there any aspect of work therapy duties that would pose a risk to the health or safety of the client?*
- *Are there any aspects of work therapy assignments that are demeaning or disrespectful?*
- *Does the institution, or do individual staff members, reap any direct financial benefits or gain from client labor?*
- *Are work assignments determined by client need for knowledge and skill development or by programmatic need (what the client is already capable of doing)?*
- *Do work therapy duties make up a disproportionate allocation of time in the treatment day compared to other more traditional therapy activities?*
- *Are the objectives—those benefits, skills, perspectives—the client is to achieve through work therapy clearly identified and communicated?*
- *Is the client's response to work therapy assignments reviewed and documented within the broader framework of treatment progress?*

Self-Disclosure

◇ ◇ **101** ◇ ◇

Jim, a recovering alcoholic counselor actively involved in Alcoholics Anonymous, is currently working in a residential substance abuse treatment program. One of his current assignments is to provide a series of lectures to clients on the steps and traditions of AA.

Discussion Questions

Is it appropriate for Jim to self-disclose his own recovering status and speak of the steps and traditions of AA from his experience as an AA member?

Would such disclosure violate the anonymity tradition of AA?

How can the agency avoid placing recovering staff in situations that might violate principles of their personal recovery programs?

The question of counselor self-disclosure encompasses practical issues (Is self-disclosure an effective counseling technique?), ethical issues (Are there circumstances under which self-disclosure would be wrong?), and personal issues (Does self-disclosure violate self-help traditions to which a counselor may be bound as part of his or her own personal recovery program?). In the above case, disclosure of the counselor's recovery status and AA affiliation would not be generally considered a breach of AA traditions as the demand for anonymity within these traditions extends only to disclosures involving print, TV, radio, films or other public media. It would be important, however, for the counselor to emphasize that he is speaking as an individual recovering person and as a professional alcoholism counselor and not speaking as a representative of or on behalf of AA. (See A.A. Guidelines for A.A. Members Employed in the Alcoholism Field available from the General Service Office of A.A.) Program managers and supervisors should be knowledgeable of various self-help traditions and guidelines and avoid assigning individuals work activities which might conflict with and undermine the staff member's personal recovery process.

◇ ◇ **102** ◇ ◇

Jack is an "old-style" recovering alcoholic who has worked for many years in halfway houses and residential treatment programs. His style of counseling involves a high level of personal self-disclosure—telling his story. Many persons have been deeply touched and personally inspired by Jack's story as it unfolded through their counseling sessions. Others were not.

Discussion Questions

Are there any ethical issues you see that could be created through such self-disclosure?

How would you distinguish appropriate from inappropriate self-disclosure?

Counselor self-disclosure has been used effectively by counselors as a relationship building tool, as a technique for reducing client resistance, and as a means of teaching principles about addiction and recovery. Some would say there has also been an over-reliance on self-disclosure at the expense of more effective counselor interactions. Ethical dimensions of counselor self-disclosure involve circumstances under which the timing or content of self-disclosure could undermine the counselor-client relationship or do other potential harm to the client. Counselor self-disclosure, for example, that was poorly timed or through its intensity created an expectation of the client to respond in like manner could so discomfort the client as to precipitate a flight from treatment. A more common concern is the danger that self-disclosure defocuses the attention of the interview from the client to the helper. Self-disclosure can represent a disengagement from the focus on client problems and needs and an over-involvement with the client to meet the support needs of the professional helper. Like the role reversal in a dysfunctional family where children take on caretaking responsibilities for their parents, here we could have the client thrust into the role of caretaker (listener, supporter) of the counselor. The over-reliance on self-disclosure as a counseling technique further violates client autonomy by inadvertently trying to program the client's experience through that of the therapist, a process that inevitably communicates: "This is the way I did it; this is the way you must do it." Developing a programmatic philosophy related to the appropriateness or inappropriateness of counselor self-

disclosure and providing training and supervision related to issues of counselor self-disclosure are recommended.

Dual Relationships

The concept of "dual relationship" embraces the existence of any relationship between the institution/worker and a client outside of the service relationship that could compromise the quality and integrity of the service process.   In   the   professional   helping   relationship,   the institution/worker takes on a special duty for the well-being of the client that assumes objectivity, honesty, advocacy, availability and continuity. Any pre-existing or secondary role relationships with the client may jeopardize these conditions, leading to a deterioration of service effectiveness and potential breaches in ethical conduct.   The vignettes below will explore a number of issues related to dual relationships.

Casual Encounters

◇ ◇ **103** ◇ ◇

Naomi, a substance abuse counselor who has worked in the same community for the past decade, runs errands for four hours on Saturday. Through the course of her tasks, she ran into five different current or former clients.

Discussion Questions

What ethical issues, if any, might arise in the following encounters?

- You have a client who lives in your neighborhood and you occasionally encounter each other while on walks and in neighborhood stores
- You have a client who has a son in the same school classroom as your daughter, creating periodic contact between you and the client at school events
- You frequent a store where one of your clients is employed as a sales clerk
- You live in a small, rural community in which you seem to always encounter clients outside the service setting

While such encounters as the above may cause fleeting awkwardness and while great care must be taken not to inadvertently violate client confidentiality (by directly or indirectly acknowledging the person's status as a client in the presence of others), these brief interactions do not usually fall within the rubric of dual relationships because the interactions possess neither the intensity nor the duration of contact to undermine the service relationship. It is best in such circumstances if the client is always in control of whether to acknowledge, address or otherwise initiate the contact. If the worker initiates contact, he may place the client in the awkward position of having to respond to a companion's query: "Who was that?"

Therapeutic Bias

◇ ◇ **104** ◇ ◇

Pam, a lifelong friend, calls you saying she feels she has a problem with alcohol and would like for you to assess her. She emphasizes how difficult this situation is for her and that she feels you are the only person with whom she would feel comfortable talking with about her drinking.

Discussion Questions

How do you respond to this request?

What are the issues to be considered in response to this request?

The primary ethical issue raised in the above vignette is whether the pre-existing personal relationship would eliminate your ability to perform your professional role. Does the intensity and duration of the pre-existing relationship destroy any pretense of objectivity? Will your prior relationship and hope for a continuing relationship with this person inevitably color your perceptions, judgements and recommendations? Are you being approached manipulatively by Pam because of what she hopes to be your lack of objectivity? Could information you have gained in the personal relationship be used in making clinical judgements and recommendations if you agreed to such an assessment? Would potential problems of role ambiguity and role conflict produced by mixing a personal and professional relationship not only undermine the personal friendship but decrease the integrity and quality of the service relationship? It is precisely the issues raised by these questions that has led to a general exclusion of service involvement with close friends, relatives and co-workers. While sharing general information about alcoholism, providing feedback on your perception of Pam's drinking, and encouraging Pam to seek assistance would all be helpful, referral of Pam to another assessment resource would be indicated.

◇ ◇ **105** ◇ ◇

You work as an intake worker at a residential substance abuse treatment program. A brother of a staff member who works as a counselor at the program is seeking admission for residential treatment.

Discussion Questions

What issues and concerns are raised by this request?

How would you respond to the request?

What guidelines should exist related to the treatment of family members, intimate partners, and close friends of staff by the agency?

See analysis after next vignette.

◇ ◇ **106** ◇ ◇

The President of the Board of your agency calls regarding the assessment of his son's apparent substance abuse problems.

Discussion Questions

Do you feel it would be appropriate or inappropriate for the agency to assess and/or treat a family member of a Board member?

What complexities could emerge from this type of dual relationship?

All of the above three vignettes represent situations in which the institutional-worker-to-client relationship could be compromised to the detriment of the potential service consumer. The ethical problems with dual relationships in these vignettes springs from pre-existing relationships with the clients that would compromise one's professional objectivity and judgement. A pre-existing relationship that elevates a client to the status of "special" almost always contaminates the integrity of clinical decision-making. In the case of the Board President seeking services for his son, there are at least two major sources of danger. The first is that the needs and interests of the child could be sacrificed to sustain a favorable relationship with the father. The father could, in such a case, exercise coercive power and control in his status as Board President to dictate clinical decisions in the service process to his son. Secondly, problems in the service delivery process could spill out to threaten the agency via arbitrary and capricious decisions of the Board President related to policies or personnel.

The potential for ethical breaches would always exist in the above described dual relationships. How programs respond to this differs widely. A growing number of programs explicitly prohibit the admission of persons who have pre-existing significant role relationships with staff persons of the agency. Other programs, particularly where alternative service agencies are not readily available, could utilize one or more of the following mechanisms to assure integrity of clinical decision-making:

- *the exclusion of the key staff person involved in the dual relationship from the service decision-making and service delivery process*
- *external clinical supervision or consultation to monitor the service delivery process so as to minimize the untoward effects of the dual relationship, or*
- *the use of an external consultant to actually conduct the assessment and provide the services required, thus providing services through the agency but outside the boundaries of the dual relationships.*

Social Relationships

◇ ◇ **107** ◇ ◇

Sherri hit it off with Renée from the second Sherri introduced herself as Renée's counselor in a 28 day residential substance abuse rehabilitation program. Sherri greatly respected the effort Renée put into treatment and found herself genuinely liking her. There were so many parallels between their lives and so many shared interests that a special bond quickly grew between them. After treatment Sherri also had continued contact with Renée through a shared twelve step program. Over the months following treatment, a special friendship developed between Sherri and Renée.

Within six months following treatment, Sherri and Renée became very close friends sharing a variety of social activities.

Discussion Questions

Comment on any ethical problems inherent within this relationship.

What special duties within the treatment relationship make social relationships with clients particularly problematic?

How would the issues be different if Sherri had met Renée while working as a secretary or outreach worker at the agency rather than as Renée's therapist?

When a social relationship is added to (some would say, replaces) a professional service relationship, the latter relationship is inextricably and irrevocably changed. Professional objectivity is lost. Professional honesty and candor is compromised because the worker does not want to jeopardize the friendship and the client's honest feedback on the service delivery process is compromised for the same reason. Both worker and client may find themselves experiencing role confusion, never being quite sure if they are interacting in the roles of helper-helpee or friend-friend. When the professional helper develops an investment and expectation in meeting his or her personal needs within the relationship with a client, the primary commitment and duty—the fiduciary contract—to care for the client has been at best weakened and at worst abandoned.

Sherri has, without conscious or malicious intent, left herself vulnerable to the charge that she has exploited the treatment relationship with Renée for her own personal needs. Both Renée and Sherri might deny such a charge, even perhaps making the points that no harm has been done to Renée and that their friendship has supported Renée's long-term recovery. By moving into a close personal relationship with Renée, Sherri has abdicated her potential to serve Renée in a professional role. If Renée should have the need to reinitiate services, Sherri's role as best friend would make it impossible to re-create their prior service relationship and would prevent Renée's access to the one professional person who could be in the best position to continue services. Future problems and conflict in this relationship could lead not only to a loss of a friendship, but to Renée's feelings of being used, feelings that could severely inhibit her willingness to enter into future helping relationships.

◇ ◇ **108** ◇ ◇

Lisa has a 16 year old son who has a different last name due to her remarriage. Lisa's son brings home his new girlfriend to meet his family. The girlfriend is a client that Lisa has been seeing in counseling for the past three months. They are both surprised to encounter each other under these circumstances.

Discussion Questions

Discuss special complications that could arise related to confidentiality, therapeutic bias and role ambiguity and confusion.

Should Lisa discontinue her clinical work with this client?

What guidelines would help staff address such difficult situations?

There are at least two types of risks posed by the above situation. The first is that the fact of the client's relationship with Lisa's son or problems which arise in this relationship could affect Lisa's professional work with the client. Problems of role confusion and role conflict may be inevitable for both the mother/counselor and the girlfriend/client. The second risk is that Lisa's knowledge of this client in their professional relationship could spill out of the professional setting to effect her relationship with her son. Suppose, for example, this young client had disclosed her past sexual promiscuity and fear that she was HIV positive. How does this privileged information not influence Lisa's communications to her son regarding this new relationship? How could the risk of inadvertent or conscious breaches of confidentiality be avoided under such circumstances? The health of all three parties in this situation may be best protected by the transfer of this client to another counselor. The general principle is: the greater the degree of intimacy in the service relationship, the greater the need for supervisory review to assure role clarity and role integrity. If the staff member in the above vignette drove a bus providing transport of the client to and from the center, there may be no significant conflict. If the staff member is the client's primary counselor, however, there is likely to be the potential for substantial conflict.

Self- help Relationships

◇ ◇ **109** ◇ ◇

You are a recovering alcoholic working as a counselor in a chemical dependency treatment program. While you are at an AA meeting, a client involved with your agency comments on his difficulties maintaining sobriety and makes references to several recent relapses and his lack of honesty with the treatment staff. The client has not disclosed this information to his counselor at your agency and the counselor is proceeding under the assumption the client has maintained continuous sobriety since counseling started.

Discussion Questions

How would you respond to this situation?

What information about this client, gained at an AA meeting, if any, would be appropriate to share back to your agency?

What ethical issues in your professional role and/or in your role as a recovering person would shape your decision?

What standard could be articulated to guide agency expectations of staff in such situations?

See analysis below.

◇ ◇ **110** ◇ ◇

A client you see has asked if you would be his/her AA sponsor.

Discussion Questions

How do you respond?

What special issues could arise in the dual roles of counselor-sponsor that could present problems for the client and yourself?

How do you feel about attending AA meetings at which clients are present or at which current or former clients are speaking?

See analysis below.

A 28 day residential chemical dependency program has all of its clients attempt to address the first five steps of Alcoholics Anonymous while in treatment. Each client is thus expected to complete a Fourth Step inventory and complete their Fifth Step just prior to discharge from treatment. Fifth Steps are usually conducted by volunteer priests and clergy but when scheduling problems occur, recovering counselors are expected to fill in for these volunteers.

Discussion Questions

What problems could potentially be created by this practice?

Should this special type of dual relationship be avoided?

All three of the above vignettes address special problems that can arise in dual relationships in which there are overlapping roles of counselor-client and self-help member to self-help member. Given the number of persons working in the substance abuse field who are involved in twelve step and related self-help programs, this is a particularly common problem area.

The guiding principle governing responses in all three vignettes is the desirability of clearly separating one's professional helping role and one's peer or helping role within a self-help structure. The first vignette tests the confidentiality of client disclosures within self-help meetings. While confrontation or encouragement for the client to initiate a more honest stance with the treatment staff would be appropriate in one's peer role as a self-help member, the disclosure of the information of the client's relapse behavior to the staff member's fellow treatment professionals would violate the tradition and expectation for confidentiality related to communications within self-help meetings. The counselor may choose to confront the client about the issue of honesty but this communication would be in the role of AA member to AA member, not counselor to client.

The second and third vignettes raise the question of whether it is ever appropriate to intensify role confusion in the helper-helpee roles by performing the role of both professional counselor and self-help sponsor and/or by mixing a professional counseling role with the sharing of a client's fifth step ritual. The concern with such situations is that the contractual relationship with the client loses its clarity through the assumption of multiple role relationships with the client, and that conflict or problems in one relationship may lead to problems in the other relationship. Folk wisdom within treatment agencies and self-help programs suggests that such dual relationships can pose risks to the long-term recovery of both the client and the staff member.

At a practical level, the recovering counselor may need to set up special guidelines for him or herself to avoid such dual relationship problems. Perhaps equally important are the special efforts that may need to be expended to sustain supports for his or her own recovery process. Many recovering counselors find it crucial to their health to find sources of support that allow them to escape the role of helper and focus on their own needs. Regularly seeking out meetings and retreats away from one's local professional helper identity and seeking peer supports from others who wrestle with such two-hat issues are examples of such personal caretaking by the recovering counselor.

Statements of belief related to this special type of dual relationship may be captured in Codes of Professional Practices as standards, aspirational values or simple statements of collective wisdom on this issue. Codes of Professional Practice can be a framework to capture collective lessons of experience, a mechanism to crystallize oral history into a form through which it can be transmitted to future generations of workers.

A new resource that tackles some of the two-hat boundary issues as well as such sensitive issues as sexual exploitation within self-help groups and ethical issues involving treatment-coerced fifth steps is Charlotte Davis Kasl's (1992) *Many Roads, One Journey.* This work is highly recommended.

Financial Transactions and Gifts

◇ ◇ **112** ◇ ◇

A worker has been patiently saving money to buy a new stereo system for several months. One of the clients in the worker's unit mentions in passing that he has a court fine due in one week and will go to jail if he is unable to pay it. The client further mentions that he will be all right if he can find someone to buy his stereo. The client is willing to sell a $1,000 stereo system for $250 so that he can pay his fine. The worker buys the stereo from the client after stopping by to see the stereo at the client's home. The client expresses gratitude to the worker for helping him out of a jam.

Discussion Questions

What issues do you see inherent within this transaction?

What problems might this transaction create for the client or the worker?

How might this transaction impact the relationship between the worker (agency) and the client?

How might the client's family view this transaction?

There are a number of potential ethical issues involved in financial transactions between professional helpers and their clients. There is the potential of a worker to exploit his or her position of power and the client's vulnerability for the worker's financial gain. There is the potential of the client's family (or members of the community) to perceive any transaction benefiting the worker in terms of manipulative exploitation, such that the reputation of the worker and/or the agency is damaged. There is the potential that the consequence of this transaction—whether good or bad—will alter the nature and integrity of the service relationship. Anyone who has witnessed the range of problems that have occurred through such transactions could speculate on the potential for such problems in the above vignette. A sample would include the following:

- *The client, though initially appreciative, quickly develops a resentment of the worker over the loss of the stereo.*
- *The worker's sense of owing the client opens vulnerability for manipulation by the client.*
- *The worker becomes quite angry and resentful toward the client when the stereo turns out to be a "lemon."*

- *The client's family perceives the transaction in terms of exploitation and discourages the client's continued service involvement.*
- *The stereo turns out to be stolen and the worker is later questioned by the police about receipt of stolen goods.*
- *The stereo turns out to be owned not by the client but by the client's parents who show up to demand the return of their property.*
- *The stereo is stolen from the worker's house a month after its purchase. The worker's suspicion of the client's involvement in the theft severely disrupts their service relationship.*

Financial transactions between professional helpers and clients (outside those involving reimbursement for professional services) in which the helper financially benefits can represent a misuse of the inequity of power in this relationship even when such misuse is unconscious or unintended. It is the client's vulnerability and the helper's power in this relationship that has led to prohibitions and restrictions on financial transactions and gifts between clients and helpers.

You have decided to buy a new vehicle and when you get to the dealer you are met by a former client now working as a salesperson. The former client is very happy to see you and expresses appreciation for your past role by offering to sell you the car of your choice at cost.

Discussion Questions

What things might be considered in your decision to accept or decline this offer?

How does this situation differ from an encounter with a client working as a cashier in a grocery store who checks out your groceries?

What standard should govern financial transactions with clients?

In an earlier discussion (of sexual relationships with former clients) in this chapter, the question was raised whether the special power of the professional helper was lost even after the service relationship was terminated. The general belief that such power is not lost is the basis for why the question of ethical conduct must be examined in the above situation. This point is further underscored in service settings that address diseases or disorders characterized by episodes of remission and relapse. All interactions with former clients must be conducted based on an awareness of the client's potential need to reinitiate the service relationship. In the grocery store situation, the worker receives no special benefit based on his or her pre-existing service relationship with the client. At the auto dealer, however, such a benefit based on the helper-helpee relationship does exist and makes the acceptance of the client's offer ethically questionable. The primary concerns are that the benefit received from such an offer could alter the client's future comfort re-initiating services and that the helper's potential acceptance of the financial benefit would represent a transformation of the relationship from the professional to the social.

◇ ◇ **114** ◇ ◇

The family of an adolescent currently in treatment at your agency hears of the agency's fund drive for a new facility and offers to donate $10,000 toward the construction of the new facility.

Discussion Questions

Would you accept this donation?

Describe the issues considered in your decision.

Are the principles consistent with the policies you would advocate governing acceptance of gifts from clients by direct service staff? If not, describe how the ethical dimensions of client-institution gifts differ from that of client-counselor gifts.

The first ethical question raised by the above incident is whether the family "hearing about" the agency's capital fund drive was, in fact, an attempt by a staff member or the institution to financially exploit the family's current vulnerability and dependence. If no such action or intent occurred, there is still the question of whether the institution's acceptance of the $10,000 will alter the service relationship to the detriment of the adolescent and/or family. Would the acceptance of the gift potentially contaminate clinical decision-making? Will the gift inevitably produce the status of "special client?" Will feedback that needs to go to the family be withheld or will clinical decisions be altered for fear of losing *the family's favor? Would acceptance of the gift influence the designation of "successfully completed treatment" if the adolescent was placed as an alternative to incarceration with the stipulation that he successfully complete treatment. Perhaps a broader issue is whether the same standard established to guide (or prohibit) financial transactions between counselors and clients also applies to the relationship between the institution and clients. One practical option might be the following: Assuming that the family's greatest vulnerability for exploitation is during the period of active service delivery, it could be explained that the program desires to avoid even the most subtle forms of exploitation and to avoid any transactions that could be perceived by other potential service consumers as exploitive. Given this desire, it would be best if the family's decision to donate to the building fund could be post-poned until after their son or daughter has completed primary treatment and aftercare. If at that time they still desire to make the contribution, their gift would be graciously accepted. It is best for the protection of clients and the agency if the roles of active service recipient and patron or benefactor are not mixed.*

◇ ◇ 115 ◇ ◇

Jason, a withdrawn adolescent who has been slowly emerging from his shell, enters your office and offers you a gift he purchased in your hospital's gift shop. The gift is a silk rose flower in a small glass vase. Jason says this is his way to say thanks for "hanging in with him."

Discussion Questions

What would be your response to Jason?

Are there any circumstances in which the refusal of a gift would be clinically or ethically inappropriate?

What kind of protocol should guide the acceptance or refusal of gifts from clients?

Agencies have attempted to address potential ethical problems related to gifts from clients through such mechanisms as the following:

- *establishing a prohibition on the acceptance of personal gifts by any agency employee*

- *establishing a value (such as $10) of a gift over which an employee may not accept, or*
- *establishing a supervisory review mechanism through which all gifts must be reported and reviewed for any potential problems.*

Barry (1983) offers seven factors that should be considered in the ethics of giving and receiving gifts.

1. *What is the value of the gift?*
2. *What is the purpose of the gift?*
3. *What are the circumstances under which the gift was given?*
4. *What is the position and sensitivity to influence of the person receiving the gift?*
5. *What is the accepted business practice in the area?*
6. *What is the company policy?*
7. *What is the law?*

Our concern in the case of Jason is the potential harm to the therapy relationship that could result from refusal of the gift. If programs implement gift policies to protect clients from potential exploitations, it is important that such policies be communicated to clients BEFORE clients extend the offer of gifts. Communicating and repeating the nature of this policy prevents clients from feeling hurt or rejected when their efforts at reciprocity in the helping relationship are met with refusal. Allowing token gifts to be accepted on behalf of the agency is a compromise position that protects the client from exploitation and the feeling of rejection that could accompany gift refusal.

◇ ◇ **116** ◇ ◇

Rick is requesting therapy services in your private addiction counseling service. He is unable to pay for these services with cash, but he has proposed a bartering of services to pay for his counseling.

Discussion Questions

Describe your response to a proposal to trade any of the following for counseling services: housecleaning services, works of art, clerical services, plumbing services , yard work, or auto repair.

What special clinical and ethical issues do you see potentially arising
from such barter arrangements?

*There are at least two troublesome issues that can arise through the use of barter
to obtain counseling services. The first is an issue of the equity and fairness in
assessing the value of labor and how misunderstandings over the barter
negotiations can spill into, and lead to a deterioration in, the helping relationship.
How does one practically compare the value of a piece of art to therapy services?
Is there a differential assessment of the value of one hour of therapy and one hour
of yard work? The therapist may be open to charges of exploitation of Rick's
vulnerability in the comparative assignment of value in the bartering process. A
second issue is the extent to which fulfilling the barter agreement leads to a
breakdown of intimacy barriers in the professional relationship. Would a client
performing housecleaning and laundry services in barter for therapy services
inevitably lead to such a breakdown? Would the regular presence of the client in
the therapist's house—the inevitable mundane social intercourse outside the
normal structure of the therapy process—trivialize and degrade the helping
relationship? Could potential disagreements over missed or poor quality cleaning
insinuate itself as a source of diversion from the helping process? While there are
potential problems in the practice of bartering, it is probably best viewed within
a cultural context. In cultural settings in which bartering is common and the
value for various products and services is clearly defined, this medium of
exchange may pose few ethical complexities. It may be important for the counselor
to explore the practice of bartering within the client's cultural context before
making a decision as to the appropriateness or inappropriateness of such an
arrangement.*

Physical Touch

◇ ◇ 117 ◇ ◇

A substance abuse agency, well known for its warm, family atmosphere,
has evolved a ritual of frequent hugging between staff members and
clients.

Discussion Questions

> Are there situations in which such familiarity could be experienced by the client as disrespectful or a violation of appropriate boundaries in the therapy relationship?

> How can we be supportive and nurturing without being disrespectful and invasive?

> Is there a value or standard that helps staff define appropriate and inappropriate touch at your agency?

> Does the value or standard explicitly define the parameters of touch as a component of counseling technique and the counseling relationship?

Values and standards related to physical touch in health and human service agencies will vary according to local community cultures, the nature of the client population, the nature of the services rendered, the education and training of staff and the unique organizational culture. Defining the boundary line between appropriate and inappropriate touch must be done with an understanding of these contexts. Jeanette H. Milgrom (1992) of the Walk-In Counseling Center in Minneapolis, Minnesota regularly conducts a workshop, "Boundaries in Professional Relationships," for a wide variety of health and human service workers. She has devised a framework for exploring personal and agency standards that goes beyond abstract philosophical discussion to examine the appropriateness or inappropriateness of specific helper behaviors. Using a three column discussion worksheet with the headings "Always OK," "Sometimes OK" and "Never OK," participants are asked to define for themselves or for their agencies under which categories certain behaviors should be placed. This structure can be used to explore a broad number of client staff boundary issues. On the following page is a worksheet through which substance abuse prevention and treatment staff can specifically explore values and standards related to physical touch. I have found this format exceptionally helpful as a training aid in helping substance abuse workers explore ethical issues related to physical touch.

There may be any number of factors that make the issue of physical touch a particularly important clinical and ethical issue within the substance abuse field. There is a growing body of evidence documenting the number of men and women entering substance abuse treatment with histories of physical and/or sexual abuse. Our clients not only have histories of sexual abuse, but have a much higher proportion of traumagenic factors associated with such abuse—factors such as early onset, extended duration, multiple perpetrators, physical violence involved in sexual violation, and failure to be believed when silence was broken to significant adults. Given the intensity and duration of such trauma, great care must be taken in protecting the physical and psychological safety of our clients within service relationships. That safety is assured through a rigorous sensitivity to actions that could be experienced by the client as a sign of imminent seduction, violation or abandonment. Physical contact of any kind—regardless of its intent—can be violating if it is made without the non-coerced consent of the person on the receiving end of such contact. Client participation in rituals of physical nurturing such as hugging should be an option rather than a mandate. Many persons, including this author, would question whether non-coerced consent is even possible given the power imbalance in the helping relationship. The greater the power differential, the less freedom available to the client to assert his or her own boundaries of comfort related to physical touch. The physical and psychological safety of clients requires great sensitivity to the multiple meanings of physical touch.

*The Boundaries of Physical Touch

Behavior	Always OK	Sometimes OK	Never OK
Frontal hug (face to face position; arms around client with bodies touching)			
Holding a client on your lap			
Kissing a client on the cheek			
Touching the client's breasts or genitals			
Asking client for a massage			
Touching a client's knee			
Side Hug (Side to side position: one arm around client's shoulder)			
Touching the client's face, as in wiping away a tear or a hand on the client's cheek.			
Brief holding of hand			
Massaging a client's face			
Massage of client's neck and shoulders			
Kissing a former client on the lips			
Sexual intercourse with a client's relative			
Patting a clients arm or shoulder			
Sustained holding of client's hand			
Giving a client a full body massage			
Asking client to remove article(s) of clothing			
Asking client for touch			

* Adapted from *Boundaries in Professional Relationships: A Training Manual,* Jeanette H. Milgrom, Available from Walk-In Counseling Center, Minneapolis, Minnesota.

Verbal Intimacy

◇ ◇ **118** ◇ ◇

Marjorie works as an outpatient substance abuse counselor at your agency. She is young, energetic and effusive in her warmth to both clients and other staff. She can be heard with great animation exclaiming or joking, "You're beautiful," "You're the greatest," or sharing other terms of affection and appreciation to staff and clients. Joshua, the other outpatient therapist in her unit, seems to spend an inordinate amount of time on sexuality issues in his counseling work with clients.

Discussion Questions

> Are there verbal intimacy barriers that can be violated in the counselor-client relationship?

> What kinds of verbal communications with clients would be considered invasive or abusive?

As noted in the introduction to this chapter, the physical and sexual abuse of clients within helping relationships is often the last step in the progressive movement of helper disengagement or over-involvement. By seeing sexual abuse, for example, as the end of a progression of violations of intimacy barriers, earlier stages can be identified as targets of intervention and prevention. Through such scrutiny, we have the capacity to not only decrease the sexual abuse of clients, but to also decrease the other boundary violations that often precede such abuse. The above vignette opens the discussion of different levels of verbal intimacy that may or may not be appropriate depending on the agency, one's role, and the characteristics of particular clients. It can be very helpful for agencies to explore values that define the boundary lines between communications that are professionally appropriate and those that violate boundaries of appropriate intimacies or are otherwise abusive to clients. On the following page, there is another worksheet using the same format developed by Jeanette Milgrom which was displayed in the last vignette. This worksheet can be used in small group discussion or individually to help staff explore boundary issues within their communications with clients.

Nature of verbal communication	Always OK	Sometimes OK	Never OK
"You're very attractive."			
Using profanity with or directed at a client.			
"We've become very close since we first started seeing each other."			
"You're very special to me."			
"There are times I forget you're a client."			
Talking with client about or inquiring about sexual topics unrelated to topics defined to be addressed in counseling.			
Answering client questions about your personal life.			
"I like you."			
Disclosing one's own intimate relationship issues.			
Increasing the frequency and duration of client interviews.			
Asking questions about the client's personal life not related to presenting problems.			
Calling the client by his or her first name.			
Using client's time to discuss helper's interests or hobbies.			
"I'll always be here for you."			
Using terms of endearment with a client, e.g., Honey, Sweetheart, etc.			
Calling the client at home.			
Meeting client outside of office.			
"I love you."			

Sexual Relationships

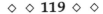

◇ ◇ **119** ◇ ◇

Robert works on the maintenance staff at your agency. He met a young woman who frequently comes to the agency for services and subsequently asked her for a date. Robert met her at the agency and asked her out while she was at the agency for an appointment with her therapist. They have become sexually involved and there is now a conflict with the woman's family because Robert has asked this client to move in with him. The family has written a formal complaint to the agency claiming that a staff member took unfair advantage of their daughter.

Discussion Questions

Did Robert's asking the client for a date constitute a breach of ethical conduct in the agency-client relationship?

Does the traditional prohibition against sexual involvements with clients extend to non-clinical staff of the agency? If so, how should such expectations be communicated?

There are a number of potential ethical issues present in the above critical incident. These would include:

- *Does Robert's sexual involvement with the client constitute an exploitive abuse of power derived from his employment at the agency? Would the situation be viewed differently if Robert knew the client in the past and the initiation of the relationship did not occur through contact at the agency?*
- *Will the client's sexual relationship with Robert pose risks to her continued service relationship with the organization?*
- *Will the perception of Robert's behavior damage the professional reputation of the agency in the eyes of the client's family or in the eyes of other potential service consumers?*

If we accept the notion that there is an institutional-client relationship in addition to a worker-client relationship; if we accept that the worker-client relationship flows out of the more fundamental contractual relationship between the institution and the worker; and if we assume that it is the institution that holds forth the primary commitment to protect the client's vulnerability through ethical and professional conduct and that each worker acts as an organizational agent bound by this commitment, then all persons who represent the organization—paid employees, board members, volunteers, consultants—are bound by this contractual relationship. For any agency representative—regardless of the role—to approach the client with the primary agenda of meeting the representative's own needs would constitute a breach in the contract governing the agency-client relationship.

This vignette offers an excellent illustration of the differences between professional codes of ethics and agency Codes of Professional Practice. Whereas agencies rely on the former to guide ethical conduct of employees, we typically find, as in Robert's case, a number of agency employees who have no such code of ethics and who quite likely have not been fully oriented to boundaries of appropriateness in their relationships with agency clients. In contrast, agency codes of professional practice cover all employees and involve all employees in training and orientation related to boundary issues in client relationships.

Verbal/Physical Abuse

◇ ◇ **120** ◇ ◇

Therapy groups within the substance abuse field have historically been much more confrontational than in any other sector of human services. Some groups—modeled on the early "Synanon game"—could potentially be viewed as almost brutal by an outsider unfamiliar with the technique and its purposes.

Discussion Questions

How do we distinguish appropriate confrontation from verbal abuse and disrespect of a client?

What standard could define and distinguish appropriate interventions from client abuse?

Like the relationship between computer hardware and computer software, treatment technology (software) must be selectively matched to the characteristics (hardware) of a client. There are ethical issues in the inappropriate use of treatment techniques when such techniques are demeaning, have little likelihood of success or pose iatrogenic (harmful) risks. The application of confrontation techniques designed to penetrate the rigid defense structure of the street/prison-hardened addict-con to the client whose defense structures are fragile and underdeveloped could pose serious iatrogenic risks. Such misapplication of clinical technique violates a number of basic explicit and implicit elements of the contractual relationship between the client and the agency/worker. It violates the commitment of the agency to base its intervention with the client on an individualized assessment of the client's needs. It also violates the commitment to not harm the client. Mechanisms to avoid ethical breaches that occur through inappropriately applied treatment technology include:

- *rigorous screening that excludes potential clients for whom a program's standard treatment protocol may be ineffective or harmful*
- *utilization of an interdisciplinary assessment and individualized service planning process that allows for the strategic deletion of potentially harmful service modalities or activities*
- *a clear mechanism (e.g., clinical supervision, team meetings) through which workers may voice their perception of client-treatment mismatch issues.*

Assisted Suicide

◇ ◇ **121** ◇ ◇

Robin went through inpatient treatment more than three years ago and has continued outpatient counseling episodically since his discharge. He has maintained uninterrupted sobriety since his admission and most of the counseling support has focused on issues surrounded the diagnosis of AIDS made during Robin's initial treatment contact. Robin's health has deteriorated significantly during the past six months and this week he announced in the counseling session that he has decided to plan his own suicide. He has been with two close friends through the final terminal phase of AIDS and has consciously made a decision to take his life before he reaches this final stage of deterioration. He has been reading about "assisted suicides" where the suicide (by drug ingestion) takes place within a ceremony in which the person with AIDS is brought together with loved ones for tribute and farewell.

Discussion Questions

Describe your response to the following:

1. Robin expresses his wish to use the counseling time to plan and emotionally prepare himself for this event. How do you respond?
2. Robin seeks your technical knowledge about drugs in the selection of an appropriate drug and dosage to assure that his death will be as quick and painless as possible. How do you respond?
3. Robin asks you if you will attend the ceremony. What factors would influence your decision to attend or not attend the ceremony?
4. You know the time and date of the ceremony at which Robin will end his life. Would you take any action to stop this event?
5. What ethical issues do you see arising in the above situations? What standards or procedures could guide staff facing such a situation?

This vignette raises some very complicated ethical issues that would have to be carefully sorted out in the process of clinical and administrative supervision. The use of counseling time to help Robin emotionally prepare himself for this ritual of suicide first and foremost raises the issue of whether the counselor would be overstepping the bounds of his or her competence to assent to this request. Assent would imply competence on the part of the counselor to both clinically understand and counsel dying persons and the ability to ascertain whether the client's exploration of suicide is being made out of free choice or compromised mental status. If the counselor's clinical training and experience does not assure such competence, then referral to other resources for these specific services would be indicated. Referral options might include hospice programs, HIV/AIDS support groups, and psychiatric/psychological consultation. Referral of Robin for mental health consultation would help assess the degree to which Robin's current suicidal thinking is being influenced by transient change in mental status, e.g., depression, that warrants active treatment. If the counselor was clinically competent to assent to this client's request, a more fundamental issue is whether the counselor could ethically support the decision of this client to take his own life. This would immediately force an examination of the values of the counselor and the values of the agency that would guide this decision. In some agencies, (i.e., Catholic social service agencies) organizational values derived from religious sponsorship would rigidly preclude any such involvement. In other agencies, the option of whether to respond to Robin's initial request would require a more involved analysis of agency policy and the values of agency staff and leadership. The obvious conflict between the value of autonomy (Robin's right to make decisions controlling his own destiny) and the value of nonmaleficence (the counselor's obligation not to harm Robin) would need to be seriously weighed.

Providing Robin technical knowledge to actually commit the suicide act would in nearly all cases fall outside the competence of the addiction counselor. Such active assistance would abdicate the counselor's role to objectively explore the client's emotional health and life options and place the counselor in the role of advocate of a particular course of action. Moving out of this position of neutrality, for example, could decrease the ability of the client to reconsider his decision at a later time. An important discussion point is whether referral of the client to a source for the information he is seeking would also abdicate counselor neutrality and loyalty to the welfare of the client. The concern is that such a referral is seen in the eyes of the client as approval and encouragement for him to proceed with his decision. There are important lines between understanding a suicide decision, providing continued emotional support to the client considering suicide, providing technical support to actually effect the suicide and advocating suicide as an option.

The decision to attend or not attend the suicide ceremony involves both counselor values and agency values and the analysis of a number of key questions. Would the counselor's presence at the suicide ceremony violate any core values of the counseling profession or the agency? If the counselor attends the ceremony, would he or she be in attendance as a private citizen or as a representative of the agency? How will the counselor's presence effect the willingness of other persons with HIV disease to seek services from the agency? How will attendance potentially effect the reputation of the counselor and the reputation of the agency? Knowledge of the time and place of the ceremony and the decision of whether to intervene would have to be carefully weighed based both on the clinical data provided by the counselor on Robin's mental status and on the values of the counselor and the organization. If the counselor judged Robin's decision as not reflecting a rational decision (the value of autonomy) but a consequence of acute depression, then he or she would have an ethical duty to protect Robin from harm (the value of beneficence).

Situations like the above raise very complex clinical, ethical and legal issues. If part of the function of professional practice codes is to protect the health and integrity of clients, staff, the agency and the community; then what is most clear is that decision-making in such situations should not be made alone and that the best resources possible are brought together to guide our responses to such situations.

Documentation

You have just finished the assessment of a client in which there was the admission of numerous acts of cocaine-related criminal activity, e.g., drug transactions, embezzlement, armed robbery and the prior physical abuse of the client's spouse. The client in reporting these incidents noted times, dates, places, and other persons involved.

Discussion Question

What would you consider in determining what, if any of this information, is recorded in the client's permanent medical record?

Numerous forces come together to shape the parameters and content of what gets documented in a client's service record. External regulatory and funding agencies dictate both elements and processes of data collection. The agency's clinical philosophy shapes the designation of what should and should not be documented. Ethical dimensions of the documentation process could involve such things as:

- *the accuracy of clinical documentation*
- *the degree to which client self-report, clinical observations and clinical judgement are clearly delineated*
- *the degree to which judgements, diagnoses, and recommendations are within the scope of the education, training and competence of each person recording such data*
- *the exclusion of material that lacks clinical relevance and could do potential harm to the client if inadvertently disclosed, and*
- *cognizance of problems related to secondary breaches of confidentiality—violation of confidentiality by persons or organizations*

to whom clinical information has been released via signed client consent.

Ethical issues in the vignette above would be influenced by one's setting and role. If this was an evaluation conducted by a forensic psychiatrist or psychologist, documentation of a high level of detail might be warranted to elucidate the client's state of mind at the time of the criminal offenses and to detail the exact relationship between the client's substance abuse and the client's criminal activity. If, however, this assessment is an intake to a substance abuse treatment program, different documentation criteria would apply. In the latter setting, it is the fact of drug-related criminal activity and the frequency, intensity, duration, and variety of criminal activity that is clinically relevant in assessing the person-drug relationship, not the details of when, where and with whom such crimes were committed. The latter detail not only lacks clinical relevance but its documentation could potentially harm the client via inadvertent or secondary breaches of confidentiality.

Staff members who have been trained to rigorously document nearly all clinical data may have difficulty understanding the need for such care related to documentation. After all, some would say, the clinical records are confidential and the dangers of secondary disclosure are remote. The following story is illustrative of the possibility and potential consequences of accidental disclosure of nonessential information.

> *John completed treatment related to his cocaine dependence in a reputable inpatient chemical dependency unit within the local hospital in his home community. During the early assessment interviews John disclosed that he had sold cocaine to fellow employees and had embezzled funds from his employer to sustain his cocaine addiction. John's primary counselor noted the details of these actions (how, when, where, to whom) as John had reported them within the "Psychosocial Summary" form used by the unit. As John's treatment progressed, he spent considerable time expiating feelings of guilt related to his drug-related criminal activity, particularly as it related to the embezzlement of funds from his employer who had been extremely supportive of John. Deciding that he couldn't have the guilt and risk of eventual discovery hanging over his head, John called and set an appointment with his boss for his first day back at work, at which time he planned to confess his indiscretion and either work out a plan for restitution or "let the chips fall where they may." John signed a release of information*

for a "Discharge Summary" to be sent to his employer which according to company policy had to accompany his release to go back to work. The release which was forwarded to the Medical Records Department of the hospital within which the unit operated found itself in the hands of a new employee. Confronted by a thick file and forms unlike those used on all the other units of the hospital, she mistakenly pulled and forwarded the "Psychosocial Summary" from John's file instead of the "Discharge Summary." John's employer, expecting to find a routine release for John to return to work, was quite shocked to find a document detailing John's embezzlement of funds. When John arrived at the meeting with his boss on his first day back, he was summarily fired and told the information had been turned over to the local police department. John was eventually indicted and the hospital was subsequently sued, choosing to settle out of court for what was an obvious and blatant breach of client confidentiality.

Cheryl has seen Gerald for the past seven months in her private practice substance abuse counseling service. The clinical record, if it were examined today, would include intake forms completed by the client and progress notes which contain only the repeated notations "client seen" following each date that Gerald has been counseled over the past months.

Discussion Questions

What kind of ethical issues do you see in this situation?

What kind of problems could arise due to the failure to document the course of treatment and the client's response to this treatment?

What special ethical issues, if any, could arise in your setting due to failure to adequately document assessment data, the course of client treatment, and the client's response to treatment?

A client's service record has multiple functions. These functions include documentation of services related to service reimbursement, documentation to meet regulatory requirements for accreditation or licensure, and documentation related to potential legal defense, in addition to its utility in the clinical service process. A primary purpose of the service record is to capture a clear synopsis of the assessment data and conclusions, treatment procedures utilized, and the client's response to various treatments for the benefit of current and future care-givers. If Cheryl would be unable to continue seeing Gerald for any reason, the next care-giver would lack much of the significant clinical data that could speed the initiation and enhance the quality of the service delivery process. The failure to document significant clinical data about a client gathered through the counseling process could pose risks to the client or others just as a medical record that failed to document medication allergies could pose risks to the life of the client. The failure to document is an abdication of one's professional duty and responsibility to protect the current and future interests of the client.

Referral

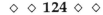

◇ ◇ **124** ◇ ◇

Scott is an intake worker at an outpatient substance abuse counseling agency. Today a 22 year old client arrives seeking counseling services which Scott is able to easily arrange through the agency. The client presents another dilemma for Scott that is more personally troublesome. The client reports that she is three months pregnant, has used massive quantities of alcohol and cocaine over the past six months and is terrified of the prospects of a severely impaired baby. Because of this fear, she reports to Scott that she has decided to get an abortion. Given that there are no physicians or clinics providing abortions in the local community, the client seeks Scott's assistance in linking her to the closest such agency. Lacking any organizational policies or procedures to guide his response to such a request, Scott is thrust back on his own discomfort. Although Scott—a practicing Catholic—is very ambivalent about many of the church's teachings, including those on abortion, his active participation in the church is very important to him. He believes he could face ex-communication if he materially aids in helping someone get an abortion.

Discussion Questions

What are Scott's choices in this situation?

What organizational policies might aid someone like Scott who find themselves in a similar situation?

Staff working in substance abuse treatment programs may encounter a variety of situations in which their personal beliefs conflict with the performance of their job duties. While it is reasonable for the agency to assume an employee would not seek a job position whose performance conflicted directly with his or her personal beliefs (person opposed to methadone applying to work in a methadone program), such conflicts can arise in isolated instances or when an employee's job responsibilities have been fundamentally altered. What is critical is the availability of a mechanism through which the employee can escape or resolve the conflict without compromising the accessibility, timeliness and quality of client services. The mechanism in most cases is that of supervisory consultation. In the case above, Scott could seek the assistance of his supervisor, explain the nature of his conflict and ask if the supervisor or another staff person could respond to the client's request for referral information. If the agency, as a matter of policy, did not provide referral information for abortion, that policy could be explained to the client with the recommendation that she discuss her concerns with her physician.

Responsibility to Terminate

Responsibility to Refer

◇ ◇ **125** ◇ ◇

Cedric, a client you have been seeing in outpatient counseling for the past four months, has prematurely terminated outpatient treatment with other therapists on two previous occasions and has experienced several episodes of relapse during this tenure in treatment.

Discussion Questions

Should Cedric's course of outpatient treatment be terminated with a referral to inpatient treatment?

When does a client's lack of responsiveness to treatment ethically require termination and referral?

Where is the line between responsibility to terminate/refer and abandonment of the client?

The mandate to terminate and refer arises when a client is not responding to a particular regimen of treatment and there exists alternative approaches or settings to treatment that have a greater likelihood of success than the treatment the client is currently receiving. This ethical mandate is intensified in circumstances where the client may be pressured into staying involved in the current treatment due to the financial or emotional self-interests of the practitioner or institution. The mandate to terminate and refer is part of a broader concern of shame-based treatment: the placement of the client in a modality that has little likelihood of success and then blaming the client when they fail to achieve change in that modality. In contrast to appropriate decisions to terminate and refer, abandonment occurs when:

- *the decision to terminate is precipitous*
- *the client is not provided a reasonable period of time to process termination of the helping relationship*
- *the decision to terminate is based not on the clients needs, but the needs of the practitioner or the institution, and*
- *there is no reasonable effort to arrange for alternative services for the client.*

This chapter has explored a number of critical incidents through which individual workers and agencies must define boundaries of appropriate and inappropriate behavior in our service relationships with clients. Individually and collectively we must do three things:

1. We must define the boundaries of abuse and declare unequivocally that such behaviors are prohibited and, if exhibited, will result in the field's most severe consequences.

2. We must define those zones of marginality that involve increased vulnerability for clients and staff and build in special supports to protect the safety of each.

3. We must define the zone of effectiveness both in terms of our mainstream clinical practices and in the articulation of our highest aspirational values.

Chapter Seven

Conduct in Professional Peer Relationships

What values and ethical standards should govern the relationships between helping professionals and helping agencies? While there is a long history of exploring ethical issues in helper-client relationships, the substance abuse field has only recently begun to fully explore the ethical dimension of the helper-to-helper relationship. The reader will find parallels between the ethical issues in these two different types of relationships. Dual relationships, boundary violations, and values of respect, honesty, and fidelity will be extended from the last chapter and applied to our examination of professional relationships. This chapter will explore ethical issues that can arise in our relationships with each other. The chapter will also explore ethical issues in professional peer relationships within two separate contexts: peer relationships inside the helping organization and relationships with professional peers and agencies external to one's primary work place. The vignettes contained in this chapter will help the reader develop a personalized version of what Haas and Malouf (1989) have called the "etiquette of collegial relationships."

Critical Incidents

Internal Professional Relationships

Management of Human Resources

Staff Hiring

◇ ◇ **126** ◇ ◇

Sue has developed a reputation as an extremely competent and charismatic leader of a local substance abuse agency. She has handpicked and recruited what many would call the "cream of the crop" of substance abuse professionals within her community. Her ability to aggressively recruit

highly capable and experienced staff has been described by some as
"management genius" while others refer to her recruiting practices
pejoratively as "raiding," and bitterly refer to their own agencies as
training centers for Sue's agency.

Discussion Questions

Are there any standards (ethical or otherwise) governing how your
agency recruits staff?

What would you consider to be unethical recruiting practices?

*Most agencies who address this issue quickly achieve consensus on two issues
First, they articulate an ethical mandate to accurately represent job duties, salary
benefits, career ladders/paths and the realistic potential for advancement during th
staff recruitment and interviewing process. Second, they articulate an ethica
prohibition against misrepresenting or impugning the reputation, salary structure
career potential, etc., of the agency in which the person being recruited currentl
works. There is less consensus on where to draw the boundary line betwee
aggressive recruiting and recruiting that is unprofessional or unethical. An eve
more complex issue is raised by the following question: Is it unethical to buil
the strength of one agency at the expense of the remaining local health and huma
service agencies? This question broadens the perspective and raises the possibilit
of practices which enhance one agency while weakening, and thus doing potentia
harm to, the whole community's health and human service system.*

◇ ◇ **127** ◇ ◇

You are a supervisor in an agency that has experienced, and i
experiencing, extreme turmoil. The agency has undergone seriou
leadership problems, been subjected to numerous reorganizations, an
experienced an extremely high rate of staff turnover. Staff morale is at a
all time low.

Discussion Question

In filling the vacant staff positions, how much information do yo
provide to perspective applicants about the agency's current intern
problems?

This vignette raises the question of whether there is an ethical mandate for "truth in hiring." There would be a breach in the ethical principle of honesty if conditions within the agency were overtly misrepresented. It creates a situation in which the foundation of the agency-worker relationship is one of dishonesty and deception. Most workers know that morale ebbs and flows within an organization. A candid description of the organization's current stage of development, while potentially scaring a few candidates away, begins the relationship between the employee and the organization on a foundation of candor and honesty. While it may not be appropriate to indiscriminately disclose an agency's internal problems to every job applicant, it would seem reasonable that all candidates being offered a particular position would be apprised of such problems. A "no surprise" policy begins the person-agency contract on an ethical foundation of honesty and fidelity.

◇ ◇ **128** ◇ ◇

A residential substance abuse program has for more than two decades recruited the majority of its staff from the pool of clients who have gone through the program.

Discussion Questions

What kind of guidelines should govern the recruitment and hiring of recovering persons?

Are there special concerns related to hiring persons to work in a program in which they were also in treatment?

There may be a number of practical concerns involved with hiring recovering persons to work in the roles of professional helpers within substance abuse programs, but the ethical issues generally involve the potential for exploitation by the hiring organization. The potential for harmful exploitation is illustrated through the following questions.

1) *Are the interests and needs of the recovering person/client compromised to meet program needs? Has the client's treatment been shortened, for example, to speed his or her movement into a staff position during a period of high staff turnover?*

2) *Is the recovering person being placed in a position that jeopardizes the stability and durability of his or her recovery? Does the recovering*

person have the length and stability of sobriety to manage the high stress work environment of substance abuse treatment?

3) Is the person's status of recovery or his or her status of former client being unduly taken advantage of via lack of equity, salary, work schedules, working assignments, etc., in comparison to non-recovering staff?

The most frequent attempt to address this potential for harmful exploitation is to establish time requirements for continuous sobriety when you consider hiring recovering persons as staff. These requirements may range from one year of continuous sobriety for detox technicians to the more typical three to five years of continuous sobriety for recovering substance abuse counselors.

Nepotism

◇ ◇ **129** ◇ ◇

You are an executive director who has been recruited from out of state to take over the management of a rural substance abuse agency with a multi-county catchment area. Confronted with your inability to recruit qualified staff into your locality, you are considering hiring your spouse to run the agency's residential services. Your spouse is academically trained, is a certified addictions counselor, and has prior supervision experience.

Discussion Questions

What problems could be created by this choice?

What ethical issues are raised via the hiring of family members?

There is a substantial amount of folk wisdom within the substance abuse field—and almost all other fields—on the risks inherent in hiring one's own family members. This wisdom posits that the selection and placement of one's spouse could prove disruptive to the organization and pose potential risks to the health of the marital relationship. In short, the folk wisdom says: "Anyone who hires his or her own spouse is just asking for trouble." A closer examination would reveal writings within the field (White, 1986) that have even generated principles like the following to predict the degree of organizational and personal impact from such situations:

- *The smaller the organization, the greater the repercussion.*
- *The closer the roles and the more functionally interdependent, the greater the conflict within the organization and the marriage.*

The major problem of such situations is similar to those described under the section entitled Dual Relationships with Clients. The dual roles of husband-wife and supervisor-supervisee contaminate the normal chemistry of team relationships. At its worst, it turns the organizational environment into a soap opera.

While the decision to hire one's own spouse in a particular situation may pose risks or be a stupid decision, that does not in, and of itself, make the decision unethical. In what way does the hiring of one's own spouse violate some ethical principle or do potential harm? The most frequent principle violated by nepotism is a generally held principle of equal access and equal consideration of all candidates. This principle of justice says that access for consideration is open and that the criteria upon which the hiring decision is made are objective—that everyone is competing by the same ground rules. Equity of access is violated when objectivity and fairness are compromised by the personal and/or financial self-interest of the person involved in the hiring decision. Even where such objectivity may lead to the selection of the director's spouse, the PERCEPTION of the hiring process may damage internal morale and the agency's external professional image. The potential for such damage must be factored into the hiring decision. The potential disruption of team relationships and the effect on the quality of service delivery must also be calculated into the decision-making process. To justify such hiring, equity of access to the position should be rigorously assured and the skills and potential contributions of the related job candidate should outweigh the potential for problems inherent in the dual relationship.

Patronage

◊ ◊ **130** ◊ ◊

As the director of the local human service center in an economically depressed county, you have become one of the largest employers in the county—a fact that has not gone unnoticed by politicians in the area. In the past five years, key members of the local political party have worked their way onto your agency board of directors and in the last year have made the following changes:

- Job applications must be picked up at the County Clerk's office rather than at the agency (the county clerk is on your Board).
- Personnel committee members participate with supervisors in the selection of which candidates will be interviewed.
- Personnel committee participate in the face-to-face interviews.
- Supervisors must recommend three acceptable candidates to the Board for each open position.
- It is the Board rather than the supervisor who makes the final selection.

Discussion Questions

What ethical issues are raised by these changes?

As the Executive Director, what recourse would you have in this situation?

There are serious management issues raised by the above vignette (e.g., boundary issues between the authority of the Board, the executive director and the management team) some of which may have ethical dimensions. Patronage is an ethical issue if, and the extent to which, it:

- *compromises or degrades standards of education, training, experience, or competence of workers*
- *injects politically-influenced coercion into the decision-making processes of supervision*
- *violates the integrity of the clinical decision-making process*
- *degrades legal and ethical practices related to the management of personnel (hiring, evaluation, promotion, firing) and the conduct of the agency's business practices, and*
- *decreases client access to services due to the deterioration in the public and professional reputation of the agency.*

Issues in Authority Relationships

Confidentiality

◇ ◇ **131** ◇ ◇

Mary reported to James, her supervisor, that she was divorcing her husband and that she would be needing some short periods away from work for meetings with her lawyer and for court appearances. Marjorie—a co-worker of Mary's—complained to James a week later that she was having increasing problems working with Mary on their team assignments. James took Marjorie into his confidence and explained to her that Mary was going through a rough time right now with a divorce and that Marjorie should be patient with Mary during this highly stressful period.

Discussion Questions

Was James' disclosure of Mary's impending divorce a breach of confidentiality?

Is there a standard of confidentiality that applies to the supervisory relationship?

Under what conditions, if any, should a supervisor disclose personal details revealed to him or her in the context of the supervisory relationship?

The structure, process and style of supervision varies greatly from agency to agency and may also vary greatly from supervisor to supervisor within the same agency. If there is an ethical mandate regarding confidentiality in supervision, it is the implicit demand that the scope and limits of confidentiality should be discussed and defined as a contractual foundation of the supervision relationship. While the scope of what is determined to be confidential communication in supervision varies considerably, exclusions nearly always include information disclosed in supervision that reveals a threat to a client or the agency and information that, if withheld in an emergency, could jeopardize the staff member's health or safety. Discussing and adhering to agreed upon boundaries of confidentiality in the supervisory relationship reflect values of honesty, trust, and respect for privacy and reinforce the general discouragement of, or prohibition against, gossip.

◇ ◇ **132** ◇ ◇

You recently terminated an employee that you supervised on the grounds of a breach in ethical conduct (a sexual relationship with a client). This former employee is communicating to other staff members and other community agencies that he was fired for the following reasons:

1. You are racially prejudiced.
2. The employee had discovered you were doing something funny with agency funds (described vaguely, but implying embezzlement).
3. The employee had confronted you about having an affair with another staff person that you supervise.

Discussion Questions

How would you respond to this situation?

What information, if any, can be shared with other staff or other agency representatives about personnel actions, e.g., the conditions under which an employee left the agency?

There are multiple interests in the above situation: potential threats to future clients of the fired staff member, the reputation of the discharged staff member, the reputation of the supervisor and the agency, and the relationship between the supervisor and other workers at the agency. While there are potential legal nuances in this vignette, the ethical challenge for the agency is to simultaneously respond to all of these interests. The manner in which the agency responds to these interests in the face of such allegations will influence future supervisor-staff relationships and agency-community relationships. Indiscriminate release of personnel actions to persons not in a need to know position constitutes gossip and violates the generally held principle of confidentiality governing supervisor-supervisee relationships. The most frequently used response is to talk about principles without talking about details of a particular personnel decision. Upon questioning by other agencies, for example, the supervisor could refuse to talk about the status under which the former employee left but could acknowledge his or her awareness of the former employee's allegations and rumors surrounding the agency and respond to those allegations and rumors.

Mandatory Training

Right to Privacy

◇ ◇ **133** ◇ ◇

A residential substance abuse program launches a new staff training program. This mandatory training program requires that all direct service staff participate in 60 hours of intensive training. The training is scheduled for one weekend a month (the training session runs from Friday evening to Sunday afternoon) and involves a training format that is highly experiential. In short, staff learn the techniques by actually experiencing the techniques in a process group with other staff. Within this group training context, there is immense pressure for staff self-disclosure. Staff who fail to get emotionally involved in the process have both their personal integrity and professional competence and commitment challenged.

Discussion Questions

What are your thoughts about this situation?

What is the boundary between therapy and training?

What kind of mandatory staff training might be considered a breach of ethics in the relationship between the institution and its staff members?

Chapter Six described a continuum of intimacy that exists in the relationship between professional helpers and their clients. There is a parallel continuum of intimacy upon which relationships between professional staff of an organization can be conceptualized. The zones of appropriateness, marginality and abuse also exist in a parallel manner between staff-client relationships and staff-staff relationships. The boundary lines delineating these zones may vary considerably by treatment setting, treatment role, and the dominant treatment philosophy and techniques. Mandatory staff training of the experiential variety described above raises such ethical concerns as the following:

- *Can experiential training be mandated, when such a mandate was not communicated to the employee as part of the contractual relationship with the organization?*
- *Does the concept of "informed consent" apply to staff members? If there are potential risks or unpleasant side effects from such mandated training, should staff be informed ahead of time of such risks and have the freedom to agree or refuse to participate?*
- *Does mandated experiential training that includes coerced self-disclosure violate the right to privacy of participating staff members?*
- *Does mandated training infringe on personal decision-making when the content of training pressures staff toward certain beliefs or decisions unrelated to their work performance?*
- *Does mandated experiential training unduly violate the boundary between the staff member's professional and personal life?*

For a personalized account of the abuse that can be masked in the name of experiential training, the reader is referred to Jeffrey Moussaieff Masson's *Final Analysis: The Making and Unmaking of a Psychoanalyst* Reading, MA: Addison-Wesley Publishing Company, Inc., 1990. Temerlin and Temerlin's (1982) paper on psychotherapy cults also provides helpful insights into such boundary violations in professional peer relationships.

Socializing Outside of Work

◇ ◇ **134** ◇ ◇

Many organizations have encountered problems related to staff relationships outside of the work environment. Such problems include:

- conflict in social relationships outside of work affecting team functioning
- internal decision-making (e.g., promotions, assignments) contaminated by external relationships
- issues of staff inclusion and exclusion (scapegoating) getting played out through social relationships outside of work
- staff developing a work-dominated social network (a factor seen as contributing to burnout)
- a process of inversion characterized by an intense focusing on the personal and interpersonal problems of staff, and

- a process of diversion through which most staff-staff communications inside work revolve around external social events.

Discussion Questions

Do we possess any collective wisdom or values related to what staff relationships should look like outside the work environment?

How would you articulate such values?

Most organizations completely ignore this issue until it detonates into some kind of crisis. Organizations that try to address the issue proactively usually do so in two ways. The first is to articulate an aspirational value or to otherwise capture and transmit folk wisdom about the advisability of such relationships. Examples would include the following:

- *Given the stressful and emotionally draining nature of our work, staff are encouraged to develop a rich network of replenishing activities and non-work oriented relationships.*
- *When social relationships with co-workers exist outside of the work environment, such relationships should supplement rather than replace outside social supports.*

A second response is to articulate a performance expectation. An example would include the following:

- *Issues and problems in outside personal relationships between staff will be confronted as an issue in supervision when, and only when, such issues and problems spill into the work place affecting either individual or team performance.*

This latter point provides a balanced approach by avoiding intrusions into the personal lives of staff while providing the organization a framework to intervene with any issue that results in a deterioration in productivity.

Role Stressors

◇ ◇ **135** ◇ ◇

T.R.I. is a community mental health and substance abuse agency with a long history of aggressive community service. T.R.I. has experienced funding cuts due to both state fiscal crises and a deteriorating local economy. In spite of more than a 30% cut in budget over two years, all service delivery statistics have stayed at the same level or have gone up during the past two years. Although the agency has been forced to cut staff, there has been no appreciable cutback in the range of services offered by T.R.I. Staff morale has deteriorated and staff turnover has begun to escalate because of unrelenting and excessively high workloads. A number of staff have begun to experience stress-related deteriorations in productivity and in their personal health.

Discussion Questions

Does sustained role overload constitute an ethical breach in the relationship between the organization and its employees?

Describe potential responses to this situation.

The ethical principles noted in chapter one—beneficence, justice, loyalty, honesty, fidelity, loyalty, nonmaleficence—apply to the agency-worker relationship as well as the worker-client relationship. Sustained conditions that undermine the health of the worker violate these principles. An agency that has not defined what it can and cannot do with available resources will inevitably have staff suffering from sustained role overload. Failure to appropriately match limitations on service provision with available resources not only threatens the health of workers, but eventually threatens the health and safety of clients due to stress-related employee impairment. Broad responses to sustained role overload include: 1) reducing role stressors (decreasing the load by redefining what the agency can realistically do with its constricted resources), 2) increasing staff supports (increased supervision, use of volunteers, improved technology and efficiency), and 3) strategic intervention with workers who become symptomatic as a result of the overload (employee assistance programs).

Obedience and Conscientious Refusal

◇ ◇ **136** ◇ ◇

Zachary has been assigned to facilitate a new aftercare group at the agency by his supervisor. Although the assignment is clearly within his job description, Zachary refuses to accept the new assignment on the grounds that he is tired of doing groups and feels some other staff member should be assigned the group.

Discussion Question

> While Zachary's refusal raises a performance and potential discipline issue, is there any ethical violation involved in this refusal?

There is a value of obedience implicit within the contractual relationship between Zachary and his employing agency. This value was part of the promissory agreement inherent in Zachary's agreement to accept employment with the agency. This value of obedience demands that Zachary follow the directives of his supervisor except when such directives demand action that is unethical, illegal or outside the scope of his professional duties. Zachary could seek to negotiate alternative duties with his supervisor or could resign to seek a position that better meets his needs, but his refusal in the above case is a breach of his promissory commitment to obedience.

◇ ◇ **137** ◇ ◇

A large substance abuse prevention agency was experiencing severe staff morale and staff turnover problems. The Executive Director and the Program Supervisor met and agreed that this problem needed to be addressed. A plan was formulated whereby the Program Supervisor would confidentially interview each current staff member and a sample of staff members who had left in the last year. The Supervisor would then compile the findings of these interviews to list the major issues contributing to low morale and any recommendations that emerged from the interviews. The Program Supervisor and the Executive Director explicitly agreed that comments contained in the report would not be attributed to particular staff people in compliance with the agreement of confidentiality. The supervisor conducted the individual interviews as planned (recording the interviews to help capture the desired information) and then prepared and submitted the report as planned to the Executive Director. The Executive Director, after reviewing excerpted quotes from the interviews that were quite critical of his management style and recent management decisions, decided that it was essential for him to listen to the full interviews. The Executive Director demanded the tapes from the Program Supervisor and responded to the Supervisor's discomfort with this request by saying that the tapes were agency property and that the Supervisor would be disciplined for theft if the tapes were not immediately turned over.

Discussion Questions

If you were the Supervisor, what would you do?

What ethical issues are raised by this vignette?

The condition that the Supervisor would be the only one who would know the identity of persons offering feedback or recommendations would be broken if the tapes were turned over to the Executive Director or anyone else. The pledge of confidentiality by the Supervisor—as a designated representative of the agency—constituted a promise of safety under which the interviews were conducted. Any alteration in this arrangement would violate both the value of honesty and the obligation stemming from the pledge of confidentiality. The normal ethical duty of obedience does not apply to conditions under which an employee is directed to commit unethical or illegal actions. In the situation like the above, the ethical mandate is for conscientious refusal of the directive, even if this refusal opens the Supervisor up to punitive action by the Executive Director. Making an ethical choice does not free one from the potential for arbitrary and unjust punishment.

Sexual Harassment

Abuse of Power

◇ ◇ **138** ◇ ◇

(The following story is taken from the author's book, *Incest in the Organizational Family.*)

Faye took a position as a secretary in a community substance abuse agency against the advice of her husband who couldn't figure out why she would want to work around crazy people. Within three years, her intelligence and organizational skills had earned her the position of administrative assistant to the Agency Director. During these three years, she'd found a whole new world of experience compared to her sheltered upbringing and married life. Her work also changed her social life, as staff socialized frequently away from work. This created some problems as her husband couldn't handle the "weirdness" of most of the staff. They reciprocated by applying a diverse range of diagnostic labels on the husband. During Faye's fourth year of employment, she was given the opportunity to participate in staff growth groups that demanded a high level of self-disclosure. The Director and others commented on her natural counseling aptitude, and it wasn't long before Faye was enrolled in college to prepare herself for a future career change. This was a very exhilarating time for Faye, but also a time of conflict as her husband was coldly unsupportive of her enrollment in school and her future plans. She increasingly sought support from the Director as conflict in the marriage increased. The Director became her trusted mentor, constantly providing encouragement and acknowledgement of her personal and professional value. Over the next year, Faye's school schedule and evening staff growth groups caused increasing conflict at home that was further complicated by her physical and emotional exhaustion. Partially through the counsel of the Director, Faye separated from her husband and got a place of her own. Faye had heard but didn't believe that the Director had been sexually involved with one of the counselors at the agency. The Director had never made sexual advances toward her, although there had been times that she wished he would. A month after her separation, Faye and the Director began their sexual relationship—an act in which she was totally willing to participate. She was in love—a fact unchanged by the Director's wife and family. Their relationship continued and became common knowledge at the agency. Other staff cooled their relationship with Faye, who found herself increasingly dependent upon the Director. After four months, the Director informed Faye in rather painful terms that he could no longer handle her demands for time, that she put too much stock in the relationship and that the relationship was over. Emotionally crushed, Faye never returned to the agency. She did not even go in to resign as she felt she couldn't face the other staff.

Discussion Questions

Is the above a regrettable personal story, but one which has no
professional/organizational implications, or does the story reflect the
abuse of power by an agency manager?

Is this a story of sexual harassment? Are there ethical issues involved
in any sexual relationship between a supervisor and a supervisee?

*The task of any helping organization is to protect clients and staff from any
situation whereby vulnerabilities could be exploited, but to provide such protection
without undermining their freedom and autonomy. It is the implicit power in the
supervisor's role and the potential for coercion and manipulation that brings
ethical dimensions into such professional relationships when they extend to social,
financial or sexual activity. In an earlier book (White, 1986) and several follow-
up articles (White, 1992), the author offered two concepts on the sexual
harassment and exploitation of workers within human service agencies. The first
concept—presumptive   vulnerability—places the primary responsibility for
defining and maintaining appropriate boundaries in the co-worker relationship on
that worker who has the greatest ascribed power. Presumptive vulnerability
suggests that the power inequity in some relationships is so great that all sexual
suggestions are by definition coercive. The second concept is that of manipulation
of vulnerability. It is the author's contention that a definition of sexual
harassment in closed systems must include the phrase "manipulation of
vulnerability." A supervisor, or other person with significant organizational
power, can isolate staff professionally and socially, overextend staff in ways that
deplete their physical and emotional energy, use his/her influence to undermine the
outside intimate relationships of staff, and foster dependency in nurturing staff
who experience conflict in their outside relationships. If the supervisor then
manipulates the vulnerability and dependency of a staff member to meet his/her
own sexual needs, then the supervisor has committed a type of sexual harassment
every bit as demeaning as the more blatant behaviors associated with this term.*

For an excellent analysis of the potential for abuse in the supervisory
relationship, see: Conroe, R. and Schank, J. "Sexual Intimacy in Clinical
Supervision: Unmasking the Silence," in Schoener, et. al., (1989)
Psychotherapists' Sexual Involvement with Clients.

Impaired Co-worker

◇ ◇ **139** ◇ ◇

You and several friends have decided to get out of town for a few days so you drive to another city three hours away. While at a comedy club, you are horrified to look across the room and see a counselor at your program—a highly visible and self-proclaimed recovering alcoholic—drinking a Budweiser beer.

Discussion Questions

What would you do?

More specifically, would you communicate directly with this staff person and, if so, what would be the nature of this communication?

Would you communicate what you had observed to anyone else, e.g., your supervisor?

To the extent that the worker's recovering status was used to obtain his or her position and has been represented to fellow workers, professional peers, clients and the community, there is an ethical breach of honesty and a misrepresentation of credentials (the status of recovery). The vignette also raises issues related to potential threats to the reputation of the agency and potential threats posed to agency clients from an impaired counselor. While the ethical responsibility to confront this situation in some manner is clear, agencies have not addressed, nor have they provided varied expectations to staff on how to handle such an incident. Whereas the decision to approach and confront the counselor at the comedy club would be a personal one, most agencies set an expectation that such incidents are to be reported in a timely fashion to the supervisor of the staff member observing the incident. It is then the supervisor's responsibility to initiate an administrative review of the incident. If both staff members in the above vignette are certified addictions counselors, there may be additional mandates to the observing counselor to report this incident to the ethics committee of the certification board. Such mandates vary considerably from state to state.

Team Relationships

◇ ◇ **140** ◇ ◇

Phil is an extremely capable staff member in an intensive outpatient substance abuse program. While technically skilled, he isolates himself from other staff and rarely participates in staff meetings or other group oriented staff activities. While he performs the elements of his own duties with great precision, Phil never asks for nor offers support to other staff. His relationships with other staff are physically aloof and emotionally cool. It is almost as if Phil is conducting his own private practice inside the boundaries of the program.

Discussion Questions

> While each of us have our own assigned responsibilities, what duties and obligations exist in regard to our relationships with one another as part of a treatment team?

> What values should govern team relationships within our agency?

Examples of the values most frequently articulated by agencies who have attempted to define this process include elaborations of the following:

- *fairness in distribution of responsibilities and rewards*
- *expectation for mutual support*
- *expectation for participation in problem identification and problem solving*
- *expectation for honesty and candor; definition of and prohibition against gossip*
- *respect for role boundaries, and*
- *respect for team decisions.*

Managing Conflict

◇ ◇ **141** ◇ ◇

Terry and Paul are two counselors who co-facilitate counseling groups within a residential halfway house program. Today, Terry and Paul go into a disagreement following group that escalated into a shouting match and a mutual vow that each would refuse to facilitate group with the other.

Discussion Questions

In this small program, where there are minimal opportunities to transfer or reallocate staff, how would you respond to this situation if you were their supervisor?

What values or preferred methods of problem solving should guide staff experiencing conflict in their relationships with one another?

The concern with this situation is that the style of managing—or refusing to manage—conflict jeopardizes the accessibility of client services and quite likely compromises the quality of services available to clients. Programs that help clients overcome chronic, self-defeating styles of living may have a greater mandate than other organizations to model healthy styles of problem and conflict resolution. There is a responsibility for staff to adhere to particularly high ideals related to conflict resolution when the manner in which staff responds to conflict is an integral part of the treatment milieu and treatment process. Conflict between staff is always uncomfortable and without an expectation and structure for problem-solving, small conflicts tend to escalate into large ones. Many agencies have attempted, in their development of a Code of Professional Practice, to articulate values related to the resolution of conflict within the agency. Such values often include:

- *the expectation that disagreement or conflict will be addressed face-to-face with the involved parties*
- *the expectation that this exploration of disagreement or conflict will occur in a timely manner*
- *the expectation that involved parties have an overriding responsibility to keep any conflict from compromising the service delivery process to clients, and*
- *the demand that conflict affecting service delivery or other aspects of team performance, if not resolvable by the parties involved, be brought to the attention of the supervisor(s) for assistance with problem-solving.*

Professional or Ethical Misconduct / Whistle Blowing

◇ ◇ **142** ◇ ◇

You have information which all but confirms that another staff member of your agency is sexually involved with a client. What complicates this particular situation is that the staff person involved is your supervisor.

Discussion Questions

What would you do?

What procedures are built into the organization through which staff can raise issues of ethical misconduct involving supervisory and administrative personnel?

What recourse would there be if the staff member attempted to raise this issue only to have the response be a perceived cover-up and lack of apparent action by the administrator/board?

Without significant structural supports for ethical conduct built into the organization, the staff member in such a situation is extremely vulnerable to be scapegoated and extruded from the organization if he or she attempts to raise the issue of the supervisor's conduct. Any organization that wishes to make the highest level of ethical conduct a crucial and visible component of its organizational culture must establish clear channels of communication and redress involving perceived ethical breaches by supervisory/administrative staff. Codes of Professional Practice or personnel policies can, for example, inform staff to move to the next highest level to report allegations of supervisory misconduct (e.g., the conduct of one's immediate supervisor would be reported to the person administratively above the supervisor, the conduct of an executive director would be reported to the Personnel or Executive Committee of the Board). While the precise procedures may vary, it is the establishment and communication of such reporting channels that is paramount.

A staff member's response to a perceived cover-up of unethical conduct by administrative/supervisory personnel could vary depending on the nature of the ethical breach and the degree of imminent threat posed to clients or the public. At a practical level, the challenge is to address any issues that compromise the quality of services by using those methods that can correct the situation with the least potential damage to the reputation of the agency. The ultimate value is not the existence of the agency, but the accessibility, continuity, and quality of client services. The consideration of external redress via reporting the allegation of misconduct to outside licensing, funding, accreditation, advisory bodies or the press can be best judged by this value. The staff member's choices in such a situation may also be tempered by an articulated organizational value that requires internal sources of redress to be exhausted before such external redress is sought.

Bowie (1982) in his excellent analysis of whistle blowing (employee disclosure to the public of institutional acts that breach boundaries of ethics and law) has defined six conditions in which whistle blowing is ethically justified. He feels the potential damage to the organization and its employees can be practically and morally justified if: 1) the motivation for whistle blowing is moral rather than personal, 2) the whistle blower has exhausted internal channels of redress, 3) there is overwhelming evidence of harmful actions, 4) action is taken only after a careful analysis of consequence of the moral or legal breach, 5) his or her action is within one's responsibility for avoiding and/or exposing moral violations, and 6) the whistle blower has some chance of success.

Staff Termination

◇ ◇ 143 ◇ ◇

Over the past four years, the Integrity program has evolved the following patterns related to staff termination. A number of staff have been fired capriciously and asked to leave immediately. Staff who resign—while paid for the required two week notice period—are given a few hours to clean out their desk and are asked to then leave and not work the remaining days. A number of staff have become extremely negative and embittered in the weeks preceding their resignation—it's as if people have to get mad and fight their way out of the organization to leave. Other staff have left precipitously with no notice—a kind of explosive, adult runaway behavior.

Discussion Question

> While these conditions are clearly far from ideal, does the vignette raise any ethical issues about the relationship between the organization and its employees?

There are ethical issues raised by the above vignette to the extent that the methods of termination violate the promises inherent within the contractual relationship between the worker and the organization and to the extent that quality of services to clients is compromised by the deteriorating morale surrounding these terminations. Ideally, the termination process should be structured in a manner that facilitates emotional closure of the employee, facilitates a smooth transfer of service responsibilities to minimize disruption and discomfort to clients, and provides rituals through which the team can positively redefine itself in the absence of the exiting member. How terminations are managed involve ethical dimensions because these processes affect the health of clients, the health of workers and the health of the organizational system. Because termination of employment can have such an effect on an employee and his or her family's economic and emotional health, particular care should be taken in managing the termination process. Continued respect for the employee even at the point of termination is reflected in psychological preparation for the prospects of termination (progressive discipline), courtesy and professionalism in the termination interview, adequate termination notice and structuring of the termination process. Some organizations supplement these efforts with outplacement counseling and job search assistance. The goal is to make the process as painless as possible for all persons involved. Principles of fairness (justice), kindness (beneficence), and honesty apply to employees as well as clients. Precipitous termination should be the rare exception reflecting extraordinary circumstances, not the norm.

External Professional Relationships

Value of External Relationships

◇ ◇ 144 ◇ ◇

Agencies, like family systems, vary in their degree of connectedness to the outside social and professional world. Some are characterized by a high frequency and intensity of boundary transactions with the outside world while others are highly isolated from external professional relationships.

Discussion Question

To what extent does this connectedness to the outside world influence the health of the organization and the ethical conduct of its members?

Sustained organizational isolation leads to a deterioration of technical skills and professional support of staff as well as a reduction in resources available to address clients' needs. The xenophobic position that there is something wrong with all other agencies and workers—that we must meet all of the needs of our clients—inevitably leads an agency staff into practicing significantly beyond the boundaries of their individual and collective competence. Some agencies attempt to articulate the value of external relationships in their Code of Professional Practice. For example: center staff shall maximize the resources available to client/families through the fullest possible utilization of other community health and social services. Valuing external resources implies a value of respect and appreciation for the knowledge, skills, perspectives and commitments of other helping persons—seeing such persons as kindred spirits rather than competition.

Multiple Service Involvement

◇ ◇ **145** ◇ ◇

Laurie arrives for an assessment seeking your advice regarding her need for treatment. She is clearly chemically dependent but is being actively seen by a psychiatrist who is promoting controlled drinking and maintaining her on high doses of minor tranquilizers and sedatives.

Discussion Question

Describe your response to: A) Laurie and B) the psychiatrist.

While there are any number of clinical issues raised by the above situation, most agencies identify four primary ethical concerns which they most often respond to in the following manner:

1. *Clients should be presented differences of opinion on treatment philosophy and technique between agencies or professionals with the greatest possible objectivity and least possible personal acrimony.*

2. *Clients receiving treatment from another professional that is both outside the mainstream of current treatment approaches and which poses risks to the health of the client should be informed of such divergence and risks by the person/agency being consulted.*

3. *Where the client faces imminent harm from the proposed treatment, the agency/professional being consulted should take whatever action is necessary to protect the client. This could range from bringing the risk to the attention of the psychiatrist, informing the family members of the client (with the client's permission), or notifying a higher authority regarding the psychiatrist's threat to his/her patients. Such higher authority could range from any administrative or clinical authority under which the psychiatrist works, the medical director of the hospital (if the services are provided through the hospital) or an external professional practice review panel.*

4. *There should be a refusal to do concurrent treatment where goals or methods conflict or where concurrent treatment would result in decreased likelihood of problem resolution. The potential risks and benefits of the alternative treatment approaches should be explained to the client and outside sources of consultation should be offered. The client should also be told that he or she must make the judgement as to which approach will be best for him or her.*

Commenting on the Competence of Other Professionals

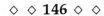

◇ ◇ **146** ◇ ◇

You are having lunch with representatives from four other agencies who you have known for quite some time. In the course of the luncheon conversation, one of them asks you for your candid opinion on a new psychiatrist that has recently begun practicing in your community. It so happens that your experience with this psychiatrist has been extremely negative and that you have stopped all client referrals to the psychiatrist until a meeting can be held to iron out what appears to be major philosophical differences related to the appropriate treatment of addictive disorders.

Discussion Questions

How do you respond to the question regarding the psychiatrist's competence?

What ethical or professional practice issues are involved in commenting on the competence or incompetence of other professionals?

At a practical level, it is probably crucial to reserve communicating one's judgement of a professional peer while there is some process continuing whose goal is to clarify and resolve professional differences. Most agencies that explore this question wish to strike a balance between two extremes. On the one hand, they want to define professionalism as it relates to commenting on the competence or approaches of others. This professionalism is usually defined in terms of objectivity or in terms of prohibitions against personalized or derogatory indictments or gossip. On the other hand, they want to avoid the criticism that professional disciplines represent closed guilds that protect through silence their least competent and their most impaired professional peers. A general guideline in commenting on the competence of another professional is to state first the nature and extent of the experience upon which your judgement is based and then state as objectively as possible your judgement of their performance.

◇ ◇ **147** ◇ ◇

Representatives from two local substance abuse programs were asked to participate in a panel discussion of chemical dependency treatment on a local television show. The two substance abuse programs had a long history of competition and mutual hostility that broke through initially during the television show in the form of attempted one-up-manship, challenges to the truth and accuracy of statements, and narcissistic posturing. In spite of the interviewer's attempts to focus the dialogue on issues that would be relevant to viewers, the discussion frequently involved a competitive bantering on arcane professional issues that the public neither cared about nor would understand. By the end of the show, the television host was barely able to keep the discussion from degenerating into personal attacks.

Discussion Question

What ethical issues are raised by the conduct portrayed in this story?

The participants in the above story—influenced by their historical relationship—defined the media opportunity as a debate rather than an informational panel. They had prepared and would evaluate their respective performances in terms of win or lose. The ethically questionable conduct involves the misuse of the media opportunity. Like a counselor letting his or her own needs and agendas interfere with effective counseling of a client, the workers above allowed institutional agendas to violate the integrity of their professional involvement in an educational forum. Time spent in competitive bantering constituted missed opportunities for public education. By failing to set aside institutional history or personal acrimony, the participants conveyed an image of the treatment field that diminished personal and institutional reputations and potentially decreased the willingness of potential clients/family members to seek services not only from the two programs but from ANY chemical dependency treatment program. To avoid demeaning the professional field of substance abuse prevention and treatment, disagreements on philosophical or programmatic issues should be presented only in forums appropriate for such communication and should be presented with the highest level of professionalism and objectivity.

Allegations of Unethical Conduct

◇ ◇ **148** ◇ ◇

A client you are currently counseling reports that she was sexually exploited by her previous therapist. The therapist named by this client is a colleague who you have met at numerous professional meetings and who is still working as a therapist in another agency within your community.

Discussion Questions

Are there any actions you would take above and beyond your clinical response to this report?

What standard would capture the essence of staff in response to such an allegation?

The response to allegations of professional misconduct involves clinical as well as ethical issues. One quite poignant concern here involves the betrayal of the client through failure to take action. This parallels the frequent experience of sexually abused children feeling betrayed because family members and others do not believe them nor protect them from the sexual perpetrator within the family once the abuse is revealed. If the client in the above vignette had a history of such abuse, this potential recapitulation of her family of origin betrayal could be particularly devastating. Options available to the therapist in the above vignette would include the following:

- *informing the client of her options of filing formal complaints or charges via the alleged abusing therapist's employer, funding sources of the agency in which alleged abuse occurred, regulatory agencies overseeing service agency, professional licensure or certification Board, civil suit or criminal complaint*
- *notifying in writing—with the client's permission—one or more of the above administrators or institutions about the nature of the allegation reported by the client, and*
- *providing on-going emotional support to the client through the formal allegation and hearing processes.*

Responding to a client allegation of sexual exploitation by a professional helper raises complex clinical, ethical, and legal issues. Most agencies require that such allegations be immediately brought into the process of supervision to assure that such complexities can be identified and responded to appropriately. The supervisory process can be particularly helpful in providing the worker a means of preparing for any communication with the person about whom the allegation has been made. Supervision can help the worker:

- *maintain the presumed innocence of the therapist by referring to the sexual activity as "alleged" or "reported"*
- *determine the desirability or necessity of communication with the therapist*
- *select the best timing for such communication*
- *explore the best structure for such communication, e.g., in writing, by telephone, or face-to-face meeting, and*
- *determine what precisely should be said to the therapist and how it could be best communicated.*

Schoener (1989) has written an excellent review of the intricacies involved in filing complaints of unethical conduct against counselors and psychotherapists and has included an insightful section on the mechanics and risks involved in filing third party complaints on behalf of clients. Haas and Malouf (1989) provide the best discussion available on the ethics of confronting and being confronted.

Chapter
Eight

Conduct Related to Public Safety

Addiction treatment professionals have always had to address issues related to public safety. However, recent changes in the psychoactive drug menu, changes in the characteristics of drug consumers, and changes in the social context of substance abuse in the U.S. have greatly intensified the public safety issues encountered by treatment professionals. The dramatic increase in predatory crime and violence and the spread of HIV infection within the culture of addiction have been supplemented by growing concerns about the risks posed by drug-impaired workers in American businesses and industries. Addiction treatment professionals now regularly face difficult ethical and legal issues surrounding the potential threats posed by clients to the health and safety of others. Treatment professionals are being called upon to assess and make judgements about a client's potential and imminent threat to public safety without either the technical training to conduct such an assessment nor training in a clinical/ethical/legal decision-making model through which such judgements can be made. The vignettes in this chapter will help agencies and staff explore the ethical issues raised by such threats to public safety.

Critical Incidents

Physical/Sexual Abuse

◇ ◇ **149** ◇ ◇

You work in an outpatient substance abuse counseling agency. Ruth, a 16 year-old client that you have counseled for presenting problems of substance abuse, runaway behavior, and sexual promiscuity, today discloses her sexual abuse by her father. Ruth reports that the abuse began at age eight and continued up until a year ago. Ruth has not been molested or otherwise abused during the past year. She has two younger siblings. She wants to talk about the abuse, but doesn't want her father reported since the abuse has stopped. She feels reporting him will "tear the family up" and make things worse for her.

Discussion Questions:

How do you respond to Ruth's disclosure?

Would these circumstances ethically and/or legally require mandatory reporting to the child protection agency within your state?

All fifty states have provisions for mandatory reporting of physical and/or sexual abuse of children. These statutes are based on the premise that the potential harm to children from abusive acts outweighs the potential harm that could occur through the violation of client confidentiality. The ethical command in the case above is to assure that the abuse of Ruth does not recommence and to assure the safety of Ruth's younger siblings (and perhaps the safety of other potential victims). How substance abuse workers and agencies reconcile their ethical and legal responsibilities differs widely. Three broad approaches are regularly encountered by the author.

The first approach takes the position that the clinician should report only those cases of abuse that clearly fall under the definition of legally mandated reporting. This option makes compliance with the law the framework for ethical conduct. The risk here is twofold: first, that cases may arise in which there is an ethical mandate to protect which falls outside the legal requirement to report, and, second, that actions taken to protect—mandatory reporting—may, due to unique circumstances, do harm to those targeted for protection.

The second approach takes the position that the clinician should report only in those circumstances where there is a legal obligation to report AND when the action of reporting is judged by the clinician to be the best available vehicle capable of protecting the innocent parties and supporting the long-term health and safety of all parties involved. A judgement to not report with this option is an implicit assumption of responsibility and liability by the clinician for the welfare of those involved, but one deemed justifiable under certain circumstances.

The third approach posits that the clinician should report not only those cases that fall under the definition of legally mandated reporting, but also cases where the clinician feels an ethical duty to protect but circumstances are not of such severity as to legally require reporting. The risk in this option is in unduly violating client confidentiality and in adding non-critical work to an already overburdened child protection system.

To reconcile the client's right to confidentiality with the duty to report, it is crucial that each agency clearly defines how it operationalizes both of these mandates within the span of the three positions noted above. Once that position has been determined, clients can be told of the exceptions to confidentiality in language precise enough to allow them to make informed choices regarding likely responses to their disclosures.

There are numerous variations on abuse situations that make it more difficult to sort out one's legal and ethical duties. The worksheet on the following page has been devised to help explore some of these variations. It is designed as a tool for discussion during inservice trainings or in staff meetings. The agency/clinician response to each situation can be discussed using the following questions:

- *Does the situation, as presented, warrant suspension of confidentiality and reporting to an outside authority? If yes, which outside authority?*
- *What actions in addition to, or as an alternative to, external reporting would enhance the protection of safety in the situation?*
- *Who will benefit and who will be potentially harmed by the proposed action?*
- *Which ethical values (See worksheet in Chapter Two) should guide our response to the situation?*

Duty to Warn (Threat of Physical Violence)

◇ ◇ **150** ◇ ◇

You work as the evening counselor in a residential substance abuse treatment program. Following a loud argumentative phone call, a client charges out of the facility threatening to kill his ex-wife and her new boyfriend.

Exploring the Ethical Duty to Report	
Situation	Action Recommended (if any) (Confidentiality Versus Duty to Protect)
Minor client reports "sexual fondling" by foster parent with whom she is currently living.	
You repeatedly observe bruises on an adolescent client's face and arms, the client denies being beaten by parents or boyfriend.	
Adult client reports sexual abuse by father when he/she was a child. There are still minor children in the home.	
A 13 year-old client discloses initiating sexual fondling of younger siblings, ages 11 and 9.	
A 22 year-old client reports being sexually abused from ages 9 to 15 by her older brother.	
A 15 year old client reports current sexual abuse by the father of her best friend.	
An adult client reports sexual abuse by the father when he/she was a child. There are no minor children left in the home.	
A minor client reports sexual abuse by a pastor continuing up to time of present treatment admission.	
An adult client reports childhood sexual abuse by a pastor still working in your community.	

Discussion Questions

Would contacting the ex-wife or the police constitute a breach of this client's confidentiality?

Would failure to warn the ex-wife constitute a breach of professional ethics?

What would you do in this situation?

In 1976, the California Supreme Court, in the now famous Tarasoff v. Regents of the University of California case, ruled that therapists have a duty to warn potential victims of a specific threat of violence made by the therapist's client, even if such disclosure is not approved by the client. The Tarasoff decision intensified the ethical discussion within the professional helping disciplines regarding the rights of clients to confidentiality and the rights of potential victims to be warned of threats to their physical safety. This tension between client privacy and community safety continues today. Since the Tarasoff decision, the "duty to warn" has become both a legal obligation and a keystone within the ethical standards of helping professions. The "duty to warn" is generally operationalized as follows:

- *All clients, as part of the informed consent process, are fully informed of both the scope and limits of confidentiality. One such exception to confidentiality noted is the obligation of the helper to notify any third party of threatened harm by the client.*
- *A reasonable assessment of the client's potential for violence is conducted as a component of the intake assessment process.*
- *"Duty to warn" is activated when a client makes a threat of physical harm to an identified individual or individuals.*
- *A more intensified evaluation of the client's potential for violence is conducted in response to the verbal threat of aggression.*
- *The warning constitutes direct contact of the threatened individual by the helper with a concise explanation of the nature of the threat that was made.*
- *The helper should initiate all other possible actions to reduce the likelihood of harm to others. These actions may include dealing with the client's anger in counseling, increasing the frequency of client counseling, referring the client for psychiatric assessment, hospitalizing the client, asking the client to relinquish weapons, and initiating a no-*

contact contract between the client and the potential victim.
(VandeCreek and Knapp, 1989).

● The details of the client's threats, the assessment findings of the client's
potential for violence, the management options considered by the
counselor/agency, and the actions taken are documented in detail within
the client's clinical record.

◇ ◇ **151** ◇ ◇

You work as a receptionist in a substance abuse treatment program.
Today a client arrives in a state of extreme intoxication for an interview.
The client becomes irritated in the waiting room because the intake
worker is running a little late for the client's appointment. The client says
he's leaving and resists your suggestion that he wait for the counselor or
talk to someone at the detox unit. Becoming increasingly belligerent, the
client walks out of the reception room with his car keys in hand saying
he's going to drive across the country to see his sister.

Discussion Questions

How would you respond to this situation?

Do the receptionist and the agency have an ethical responsibility to
protect the public from this client?

*The challenge in this situation is how to protect the public from the impaired
driving of the intoxicated client without violating the client's confidentiality.
Responses could include the following:*

● *seek the assistance of any other available staff person to help you assess
and respond to the situation*
● *communicate to the client that he is too intoxicated to drive and that
if he gets in his car you will have no recourse but to call the police,
and*
● *call the police informing them of your observation of an intoxicated
person getting into an automobile, with the car's description, license
number and location, without identifying the person as a client of your
agency.*

If there was an extreme situation where the only way to protect the public was to acknowledge the person's status as an agency client, then such disclosure could be made on the grounds that the imminent threat to public safety outweighed the client's right to confidentiality.

Allegations of Misconduct

◇ ◇ **152** ◇ ◇

You are at a social function with 50 other people. While in a small group of five to six persons, you mention in casual conversation that you work at the local substance abuse counseling agency. One of the other people says, with sarcastic amusement, that it must be a real interesting place to work because her neighbor who is receiving counseling at your agency has been describing to her the ongoing affair the client is having with her therapist (mentioned by name) at the agency.

Discussion Questions

How do you respond to this immediate situation as the five to six persons turn to you with great anticipation of your response to these comments? What do you say?

Do you share this information with the therapist about whom the allegation was made?

Do you share this information with administrative/supervisory staff at the agency?

Do you share it with other staff of the agency?

The staff member in a vignette like the above is instantaneously thrust into potentially conflicting interests. The allegation raises concerns regarding the potential exploitation of clients as well as threats to the reputations of the individual staff member named in the allegation and to the agency as a whole. Discussions of this vignette most often raise the following points:

Immediate Response: The goals in responding to this allegation at the party are: 1) to obtain the necessary information that will allow a subsequent investigation of the charge (protection of client) and 2) to express that such a behavior, if true, would constitute a breach in both professional ethics and agency policy (protection of agency). The first goal requires that the staff member at the party get the name and telephone number of the person making the allegation and the name of the person who is alleging the sexual involvement with the therapist (without acknowledging this person's status as an agency client). The second goal requires expressing the organizational value about sexual involvement between therapists and clients and bringing the discussion to closure as rapidly as possible to minimize damage to the reputation of the agency and the worker.

Communication to Person Accused: Staff vary in their responses to whether the person hearing the allegation should report it to the person about whom the allegation was made. Most are struck by how uncomfortable it would be to communicate this information to another staff member. But most respond affirmatively to the question: "Would you want to be told immediately if such an accusation was being made about you?" What is helpful to the person in the quandary of how to respond to their awareness of an allegation of misconduct is that some consensus or standard has been defined within the agency as to the desired professional response in this situation.

Communication to Supervisor: Most agencies define in their Code of Professional Practice the expectation that all staff shall convey to their direct supervisor any allegations of ethical misconduct made toward a staff member or the agency as a whole. Many staff when they first brainstorm their response to this vignette respond that they would not want to communicate the allegation to their supervisor unless they were sure the allegation was true. After continued discussion, they usually realize the enormous burden this position places on them to determine the guilt or innocence of a co-worker and the enormity of the consequences if they misjudge the situation. The mandatory reporting to a supervisor is as much for the protection of the worker who hears such allegations as it is for the protection of the client. It also assures that the accused staff member is given full procedural rights in responding to the allegation.

Communication to Others: What happens when you walk into the staff lounge for a cup of coffee Monday morning following this incident and everyone wants to know, "How was your weekend? Did you do anything exciting?" How do you respond? Most agencies try to incorporate into their Code of Professional Practice not only a mandate to report allegations of misconduct, but go further in restricting the range of subsequent disclosure of the allegation. Sometimes referred to as a "gossip clause," staff are prohibited from casual reporting or discussion of such allegations with others on the grounds that such communication is a form of professional gossiping that could damage both the reputation of the agency and the worker about whom the allegations have been made.

◇ ◇ **153** ◇ ◇

You are in a state that has recently implemented a mandatory alcoholism assessment for all persons arrested for driving under the influence (DUI). This change has led to the rapid proliferation of DUI assessment programs and intense financial competition between the various agencies for DUI assessment referrals. One new agency in your community, whose whole business is DUI-related, has slowly evolved into a "hired gun" working closely with local defense attorneys to provide assessment conclusions and recommendations desired by the DUI offender and his/her attorney. It is your belief that this practice both hurts the reputation and integrity of the substance abuse assessment/treatment field and poses a significant risk to public safety by its failure to identify and divert alcoholics into treatment or, at a minimum, play a supportive role in depriving actively drinking alcoholics of their right to legally drive.

Discussion Question

What would you do in response to this situation?

Most of us would agree that substance abuse agencies and professionals have a responsibility to identify and, when possible, respond to threats to public safety. The potential threat to public safety and the alleged professional misconduct implicit in the above vignette should be brought into the process of supervision for review and strategy development. One's response in this situation must be measured to avoid the appearance that the agency is acting out of "sour grapes" in response to the other agency's financial success. Having the whole issue discounted as one of competitive back-biting will help no one. Responses could range from:

- *communicating to the director of the other agency feedback about their "hired gun" reputation,*
- *communicating your concerns to the presiding judge in the circuit in which the agency's DUI evaluations are being submitted*
- *expressing concern to the state licensing authority regarding the agency's conduct, and/or*
- *expressing concern to the state counselor certification body that counselors may be compromising professional judgement in DUI evaluations for the financial benefit of their agency.*

AIDS and Risks to Third Parties

◇ ◇ **154** ◇ ◇

Tomas, a client in outpatient treatment who knows he is HIV positive, has not yet informed his partner of this fact, in spite of their continued involvement in unsafe sexual activity.

Discussion Questions

As Tomas' primary therapist, do you have any ethical or legal responsibility to convey this information to his partner?

What would you do in this situation?

Laws governing this situation vary from state to state and consensus is not easy on the conditions under which professionals may inform, or have an ethical duty to inform, third parties of their exposure to HIV. The professional, in balancing the client's right to confidentiality and the public's—or particular injured parties'—right to protect itself, may consider several possible courses of action:

- *convincing Tomas to directly inform his partner regarding his HIV status and his or her potential risk—validating that such communication did occur and linking Tomas' partner to antibody counseling and testing*
- *conducting a joint session with Tomas and his partner to help to provide support and assistance as he informs his partner*

- *informing Tomas' partner of Tomas' status and his or her risk of HIV infection in spite of Tomas' refusal to grant permission—such decision reflecting a judgement of an ethical duty to inform*
- *informing the third party (if it was someone other than the partner) of their exposure to HIV without informing them of the identity of the client*
- *inviting and involving John's family, intimate partners, and needle-sharing partners to HIV/AIDS education programs offered by the agency*
- *discussing consequences of possible pregnancy (if partner is female).*

◇ ◇ **155** ◇ ◇

Jessie is a client with AIDS who is participating in the intensive outpatient component of your treatment program. In spite of—or in reaction to—his AIDS diagnosis, Jessie is continuing a very sexually aggressive lifestyle, is consistently refraining from disclosing his infection status to his sexual partners, and refuses to use condoms. Jessie is being sexually aggressive (seeking sexual activity) with a number of other intensive outpatient clients.

Discussion Questions

- How would you intervene in this situation?

- Do other clients have a right to know of Jessie's medical condition or would the communication of that knowledge be a gross breach of Jessie's right to confidentiality?

Under ordinary circumstances, Jessie's medical history, including his HIV status could not be disclosed without Jessie's written consent. The ethical concern here is the extent to which other clients' reasonable expectations of safety and protection from communicable disease in the treatment environment is being jeopardized by Jessie's actions and whether this threat supersedes his right to confidentiality. Balancing these conflicting rights and duties, staff might consider the following options:

- *confront the inappropriateness of Jessie's behavior in the treatment environment,*
- *define and contract for restraint of sexual behavior in the treatment environment with clearly defined consequences for failure to comply, e.g., discharge from treatment, even though such contracting may have only minimal deterrent effect on Jessie's behavior,*
- *intensifying HIV/AIDS education to clients, to include warnings of the high risk of sexual activity with other clients, and*
- *disclosing Jessie's status to a public health agency with expressed concerns about his knowingly infecting other persons.*

Threats to Public Safety

◇ ◇ **156** ◇ ◇

You work as a substance abuse counselor in a local treatment agency. In the past two months, you have seen innumerable clients who report the same source for the enormous quantities of amphetamines they have been consuming. In each case, a local physician was named who is indiscriminately prescribing large quantities and varieties of psychostimulants and amphetamines. You know from personal contact with this aging physician that he has become increasingly impaired and has lost much of his traditional medical practice.

Discussion Questions

Does this physician constitute a threat to public safety?

Do you have an ethical responsibility to convey the information about this physician's prescribing practices to an appropriate public authority?

Would the disclosure of this information constitute a violation of confidentiality since it was derived from treatment interviews?

What would you do in this situation?

What standards would serve as a guide to staff facing such dilemmas?

Data from multiple client interviews suggesting the escalating impairment of a physician raises concerns about threats to public safety both in terms of the doctor's contribution to local substance abuse and the potential errors in professional judgement that may pose equally dire consequences to his or her other medical patients. Responses to this threat might include one or more of the following:

- *informing your immediate supervisor of the information obtained from the clients, expressing your sense of ethical concern about the physician's actions, and seeking consultation from the supervisor on potential courses of action*
- *involving the medical director of the agency as a consultant on potential courses of response*
- *approaching the physician directly with expression of concern about the ease with which he or she is prescribing and dispensing abusable drugs*
- *expressing concern about the situation to the physician's professional peers, if he or she is in group practice*
- *contacting the ethics committee of the local medical society and*
- *notifying local law enforcement authorities, if all other courses of resolution fail.*

All communications in the above circumstances must involve a summary of findings reported by many clients and must be done in a way not to directly or inadvertently identify any persons as clients of the agency.

◇ ◇ **157** ◇ ◇

Lucinda works as a registered nurse in a hospital-based chemical dependency unit that utilizes multiple admitting physicians. A physician calls in an order for a medication that is both contraindicated for the particular patient and has been ordered at an excessively high dosage. After reviewing the client's medical history and reconfirming her understanding of the drug through reference texts in the nursing station, Lucinda is convinced that the administration of the medication could jeopardize the life of the client. When she calls the physician to express her concern, the doctor asks where she went to medical school and hangs up on her. The medication is scheduled to be given in one hour.

Discussion Questions

If you were Lucinda, what would you do?

How can Lucinda reconcile the duty to comply with directives from her superiors with the imminent threat to the safety of a client?

There are two ethical values that apply directly to this situation: nonmaleficence and conscientious refusal. The former demands that we not hurt anyone; the latter demands that we disobey illegal or unethical directives. While the doctor is demanding obedience to the order, the ethical obligation of obedience only extends to legal and ethically permissible directives. Lucinda's ethical recourse is to report the order of a medication that she believes will harm the patient and seek administrative review of the situation by soliciting consultation through the chain of command, e.g., nursing supervisor, director of nursing, chief of the medical staff.

◇ ◇ **158** ◇ ◇

Describe how, as an employee assistance program (EAP) counselor, you would balance or reconcile the protection of client confidentiality with the protection of public safety in the following situations:

A. An inspector at a nuclear power plant admits falsifying safety inspections due to his inability to keep up with the escalating requirements of his job.

B. A pilot for a major commercial airline self-reports flying repeatedly while being hung over and using cocaine and other stimulants to compensate for her alcohol-impairment.

C. A nurse, who has been referred to the EAP because of performance problems, breaks down in the second interview and spills out the scope and intensity of his current drug involvement. The nurse discloses in tears his guilt over theft of drugs from the hospital, including the use of drugs ordered for patients.

D. A young police officer has been recalled to uniform following four years of undercover vice work. Referred because of suspicion of psychiatric impairment, you discover a cocaine addict whose paranoia is increasing daily. He is hypervigilant and delusional—capable of misinterpreting very harmless cues as very threatening—and carries a gun around-the-clock.

There are numerous issues in these situations: the confidentiality of EAP service consumers, the vulnerability and reputation of the EAP counselor, the reputation of the EAP agency and the contracting company, and threats to the safety of parties outside the EAP helping relationship. Because of the ethical, legal and clinical complexities of cases like the above, the first goal is to keep the individual EAP practitioner from having to make and bear the brunt of such judgements by themselves. The first rule of action in such ethical complexities is to seek consultation. The goal is to bring the best collective judgement of agency personnel to bear on the situation. There are threats to public safety implicit within each of the above vignettes. The degree of imminence of harm and the degree of imperative for action varies. There is a mandate in each of the situations to collect sufficient information to determine the degree of threat to public safety. The first pathway of problem resolution is to seek an answer that allows the EAP counselor to uphold client confidentiality and protect the public safety. Such avenues could include enlisting the client's cooperation to disclose their status or actions to their supervisors, via a request for personal leave or medical leave to enter treatment, or to give the EAP counselor permission to speak with his or her supervisor. Offering to arrange, host, and support the client through such a meeting may increase the likelihood of this option being chosen by the client. Some EAP counselors use an either/or option to pressure the client to take action in order to remove the threat to public safety: "Either you talk to your supervisor and take a medical leave to enter treatment now or I will be ethically bound to report the theft and use of patient medication." The ethical value of self-interest not only demands that the EAP counselor seek consultation through this ethical quagmire, but also that the whole process be rigorously documented for the protection of the counselor and the agency. Such documentation should include:

- *details of the nature and intensity of the threat to public safety*
- *identification of the ethical issues involved, e.g., client confidentiality and duty to protect public safety*
- *the solicitation of consultation, the identification of the consultation resources used, and the nature of the advice given*
- *the clinical data that was most critical to the decision made*
- *the nature of the decision and how it was implemented and*
- *the client's response to the action taken.*

◇ ◇ **159** ◇ ◇

An employee of your agency who you supervise—a certified addictions counselor—was just dismissed following the finding (in an internal administrative hearing) that he had sexually exploited a client in treatment.

Discussion Questions

Does the agency have any ethical responsibility to communicate its findings to anyone outside the agency?

Should the agency notify the state certification board for addictions counselors?

Do you feel that there is an ethical mandate to communicate such information or would an agency be overstepping its boundaries and responsibilities in making such a communication?

Does the employee have a right to privacy regarding personnel actions of the agency under these circumstances?

While employees do have some claim to rights regarding the confidentiality of personnel actions in the employee-employer relationship, there are other interests involved in this situation: protection of service consumers, protection of the reputation of treatment agencies, and protection of the integrity and reputation of the profession. The ethical duty to protect clients and the profession is not fully met by discharging the employee. The employee may simply seek re-employment and continue the pattern of sexual exploitation. As a supervisor, there may be a number of actions to consider including the following:

- *inform the abused clients of their rights to seek civil and criminal redress against the counselor,*
- *encourage the counselor to seek treatment and/or leave the field,*
- *notify the state counselor certification board of the ethical breach by the counselor and the actions taken by the agency (If you are certified, you may be ethically bound by your own certification to report this breach to the certification board.), and*

- *provide a strong recommendation for "no hire" to any future employer in the field contacting the agency for verification of employment.*

There may be some conflict between what a person feels is his or her ethical duty and what one is informed are his or her legal vulnerabilities. One supervisor, confronting the systematic sexual exploitation of many clients by an agency counselor, discharged the counselor and took numerous steps to decrease the likelihood that the counselor would be able to stay within the field. When the supervisor was informed that he might be opening himself up to a suit by the now former employee, the supervisor responded: "Let him sue. I couldn't stay a supervisor in this business another day if I thought I hadn't done everything possible to protect other clients from that man's sickness. I will wear as a badge of honor having been found guilty of destroying his chances to ever make a living in this field!"

Substance abuse-related threats to public safety are likely to increase in their severity and visibility within the coming decades. These threats will require an improved clinical technology in assessing the potential for violence and other behaviors that pose risks to the safety of individuals and communities. Substance abuse agencies and direct service practitioners will also need to come together to improve our ethical decision-making abilities in the midst of conflicting interests. Our best talents are needed to prepare us for this future.

Professional Standards Related to Special Roles

The bulk of professional standards in the helping professions in general, and the substance abuse field in particular, have focused on ethical issues in the relationship between a therapist and a client. While these standards have been very valuable, there are many specialty roles within the substance abuse field to which these standards are inappropriate or not easily applied. This chapter will explore some of the ethical issues encountered by workers who are not in a traditional counselor-client relationship within a substance abuse treatment program. The chapter will also explore ethical dimensions of role performance in the areas of prevention, employee assistance, student assistance, outreach, training and research. The exploration and understanding of the growing ethical complexities that can arise in the performance of these roles within the substance abuse field are just beginning.

Critical Incidents

Prevention

Personal Conduct

◇ ◇ **160** ◇ ◇

John is a youth prevention worker involved in drug education and alternatives programming in his local community. John smokes!

Discussion Questions

What ethical issues are raised by this behavior?

Given that so much of the focus of prevention programming is the teaching and promotion of principles of physical and emotional health, are there personal standards of conduct (related to physical and emotional health) to which prevention staff can and should be held accountable?

How would you articulate such a standard? What standard, if any, would apply to personal use of psychoactive drugs (nicotine, alcohol, etc.), obesity, workaholism, or other issues of personal lifestyle that may be highly incongruent with the prevention message?

See following vignette for analysis.

◇ ◇ **161** ◇ ◇

Tasha is the coordinator of a local prevention project. She inherited stock from her grandmother, among other things, a distillery and in one of the major tobacco companies.

Discussion Question

Do Tasha's personal investments represent an area of her personal life unrelated to her professional role or does her ownership of this stock potentially conflict with or compromise the performance of her professional role?

Both of the vignettes above implicitly ask whether there must be reasonable congruence between the life lived and the message preached and yet each also raises the question of the appropriate boundary line between the professional and private life of the prevention worker. Prevention professionals, because of their visible advocacy of practices which promote individual and community health, may inevitably be held to a high standard of personal conduct. There would be ethical dimensions to any personal conduct which compromised one's ability to perform assigned role responsibilities within a prevention program. The private behavior of a prevention worker could involve breaches in ethical conduct to the extent that:

- *private behavior was so incongruent with the prevention message that the person's ability to carry this message was fundamentally negated*
- *private conduct in violation of prevailing moral and legal standards impugned his or her reputation to the degree it was no longer possible to effectively perform professional responsibilities, or*

- *financial relationships in one's private life posed conflicts of interest and loyalty that could influence one's professional judgement and decision-making.*

The potential development of an ethical code of professional conduct for prevention workers must inevitably confront the visibility and power of these roles and the need for reasonable congruence between personal lifestyle and the prevention message. To choose to be a change agent within the context of prevention work may demand a higher and more rigorous standard of personal conduct than is inherent in other roles within health and human service systems, or even within the substance abuse field. Some even believe that those who are promoting health have a higher obligation as a role model than those who are treating illness. The standards of prevention agencies may inevitably be more rigorous than agencies without the prevention-focused mission. Prevention workers will quite likely continue to be held to a rigorous standard of personal conduct like other models of community propriety, e.g., the clergy and teachers.

Conflict between privacy rights and organizational accountability are likely to escalate in the coming decade. Both rights spring from legitimate foundations. The individual has a right to a private existence outside the reach of employer infringement. The organization has a right to protect itself and advance its interests by reasonably assuring that its employees exemplify character and actions congruent with the organization's mission. Reasonable people support both of these rights and have different opinions on how to reconcile them when they come into conflict. Each prevention organization must reach into the collective will of its members to forge a position that supports and protects both the individual and the organization. The articulation of rights and accountabilities in the form of values and professional standards will do much to insure the vitality and protection of the field.

It is the field's zeal for excess that poses dangers. We all have imperfections and fall short of complete adherence to our aspirational values. If a campaign were launched to "purify" the field with perfection as its criteria of inclusion, there would be no one left to work in the field. Someone once noted that programs which set out to stamp out sin usually end up stamping out sinners. Defining the line between privacy rights and organizational accountability as it relates to lifestyle must be done with great care and support to help people be included rather than self-righteously excluded. While the value of honesty demands reasonable congruence between organizational values and personal actions, the value of loyalty demands that we help persons achieve newly defined standards of professional propriety.

Role as Change Agent

◇ ◇ **162** ◇ ◇

Some persons, with a great deal of encouragement from the alcohol and tobacco industries, have launched an attack against prevention programs and workers. Today in your local newspaper there appears such an attack claiming that prevention professionals have become health police—seeking to suppress freedom of speech and action—in the name of some arbitrary standard of health purity.

Discussion Questions

How would you respond to this charge?

What is the boundary between educating a community and imposing one's beliefs on a community?

If the primary thrust of prevention activities is community change, what standards of ethics and values should govern our roles as change agents?

The ethical value of autonomy demands that prevention and treatment professionals not deplete the rights and freedoms of its consumers except under extraordinary circumstances, e.g., threats to the health of others. Each prevention program will evolve implicitly or explicitly a philosophical position on the question of autonomy that will define the boundary between appropriate and inappropriate strategies for social change. What would be, for example, the line between advocating and dictating a health standard related to smoking? How far can one go in promoting attitudes and behaviors conducive to personal and community health? What would be "too far?" How does the question of autonomy differ in our approaches to legal versus illegal drugs?

Relationship Boundaries

Barry, in his role as a prevention specialist in a local substance abuse prevention program which you supervise, has been involved for the past three years in organizing alternative activities for youth that have included weekend retreats, educational and recreational trips, and prom and graduation sleep-ins. A local teen advisory group has served as the primary planning vehicle for these activities. Today you receive a call from an irate father of an 18 year old graduating senior who has been president of the teen advisory committee for the past two years. He is irate over his discovery of a sexual relationship between Barry and his daughter. The father says that he will file statutory rape charges against Barry if he can find any evidence of sexual activity before his daughter's recent birthday. He is extremely concerned that his daughter was taken advantage of because of Barry's leadership of the teen advisory group and he wants to know what you, as Barry's supervisor, are going to do about it.

Discussion Question

How would you respond to this father and to Barry?

Much of the ethical standards development governing substance abuse treatment is based on the imbalance of power in the counseling relationship—power which the helping professional could exploit to the detriment of the client. Some prevention workers would attack the applicability of this model to prevention work, suggesting that the "professional-client" model smacks of classism and elitism and that no such power differential exists in the relationship between prevention workers and the people with whom they work. This position would raise some of the following questions that may be at the crux of any discussion of ethical issues in prevention. Are there any roles assumed or activities performed by prevention workers in which such power exists? Are there conditions under which prevention service recipients are vulnerable due to their special characteristics or the nature of the prevention service context? If professional magic is eschewed and the status of client abolished, are there any standards of appropriate or inappropriate conduct governing relationships between prevention workers and their various constituencies? Does the prevention context lack the exploitive possibilities to which ethical standards are directed in the treatment context?

Assuming for a moment that the accusations of the father in the above vignette are true, let us explore what, if any, ethical issues are raised by the sexual relationship between Barry and the president of the teen advisory council. Is the sexual relationship a matter of free choice between two consenting adults that is none of the agency's business or does it constitute an ethical breach of job performance subject to disciplinary review and/or action? Factors that may have to be considered in weighing these questions include the following:

- **Context**: Did the alleged exploitation occur during a prevention activity, e.g., retreat?
- **Age of the Service Recipient**: While the age of 18 may have arbitrary status under the law, the status of vulnerability—so critical to the discussion of ethical issues—may not be so arbitrarily determined. Would the potential ethical issues be viewed differently if the young woman was 16 or 14? Would it be viewed differently (based on the issue of age) if the sexual involvement was with the young woman's mother?
- **Maturity and Mental Status**: Does the cognitive and emotional functioning of the service recipient allow for informed (ability to anticipate pleasant and unpleasant consequences) choice and consent? Are there special vulnerabilities that must be recognized in prevention work with the mentally ill or developmentally disabled?
- **Coercion**: Was there coercion or duress involved in the initiation of the sexual relationship? Was there deceit or manipulation involved in the initiation of the relationship?
- **Service Intensity**: What was the nature and duration of the service relationship?

Questions like the above help us explore two dimensions that open up the potential for exploitation: the power of the service provider and the vulnerability of the service recipient. If we look at the whole continuum of prevention services, these elements of power and vulnerability differ greatly. The prevention specialist has less power presenting information for 60 minutes to a group of 100 adults than in a two-year relationship with the president of a teen advisory council. The vulnerability of service recipients in these two situations would also differ greatly.

Issues of dual relationships and issues of social, sexual and financial exploitation could be raised in the prevention context anytime:

1. *constituent characteristics potentially compromise free choice, e.g, the developmentally disabled*
2. *constituent characteristics create special vulnerabilities, e.g., children*
3. *there is an imbalance of power between the prevention service provider and the service recipient or*
4. *the service delivery is of sufficient intensity or duration as to enhance emotional dependency even where no formal "treatment or helping relationship" has been defined.*

Due to the vulnerability for exploitation that exists when these conditions are present, there may need to be a particularly strict definition of boundaries governing social, sexual and financial relationships between service providers and service recipients.

Confidentiality and Limits of Competence

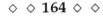

◇ ◇ **164** ◇ ◇

Alan functions as a prevention specialist assigned by a community substance abuse treatment and prevention agency to work full time within county schools. Through Alan's classroom activities, leadership roles in a broad spectrum of alternative activities, and general availability, he frequently finds himself with kids who share personal confidences or seek his advice on personal problems. Since most kids will not accept a referral for counseling, Alan often finds himself involved in informal counseling relationships. In the course of the last month, Alan has interacted with a number of individuals who have shared information of varying levels of intimacy. Among these disclosures were the following:

1. A young neighbor approached Alan following a school presentation and disclosed her parent's intention to get divorced.
2. A school principal confided to Alan his concerns about allegations of sexual misconduct a student recently made against one of the most popular teachers.

3. A jr. high student disclosed to Alan that crack was being sold for the first time at the school.
4. A professional peer disclosed to Alan her decision to enter an eating disorder program.
5. A young student disclosed her sexual abuse by an older brother and his threat of violence if she told anyone.

Discussion Questions

Alan is not a therapist or counselor, the students are not clients in any formal sense of this word, and there is no defined treatment relationship. To what extent do the normal rules of confidentiality within counseling relationships apply to Alan's relationships with students?

How does Alan appropriately determine the line between informal counseling and his need to refer a particular student/family for structured and on-going counseling services.

Are there any ethical restrictions on Alan's communications to parents, teachers, administrators, or community human service representatives regarding the status of a particular student that Alan knows through his prevention role?

Without the benefit of a formal counselor-client relationship, clearly codified confidentiality, informed consent, and clinical supervision, how does the prevention professional operationalize the value of confidentiality?

In which of the above situations would subsequent disclosure be a breach of confidentiality?

In which of the above situations, would there be an ethical mandate for subsequent disclosure to a third party?

The danger of informal counseling or advice-giving in the prevention field is that it lacks some of the specific safeguards of the formal counseling relationship: worker credentialing to conduct the counseling activity, informed consent, confidentiality, clinical supervision and continuity of contact. To the extent that

Alan is involving himself in activities for which he has not been trained and for which he is not supervised, he is breaching the ethical principle of competence. This principle demands that we limit our activities to conduct for which we have been trained and which we are competent to perform—a demand that is particularly compelling in situations where lack of knowledge and skills could result in harm.

The scope and limits of confidentiality should always be defined, even in the most informal of counseling events. The concern is that the same kind of harm can be done through the sharing of a confidence—or the failure to report that confidence under certain circumstances—in the prevention setting as can be done in the treatment setting. Each prevention agency should define and communicate to its staff and its service recipients the scope and limits of confidentiality within the various prevention service relationships. It is also essential that prevention workers have access to supervision through which they can sort out their responsibilities to refrain from any subsequent disclosure of information versus their duties to disclose in certain situations.

Alliances

◇ ◇ **165** ◇ ◇

You are president of a local grassroots substance abuse prevention task force that has been organizing and supporting a wide spectrum of local substance abuse prevention activities during its five years of existence. You are currently staging a fund-raising campaign to raise money for scholarships to send 50 inner-city youths to a prevention leadership camp. As the deadline for registration arrives, you have raised only enough money for 21 scholarships, due primarily to severe economic cutbacks that have hit local businesses and industries in the past year. A local business, reading of this dilemma in the paper, approaches the task force and offers to donate the $3,900 to reach the goal of financing 50 youths' attendance to the camp. The local business offering this financial support is the regional distributor for a national company whose primary product is beer.

Discussion Questions

What potential ethical issues, if any, would be raised by acceptance of this donation?

What course of action would you recommend to the task force as their president?

Ethical questions raised by acceptance of the above contribution would include the following:

- *What would it mean to the children to know that a brewery was sponsoring their participation in the camp?*
- *Would financial ties to the alcohol industry damage the reputation of the task force and decrease the potency of its prevention message?*
- *Would acceptance of the gift influence the task force's stand on labeling of alcoholic products or other issues related to promotion and distribution of alcoholic products, e.g., targeting?*
- *Would potential publicity noting the brewery's contribution to support prevention activities divert public attention away from the fact that this company spends more than $1 million a day promoting their alcoholic products? Would acceptance of the gift by the task force create complicity in this diversion?*

A growing number of prevention organizations are taking the position that it is an ethical conflict of interest for a prevention program to accept funds from the alcohol industry at the same time it lobbies for or against issues that effect the economic interests of that industry. Groups like the National Association of Children of Alcoholics and Remove Intoxicated Drivers have adopted policies that prohibit acceptance of contributions from the alcohol industry. Groups like the National Council on Alcoholism, Mothers Against Drunk Drivers and Students Against Drunk Drivers that once accepted such contributions have adopted policies to discontinue this practice.

◇ ◇ **166** ◇ ◇

A local citizen, publicly notorious for his role in opening the first adult book store in your community, calls your local prevention program with the following requests. First, he has seen a number of your agency's prevention posters around town and would like to get some to put up in his store. Secondly, he is very concerned about the drug abuse problem and was just made aware of the program through which you utilize local citizens as volunteers to support various prevention activities. He would like to know how he could become a volunteer.

Discussion Questions

How do you respond to these requests?

How would the situation differ, if any, if the person wishing to volunteer was the single person most associated with an anti-abortion (or pro-choice) campaign in your local community?

In sorting through its choice of alliances, each prevention agency through the deliberation of its board, managers and staff must address such questions as the following:

- *Is the person/agency seeking to use the affiliation with the prevention campaign in order to divert the community's attention from or to compensate for other exploitive or unscrupulous practices?*
- *Will affiliation with the person/agency compromise the agency's effective delivery of prevention services?*
- *Will affiliation with the person/agency involve the agency in controversy that will divert it from its primary purpose?*
- *Will affiliation with the person/agency weaken the moral and professional authority with which it speaks in the community?*

In many cases, the question will be the CONDITIONS under which affiliation would be appropriate or the DEGREE of affiliation which would be appropriate. For example, a prevention program in the above vignette whose posters were primarily targeted at youth might find placement of their posters in an adult bookstore highly inappropriate; a prevention program whose posters dealt with AIDS awareness might find placement of their posters in adult bookstores quite appropriate.

Iatrogenic Effects

Many criticisms of drug education approaches over the past twenty-five years have suggested that some of these approaches may have stimulated, rather than prevented, drug experimentation. If an ethical premise of substance abuse treatment (borrowed from a sister profession) is "First do no harm," how can any potential iatrogenic effects of prevention programs be minimized? What standards could help prevent unintended, but untoward, effects of prevention interventions? The next several vignettes will help explore approaches to avoiding such unintended effects of prevention services.

◇ ◇ **167** ◇ ◇

You work in a youth-oriented substance abuse prevention program serving a predominantly rural county that has experienced a dramatic rise in drug-related adolescent deaths during the last six months. Today you are speaking to an 8th grade class as a component of a comprehensive substance abuse curriculum used at the middle school. You discover shortly into your presentation that 5-6 students in the class have had significant drug experiences. The nature of their questions and comments suggests that they are into extremely high-risk drug choices and high-risk methods and patterns of drug use. Although your task was to talk about drug abuse and self-esteem, this small subgroup of students are asking very specific questions about drug dosages, drug effects, and the dangers of certain drug combinations.

Discussion Questions

How would you respond to this situation?

Is providing such information—which could reduce drug-related casualties among the users—a legitimate "prevention" activity?

Is there any danger that providing this information within the context of the classroom could have unintended effects upon those students who have not experimented with drugs?

The situation above poses potential risks to all parties—the using students, the non-using students and the prevention worker. The drug-experimenting students are involved in drug choices, the use of drug combinations and drug dosages that could be debilitating or lethal. The prevention worker, if he or she provides detailed aspects of drug pharmacology to reduce the risks of toxic-lethal drug reactions, may inadvertently convey permission for their drug-using activity. If such information is withheld, the prevention worker may feel an accomplice in any subsequent drug-related injury or death of the involved students. If the worker provides the detailed information in the classroom, there could be unintended effects upon the non-drug-using students, e.g., stimulating curiosity about drugs, decreasing student fears about particular drugs. The prevention worker is also potentially vulnerable in this situation to challenges to his or her professional integrity through charges that he or she is "teaching kids how to use drugs." The prevention worker must find a way out of this quandary that resolves all of these potential vulnerabilities. Options that might be used to achieve such resolution would include the following:

1) *refrain from responding to the needs of a few students in a manner that could have negative effects on the majority of students, e.g., not provide the information in the context of the class presentation, and*
2) *respond to the needs of the drug-experimenting students by*
   a) *meeting with them at a later time to discuss their information needs, e.g., after class*
   b) *referring the students to early intervention groups that may address their information needs, or*
   c) *referring the students to an SAP counselor or school counselor to provide an avenue for intervention into their drug experimentation via their desire for information.*

Social policy on illicit drugs in the United States has been to withhold information and technology (access to quality-controlled drug supplies, sterile syringes, etc.) that would reduce the risks associated with consumption of the drugs. The subsequent high risks associated with such use, it is believed, will serve as a deterrent to drug experimentation. Persons representing the extreme end of this policy would say that the provision of any information and assistance that increases the ability of the potential or actual drug consumer to use without these severe risks is promoting drug use and is unethical. At the other end of the continuum, one could posit to having information that can reduce the risks of injury or fatality and not providing such information is a breach in ethical responsibility. The conflict occurs when actions designed to achieve a public good might, through their rigid implementation, compromise the health of some individuals. Each prevention agency should define its own position on the ethics of providing or withholding drug information and explore ways in which the interests of the society and the interests of individuals can be best reconciled. What do you think this position should be?

◇ ◇ **168** ◇ ◇

You are responsible for coordinating a community-based substance abuse prevention program whose primary focus is public information, drug education in the schools and the coordination of a number of adolescent alternatives projects. During the past year, a number of newly recovering adolescents have approached you offering to serve as prevention program volunteers. They are particularly interested in opportunities to speak to younger children and other adolescents about their life experiences. They feel their experiences can be used to help others avoid the problems they encountered and that the opportunity for such public witnessing will be an important support for their own ongoing recoveries.

Discussion Question

Describe any ethical issues potentially involved in this situation.

Whether working with recovering volunteers who are youths or adults, the prevention program has a responsibility to assure the integrity of persons publicly identified with the prevention message. The practice of placing alcohol/drug offenders with minimal or no sobriety time at podiums in elementary and secondary schools or in other highly visible prevention roles is viewed by many prevention professionals as highly questionable. One concern is that the image or charisma of the presenter and elements within his or her presentation may inadvertently glamorize or otherwise increase the appeal of drug experimentation. The person with minimal sobriety time is probably much more an expert on the drug experience than on the recovery experience. Another concern is that any highly visible arrest or relapse of this person weakens the reputation of the prevention agency and the integrity of the prevention message. There may be roles and activities within the prevention field for persons at early stages of addiction recovery whose potential relapse would not have such harmful effects to the effectiveness or reputation of the program. Prevention programs have a responsibility to protect their reputation and their capacity for continued service to the community.

Honesty

◇ ◇ **169** ◇ ◇

A biology teacher who is involved in teaching her portion of a K-12 drug education curriculum seeks out your advice as the local prevention specialist. Her concern has to do with the potential effect of honest answers to questions posed by freshman and sophomore students during discussions on various drugs and their effects. The teacher offers the following example to illustrate the point. If the teacher responds to student questions as to why cocaine is so popular or why it is so addictive with a discussion of cocaine's euphorigenic properties, won't this lead to increased curiosity and potential desire to experiment with this drug in spite of warnings of its addictiveness. If the teacher says: "This drug, in its current form, may be so powerful, humans may not be able to say no to it once exposed," won't this statement potentially incite the adolescent to test the boundaries of his or her own power and control? The teacher ends her presentation of her concern with the words: "Quite frankly, I'm concerned about how to talk to sixteen-year-old kids who think they are immortal about the long-term effects of anything."

Discussion Questions

Discuss the ethical principle of honesty as it relates to drug information dissemination.

What options are available when a straightforward presentation of factual information may increase rather than decrease drug experimentation?

Is it ever okay to lie, distort the truth or withhold the truth with the intent of preventing youthful drug experimentation?

There is much in the discussion of honesty and deception in the treatment context (Chapter Six) that is applicable to prevention activities. The value of honesty constitutes the ethical foundation upon which any healthy service relationship can be based. As such, any deviance from this stance must be ethically justified. The issues of honesty, deception, and discretion are important to address in the prevention context because of their potential effect on people's decision-making.

The danger of dishonesty and deception is evident in early prevention programs that seek to utilize fear as a force to prevent drug experimentation among youth. These programs, designed with the most benevolent of intentions, would progress to the routine use of deception and lies in the effort to prevent drug experimentation. As often happens with such benign deception, there are unanticipated and untoward side-effects. The exaggerated and fabricated information used to scare youth from marijuana in the late 1960's all but destroyed the credibility of prevention workers to inform youth about drugs of much greater risk and may have contributed to youth extending experimentation beyond marijuana. What followed was a commitment to the dissemination of factual information that would also be discovered in many cases to have unanticipated and undesired consequences. If unedited honesty is at one end of a continuum and outright, intentional lying is at the other end, the value of discretion represents the center. Discretion demands that the communicator understand the kind of developmental filter through which information will be received. It demands that the communicator understand the meanings which the listener is likely to attach to information. It demands that the communicator recognize the applicability of the concept of iatrogenic (treatment-caused) illness to prevention activities.

Social Action / Civil Disobedience

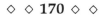

◇ ◇ **170** ◇ ◇

Shelly works in an urban prevention project that has worked intensely for more than two years to develop and implement culturally sensitive and competent prevention programming in a predominantly African American and Latino community. Today Shelly along with two other community activists (a priest and an elementary school teacher), were arrested for criminal destruction of property for defacing billboards throughout the community that promoted alcohol and tobacco products. The "criminal" acts were committed by Shelly on work time at the prevention project.

Discussion Questions

What should be the agency's response to Shelly's conduct? A memo of censure? A memo of commendation?

What ethical issues are raised by this situation—both the targeted promotion of legal drugs and the destruction of the media of such promotion?

Should Shelly be paid for the time (three hours of regularly scheduled work time) that she was involved in the above activity or for time lost while in jail, visiting her attorney, appearing in court?

What organizational values should guide our response to a worker involved in such activity?

The response to Shelly's activity would vary depending on the values of the organization and the extent to which social action and civil disobedience are a reflection or a violation of those values. As social action escalates in the prevention field, it will be increasingly important for prevention organizations to define if, and under what circumstances, civil disobedience will be viewed as a legitimate professional activity. As discussions about the use of civil disobedience increase, organizations may be able to more fully articulate if, when, and how prevention workers should be involved in such actions. There are likely to emerge parallels to the civil rights movement in which there will be ethical issues raised for individuals and for organizations both by participation in acts of civil disobedience and by the failure to participate in such acts.

Freedom of Access Versus Harmful Use of Information

◇ ◇ **171** ◇ ◇

You supervise a private not-for-profit substance abuse prevention information clearinghouse which provides library and literature search services. You have an extensive collection of audiovisual materials, curricula, books, journals and reports that serve the clearing house's mission of providing support to substance abuse prevention efforts in local communities. You have been the repository of the raw data from two alcohol and drug abuse surveys conducted within your state. These two studies, which document recent changes in attitudes and behaviors related to drinking, smoking and drug use, have received nationwide attention and many persons have come in to investigate findings in the raw data that were not published. For the past week and a half, two persons have been at the clearinghouse daily pouring over the study data. Today one of their notebooks was inadvertently returned with an assortment of research materials. When you open the notebook to discover its owner, you see a page headed with the notation "DIST. SPIR. COUNCIL ACCOUNT" with notes scattered below it under the two headings: "Who doesn't drink and why" and "Why people choose to drink beer and wine over distilled spirits." You then notice a business card stapled to the inside of the notebook—the card bearing the name of a national advertising firm. It appears that the two regular visitors have been using the latest research data to help prepare a new marketing campaign for the promotion of alcoholic products.

Discussion Questions

How would you respond to this situation?

What ethical issues are raised by the use of the clearinghouse for purposes diametrically opposed to its mission?

Discussion of this vignette with prevention workers quickly generates a divergence of opinion that roughly splits into two camps. The first of these camps is reflected in the following argument:

> *The ethical issues in this situation may be elucidated by contrasting the public library with the clearinghouse of a not-for-profit agency prevention agency. Both the library and the clearinghouse open their resources to the public as long as the guidelines of each are followed. One interesting difference has to do with the motivations of the consumers—how the consumer intends to use the information they are getting. In the case of the library, there is no inquiry as to WHY the consumer wishes to check out a particular book—such an inquiry would be seen as intrusive and invasive. While the same principle is generally true of the clearinghouse, the clearinghouse differs from the library in one important respect. The clearinghouse offers information services specifically to enhance the prevention of substance abuse. If the clearinghouse discovers persons who are obviously using the agency's information services to promote alcohol or drug consumption, then those persons' rights to access to those services could, and some would say should, be ethically revoked. This action would reflect the position that the agency's resources will not be used for purposes or activities incompatible with the agency's mission.*

A second camp argues from a very different position.

> *Restrictions on freedom of access to information from public library and clearinghouse services is unthinkable. The administrative definition of who can and cannot use reference information violates the value of autonomy. Even where some harm could result from access to this information, the restriction of access to information poses a greater evil than does the potential misuse of the information. Professional libraries and clearinghouse services tend to support this latter position, particularly those who see themselves bound by the Code of Ethics of the American Library Association. This code's adamant stand against censorship would make it difficult, if not impossible, to ethically justify selectively controlling access to library holdings based on the purposes for which such materials were to be used. This side is also supported by the fact that most libraries and clearinghouses who receive state or federal funds are contractually prohibited from denying the public access to their information. Even if such denial was legally or ethically justified, the selective denial of access is practically impossible when library and clearinghouse holdings are open to the public.*

Restriction on Speech

◊ ◊ **172** ◊ ◊

You have applied and received a prevention services grant but have just been informed that there are contractual restrictions only allowing funds to be dispersed to agencies who take an adamant stand against the concept of responsible drug use.

Discussion Question

Are there any ethical issues that could influence your consideration of the acceptance of these funds?

While the potential ethical issues that spill out of the "responsible use" controversy cannot be adequately summarized here, the principles of honesty and fidelity may prohibit the abdication of organizational values for transient gain. The ethical command of honesty demands congruence between word and action and that the values implicit in those words are not sacrificed for expediency or profit. If the prohibition against use of the concept of "responsible use" is congruent with an agency's historical philosophy, then there would be no contradictions in their acceptance of the grant award. If the agency's philosophy conflicts with this required position, then the agency would need to seriously consider refusal of the grant with the contractual restrictions.

Intrusive or Abusive Interventions

◇ ◇ **173** ◇ ◇

Following the drug-related deaths of two students, a newly formed parents group presented a petition to the school board calling for mandatory random drug testing for all students along with letters of commitment from local business and industry to pick up the costs associated with this testing. The school board, in considering this proposal, has solicited your opinion as the local substance abuse prevention expert.

Discussion Questions

Separate from issues of practicality and effectiveness, what ethical issues, if any, do you see in mandatory testing of minors within a school system?

Are any of the ethical principles outlined in Chapter Two potentially violated through such testing?

There are a number of ethical issues that might be raised in the exploration of random testing of minors within the school environment. Proponents of such a proposal would have to address some of the following concerns:

Autonomy:	*Does the mandatory solicitation of body fluids from children and the supervision of "urine drops" constitute an unacceptable invasion of personal freedom and privacy?*
Justice:	*Would the procedural rights of students be rigorously protected through both the testing process and any subsequent disciplinary action?*

Nonmaleficence: *Are there unforeseen and unintended harms that could occur through the implementation of the program?*

Stewardship: ˙ *Is the expenditure of funds to pay for laboratory testing of urine the best potential investment of community resources in substance abuse prevention?*

Proponents of testing programs would contend that the potential of testing to serve as a deterrent against drug experimentation outweighs any concerns raised by the above questions. What is your view?

◇ ◇ **174** ◇ ◇

Nearly everyone is familiar with the "Scared Straight" program and the more recent advent of "Bootcamp" programs for first-time juvenile offenders. A principal in a middle school launched his own version of the "Scared Straight" approach which he affectionately referred to as "my prevention program." Youngsters, who the principal determined to be at high risk for trouble (e.g., drugs, delinquency, and attitude), were removed from the school and taken on a tour of a nearby prison. The program had been especially planned by the principal. When the inmates asked at a planning meeting what their role was, the principal responded, "Scare them to death!" The youngsters taken through this program were subjected to intense verbal abuse and intimidation. The first two groups of youngsters who experienced this tour were terrified into at least transient meekness and compliance and most of the parents responded positively to its observed effects. Immediately following the second tour the parents of one of the participants complained that their son was emotionally anxious, had been having terrible recurrent nightmares, and had begun bedwetting since his trip to the prison.

Discussion Question

Comment on the ethical issues raised by the principal's prevention program.

There are multiple risks associated with programs whose methods are invasive and potentially abusive. One involves the failure to get the informed consent of the parent or guardian for the participation of a minor. Another issue is the effect of labeling. What effects would accompany the youth's selection to be a participant in the principal's prevention project? Would the participant's perception of himself or herself change as a result of his or her selection? Would any changes in how he or she was seen by his or her peers enhance rather than decrease social deviancy? Another risk is the potential untoward effects of the invasive or abusive experience. Even where such harshness of methods could be justified, there must be careful scrutiny in the selection process. The selection process should include screening devices to divert persons who might be potentially harmed by the experience. Where no such screening technology exists, serious consideration must be given as to whether the potential benefits of the program outweigh the program's potential risks. Even where the general effects of such programs are described positively, the potential for severe iatrogenic effects to a small number of students must be carefully weighed.

Early Intervention: Employee Assistance Programs (EAP) and Student Assistance Programs (SAP)

Integrity of Organizational Structure

◇ ◇ **175** ◇ ◇

A substance abuse treatment program that offers EAP services contractually through a thinly-veiled sister corporation consistently and significantly underbids its EAP competitors on the assumption that money lost through lower per capita fees paid by companies will be made up through increased treatment revenue generated through a pattern of preferential referral.

Discussion Questions

What ethical issues are involved in this practice?

What conflicts might arise for professionals working for this EAP?

There are ethical issues anytime the referral of an EAP client is based on anything other than the independent and objective assessment of a client's needs and where those needs can best be met. Conflicts of financial interest that can bias the assessment and referral process are a growing concern in the EAP field. Jim Wrich (1990) has painted a poignant picture of these potential conflicts by holding up the specter of a future in which half the EAP providers will be bought out by insurance and managed care industries in an effort to keep everyone out of treatment while the other half of the EAP providers will be bought out by treatment programs trying to get everyone in to treatment. The ethical mandate for the EAP counselor is to avoid both real and perceived conflicts of interest in the assessment and referral process.

Independence and Objectivity of Professional Judgement

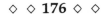

◇ ◇ **176** ◇ ◇

Maya works for a freestanding EAP program that provides EAP services contractually to a wide variety of public and private sector organizations. Maya just been contacted by a private treatment program that specializes in inpatient psychiatric and substance abuse services for adult and adolescent clients. To acquaint Maya with their services, they are offering to pay all expenses to fly her in to visit their facilities for two days. Maya's sister, who she hasn't seen in over a year, lives 30 miles from the treatment facility site.

Discussion Questions

How should Maya respond to this offer?

How would accepting this trip (valued at $700) differ from accepting $700 in cash as a "gift" from this program?

The above vignette raises the question of appropriate boundary issues in the relationship between an assessment and referral service and the organizational resources to which it refers. The first concern in this situation is whether acceptance of the "free" trip will create a sense of obligation or duty to return the gift of the trip with client referrals. A second concern is whether or not the proximity of Maya's sister to the treatment agency and the desire to see her sister would unduly influence her decision to go or not go. Would this simply be mutual needs being met or would this be mutual exploitation: the program seeking to exploit the referral potential of the EAP counselor and the EAP counselor exploiting the offer of travel to visit her sister. There are ethical issues involving the twin commands of beneficence and nonmaleficence that must be addressed. Acceptance of the trip would be a breach of ethical conduct to the extent that it influenced and contaminated the objectivity of the EAP counselor in the client referral process. The same would be true of acceptance of money, gifts, free meals, or other goods or services provided by a service agency seeking the favor of the EAP counselor.

Definition of Client / Conflicts of Loyalty

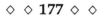

You provide contractual EAP services to a local company with 3,000 employees. An employee of this company in seeking counseling services, describes as part of her current problems the unwanted sexual advances made by the Director of Human Resources. This employee is unaware of, and you are acutely aware of, the fact that this is the person within the company who awards the EAP contract and to whom the EAP contractor reports.

Discussion Questions

Would you inform this employee of the legal redress that may be available to her due to sustained sexual harassment and would you strongly encourage her to seek such redress?

Would you attempt to approach the Director of Human Resources and resolve the problem directly?

Would you become an advocate on behalf of this employee by supporting the submission of a formal complaint of harassment to the Vice President to whom the Director of Human Resources reports?

Who is your client in this situation?

How would you respond to this situation?

There is an enormous potential for conflicts of interests and conflicts of loyalty in this situation. The first responses of the EAP counselor should be a recognition of these potential conflicts, an acknowledgement of these conflicts to the client and an exploration of the most appropriate counseling resources within or outside the framework of the employee assistance program. Potential intervention steps could include:

- *advisement of the client that there are administrative and legal channels of redress*
- *advisement of the client that she could use emotional as well as legal counsel to explore her options and to proceed through a course of action*
- *advisement of the client of the relationship between the employee assistance program and the Director of Human Resources with assurances that her discussions will remain confidential*
- *advisement of the client that this relationship poses a conflict that could jeopardize the objectivity of the EAP counselor, and*
- *referral of the client to an outside resource that could provide the needed emotional support and legal advice.*

Where no viable outside options for counseling exist, it would be advisable for the EAP counselor to seek external consultation to assure that the needs of the client are not being compromised by the financial interests and personal relationships of the employee assistance program personnel.

For a discussion of threats to public safety encountered in the EAP role, see Chapter Eight.

Environmental Stressors

 ◊ ◊ **178** ◊ ◊

You conduct assessment and referral services for a private EAP contractor. In the past six months you have assessed five employees who work within the same unit of the same company. All five were suffering from severe stress reactions generating not from stress in their personal lives but from the stress experienced within the work environment of this unit. Although the stress reactions differed for the five employees, all reported the same stressors: staff shortages due to high turnover, excessive work demands, mandatory overtime, inadequate equipment, and an alcohol-impaired supervisor who is verbally abusive.

Discussion Questions

Do you have a responsibility to report these conditions?

Should you try to work through the company in order to change these conditions?

What ethical responsibility does an EAP professional have to his or her client(s) in this situation?

See analysis after next vignette.

◇ ◇ **179** ◇ ◇

EAP professionals are in unique roles to identify the incidence and prevalence of toxic working conditions within the companies for whom they work. What ethical responsibilities does the EAP professional have when he or she discovers such conditions as:

- conditions or practices that pose a threat to worker safety or public safety
- discrimination based on age, sex, race, religion, or sexual orientation, or
- business practices that are a violation of law?

If the company is the "client" of the EAP contractor, is the EAP professionally bound to keep confidential knowledge about company practices obtained through the EAP role?

Let's explore four different potential points of view that would influence the EAP counselor's response to the above vignettes.

Position One: The ultimate responsibility of the EAP counselor is to the needs of the individual employee being assessed. The source of stressors in the above situation is not important. What is important is the EAP counselor's ability to counsel and/or refer the above employees with the goal of decreasing the stress-related impairment to their personal health and job functioning. Getting caught up in politics of trying to change the work environment should be avoided because such efforts will serve as a diversion from the individual needs of the employees and will threaten the continued accessibility of EAP services to the employees of this company.

Position Two: *The EAP counselor has a moral obligation to confront any organizational conditions that compromise the health of employees seeking services through the employee assistance program. Advocacy to alter toxic working conditions is an integral part of the EAP counselor role.*

Position Three: *The primary contractual obligation of the EAP counselor is to the company. While the needs of the individual client should be addressed to the greatest extent possible, the obligation of loyalty would not allow the EAP counselor to take any action which would harm the company. The EAP counselor is bound by confidentiality not to disclose information gained through EAP interviews in a manner that would do harm to the company or its representatives.*

Position Four: *The EAP counselor has a duty to uphold ethical and legal standards of professional conduct regardless of the needs or demands placed upon him or her by the individual EAP client or the company which contracts for EAP services. The ultimate loyalty of the EAP counselor should be to the profession. The EAP counselor cannot become an accomplice to illegal activity through his or her silence.*

The two vignettes involve potential conflicts of loyalty—loyalty to individual EAP clients and loyalty to the organization for whom EAP services have been contracted. The four positions above represent the fixed points within which the EAP counselor must seek an appropriate course of action. It may be helpful whenever possible for the EAP counselor to see these as concurrent rather than competing loyalties and seek diplomatically to find areas of compromise in which the needs of employees seeking EAP services and the needs of the company can be mutually satisfied. General guidelines on the resolution of conflicts of loyalty include the following steps:

1.   *identify and clarify the nature of the loyalty conflicts*

2. *communicate the nature of the conflict to all parties involved*
3. *seek mutually agreeable solutions that can meet the needs of all involved parties, and*
4. *where parties interests are so incompatible as to make compromise impossible, seek clinical and legal consultation.*

In the first vignette, the EAP counselor could recommend that the individual employees develop more effective means of coping with the high stress work environment; At the same time, the EAP counselor could seek to positively effect the working conditions within this particular unit. The long-term interests of the employees and the interests of the company would both be met by the EAP counselor utilizing the chain of command—within the EAP and between the EAP and the company—to acknowledge the existence of specific conditions that compromise the health of employees. Such conditions will inevitably do harm to the company via employee turnover, increased absenteeism, stress-related health care costs, and poor employee morale.

In the second vignette, the EAP counselor will again have to utilize the process of supervision to determine the best course of action—whether to take no action, whether to work within the company to get the illegal practices stopped, or to notify some external authority of the illegal activity. In making his or her decision, the EAP counselor will have to consider such issues as the following:

- *Does the context in which the EAP counselor obtains information of the illegal activity fall within the normal confidentiality restrictions?*
- *Do the company's practices pose imminent or long-term harm to employees or the public?*
- *To what extent will the EAP counselor's failure to notify authorities of the illegal activity make him or her an accomplice to the action?*
- *Will the failure to act, or the act of disclosure, damage the reputation of the EAP counselor and the employee assistance program?*
- *How will disclosure affect employees' future accessibility to EAP services?*

Confidentiality

◇ ◇ **180** ◇ ◇

You are a Student Assistance Program (SAP) counselor working contractually through your agency with a local middle school. Many students who have met with you to discuss issues related to their drug usage have all named a single supplier of their illicit drugs. The supplier is reported to be aggressively distributing drugs to middle and high school students. From the accounts of students, you also suspect that the dealer is trading drugs for sexual favors from some of the students.

Discussion Questions

What would you do, if anything, in response to this situation?

What ethical issues would dictate, or prevent, your taking action on this situation?

Can information be disclosed which was obtained from multiple interviews with different sources as long as the persons who made the disclosures are not identified? Would disclosure under these circumstances be a breach of confidentiality?

Many counselors in the above situation would find themselves torn between the normal strictures of confidentiality and the desire to stop the victimization of students via exploitive and predatory behavior. SAP counselors who have carefully weighed their responsibilities in this situation have drawn different conclusions. Some have taken the position that the risk of imminent harm is not specific enough to justify a breach of confidentiality and that any disclosure of information obtained in the counseling session without the client's permission is unethical. Other SAP counselors, aware of the risks associated with acting and the failure to act in the above circumstances, have sought some middle ground. Some have sought confirmation of the information with other students outside the context of counseling—information that could be shared without violating confidentiality. Some have sought permission from students to identify the supplier—without disclosing the identity of the students—to authorities who could investigate the situation.

In sorting through one's professional responsibilities in the above situation, the appropriateness of any proposed action could be assessed by the following questions:

1) *Will the proposed course of action increase the vulnerability of one or more students to harm?*

2) *Will the proposed course of action undermine the current relationships between the SAP counselor and students who are involved in counseling?*

3) *Will the proposed course of action potentially damage the reputation of the SAP counselor—decreasing the attractiveness of the Student Assistance Program to other students who might need the program's services in the future?*

4) *Does the proposed course of action intervene to prevent imminent harm where such harm is identifiable?*

Disposition of Contraband

◇ ◇ **181** ◇ ◇

You are a SAP counselor at a high school working under a contract between a local substance abuse prevention agency and the school district. Sharon, a student who recently went through an inpatient addiction treatment program, enters your office wanting to give you drugs that she just purchased. Sharon reports that she bought the drugs on impulse and knows she will use them if you don't take them.

Discussion Questions

Do you take possession of the drugs as requested? If so, what would you then do with them?

Would the confidentiality of the student be protected in the above situation in light of her illegal possession of drugs and the prohibition against possession of contraband on school property?

Is the fact that Sharon bought the drugs from someone on the school grounds a concern for the SAP counselor? Is it the counselor's job to seek the identity of the persons who sold the substance?

What policies exist regarding the receipt and disposal of drugs and other types of contraband?

There are three inter-related issues and interests woven through the above situation: the protection of the student, the protection of the SAP counselor, and the protection of the reputation of the school (and if applicable the external agency contractually providing the SAP counselor). To protect students, there needs to be mechanisms through which drugs or other contraband such as weapons can be received by staff from students. In the above case, for example, being able to receive the drugs and provide immediate counseling may clearly avert what would have been imminent relapse. At the same time, it is crucial that there be clear protocol established for the transfer and disposal of contraband once it is received. The lack of or disregard of such policies can lead to any number of potential problems. Other students could witness the presence of contraband in the SAP counselor's desk and rumors could fly about the SAP counselor's own drug use. In the midst of such rumors, a principal or local police could investigate and find illegal substances in the possession of the SAP counselor. Those are just a few possibilities. The establishment of clear policies on the receipt, transfer and disposal of contraband can protect the personal, professional and institutional interests of everyone in incidents like the above. Protocol regarding confidentiality would need to be explicitly defined as part of the planning process for the SAP.

Outreach

Confidentiality/Duty to Disclose

 ◊ ◊ **182** ◊ ◊

Outreach workers are often exposed to and must work/live in very dichotomous worlds. In this marginal role, they sometimes see an underworld of a community through which they may become privy to a wide assortment of discomforting information. Andy works as a detached "street worker" out of a community-based substance abuse prevention program. In the past week, through the normal working of his information networks, he has heard numerous personal confessions, several references to an impending rumble between two gangs, preparations for numerous criminal activities, reports of a prominent physician who has been purchasing enormous quantities of cocaine, and reports of two separate adolescents who have been rumored to have begun talking of killing themselves.

Discussion Question

Which ethical standards should guide what actions Andy takes in response to this information and to who else Andy communicates such information?

The outreach worker operates in professional terrain for which ethical issues remain largely uncharted. How does one operate in helping relationships that fall outside of the traditionally defined "counselor-client" relationship? Andy's role in information dissemination, case-finding, informal referral for services with persons not formally defined as agency clients leaves open to question what rules of confidentiality govern such relationships. In weighing what, if anything, he needs to do with the information above, Andy may need to consider some of the following ethical principles and questions:

- *Discretion: What information would a reasonable person in Andy's position keep confidential out of respect for the privacy of the person who shared the information? Should personal confidences that pose no threats to others be treated with the same strictness of confidentiality as the counselor-client relationship?*
- *Honesty and Fidelity: What expectations of confidentiality have been communicated or implied to those persons from whom the information was received? Was the information passed to Andy specifically for the purpose of some action being taken?*
- *Beneficence: What action could be taken to protect, support, or prevent harm to persons referenced in the information received? Do the stories of the two adolescents considering suicide warrant immediate disclosure and intervention?*
- *Nonmaleficence: What actions by way of information disclosure could result in harm being done? What inadvertent consequences could proceed from the act of disclosure? What imminent harm is likely to occur if no disclosure is made or no action is taken? Does the potential threat to public safety of a cocaine-addicted physician demand disclosure and supervisory review of potential courses of action?*

- *Loyalty*: Could Andy's and the agency's ability to continue service to this client population be harmed, via damage to reputation, by disclosure or failure to disclose.
- *Self-interest*: What actions might be necessary for Andy to take in order to protect his own vulnerability and liability resulting from having received the above information? Through what mechanisms are decisions to disclose or not to disclose, including the supervisory review process, documented?

The fact that such issues are complex and raise conflicts over competing duties makes access to regular and rigorous supervision essential for outreach workers. Charting an ethical course of action through supervisory consultation represents more a process of reaching best mutual judgement than a process of applying arbitrary rules or prescriptions.

Worker Vulnerability

◇ ◇ **183** ◇ ◇

You have just been funded to begin an innovative outreach program aimed at reducing HIV transmission among IV drug users. The project calls for a cadre of outreach workers to penetrate social networks of drug users and attempt to shift these individuals from high-risk to low-risk methods of drug ingestion via education and personal persuasion. Two of the finalists you are considering for an outreach worker position are recovering addicts with less than one year of recovery time.

Discussion Questions

What ethical issues are involved in sending addicts early in recovery into social networks of active drug users?

Would you hire these individuals? If so, how might you structure this job so as to reduce the personal risks of relapse?

What ethical responsibilities does the agency have to address "occupational safety and health" issues of outreach workers who will be paid to work daily in a predatory and increasingly violent subculture?

Placing addicted persons with minimal recovery time in professional roles that expose them to environments saturated with drug-enhancing sensory cues is a highly questionable practice. The stories of relapse which emerge from such experiments are prolific. Recovering persons may be high-risk for such environments regardless of the duration of continuous sobriety. The ethical mandate to the program is to refrain from placing any employee into situations likely to compromise their health and safety. Compliance with this mandate requires careful screening of job candidates and the development of significant support structures for the outreach worker.

Screening of candidates might include a review of such factors as:

- *the vulnerability—naivete, curiosity, immaturity—for substance abuse through exposure to the culture of addiction for those candidates without adequate addiction/treatment recovery histories*
- *the duration and stability of the candidate's program of personal recovery for those who present with addiction/treatment/recovery histories*
- *the candidate's familiarity with "street" culture, e.g., knowledge of culture of addiction, ability to accurately read verbal and non-verbal cues related to safety*
- *vulnerabilities of physical and emotional health that might be compromised in the outreach worker role and*
- *the scope and intensity of the candidate's social replenishment network.*

Practices which can support the health and safety of outreach staff working within the culture of addiction would include the following:

- *utilizing two person outreach teams as opposed to individual assignments*
- *detailed training related to assessing and managing threats to physical safety*
- *permission to not enter or immediately leave any environment that poses a risk to the physical/psychological safety of the worker*
- *creating an emergency response protocol for a worker in trouble in the field*
- *mandatory supervisory debriefing on almost a daily basis*
- *access to other outreach workers for personal and professional support*

- *strong encouragement and support for personal programs of recovery, e.g., not scheduling work assignments to conflict with self-help meetings*
- *utilization of staff meetings, training opportunities, professional meetings as a means of support and replenishment, and*
- *active support of the treatment of any persons who relapse while in an outreach role.*

Relationship Boundaries

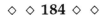

◇ ◇ **184** ◇ ◇

Ricky is an outreach worker who has become well known in the Gay community for his long history of service working in projects sponsored by the community AIDS foundation. For the past two years, Ricky has worked in AIDS education serving as a point of contact for information, service referral, crisis management and informal counseling. His office is the streets and bars and other gathering places within the Gay community. He is a one-man campaign on the role of alcohol and drug use in the continued spread of HIV within the Gay community. Ricky's work-life and lifestyle are almost inseparable. The world of his work and the world of his personal life share the same physical and social space. His clientele are part of a voluntary community to which Ricky also claims membership.

Discussion Questions

When indigenous persons are recruited to work professionally within such communities, what distinguishes lovers, friends, and acquaintances from "clients?"

How could Ricky separate, for example, information received as a member of this community versus information he received in his work role?

What, if anything, would separate appropriate from inappropriate social or sexual relationships between Ricky and his clientele?

The outreach worker is in a particularly nebulous ethical quandary if he or she is a highly visible member of the community which he or she serves through his or her professional role. In such circumstances, the line between one's personal and private life becomes particularly difficult to define. An essential step in providing some degree of role clarity for the outreach worker would be to answer at the agency or project level the following questions:

- *Is the outreach worker-client (or whatever name we give to those who are the consumers to which outreach services are directed) relationship characterized by an inequity of power and/or emotional vulnerability that could result in harm or exploitation?*
- *Are there special duties and obligations inherent in the relationship between the outreach worker and his or her individual service constituents?*
- *Is the effectiveness of the service relationship between the outreach worker and client compromised by concurrent social, sexual, and financial relationships as would be the case in a counselor-client relationship?*
- *What boundaries of appropriateness will the outreach worker be held accountable to in his or her relationships with clients/constituents/consumers?*

Compensation

◇ ◇ **185** ◇ ◇

A pilot project designed to work with chemically dependent women and their children is about to be replicated through all regions of the state following the very positive evaluation of the pilot service sites. The five-year evaluation report as well as everyone associated with the project attribute much of the program's success to an aggressive and innovative approach to in-home services provided by outreach workers indigenous to the community areas from which clients were drawn. The outreach workers throughout this project were known for the skill and tenaciousness with which they initiated and sustained client involvement in the treatment process. In spite of the praise of the outreach workers, a close scrutiny of the project budget reveals that the outreach workers were often paid as little as one third the salary of "professional" staff working on the project.

Discussion Question

Comment on any ethical issues inherent within such differences in compensation.

There is a concern that indigenous outreach workers within health and human service agencies—among whom women and people of color are highly represented—are exploited for their talents through unjust compensation. There are many projects whose success is attributed to the skills and passionate involvement of outreach workers. Yet their salaries are markedly less than other staff, there exists no supports for their continued education, and there are no structured career ladders or paths to provide for their future. In short, their importance is matched by their expendability. Under such circumstances, it is little wonder that an outreach worker cast aside in a funding cut or at the end of a grant has the sense of having being used. The ethical principle of justice calls for the distribution of rewards by merit. In the case of outreach workers, it may be time that the factors used to determine merit are reassessed. It is of particular concern that people whose life circumstances have precluded access to education and whose successful job performance involves knowledge and skills not achieved through traditional education, should have their value judged so arbitrarily. The principle of fairness calls for the careful review of systems of compensation and the extent to which such systems may have been unduly influenced by classism, sexism, and racism.

Training

Use of Agency Resources for Personal Gain

◇ ◇ **186** ◇ ◇

Jerome delivers substance abuse workshops and seminars throughout the United States as an employee of a training institute.

Discussion Questions

Comment on the following practices.

A. Jerome accumulates a considerable number of free trips through frequent flyer programs sponsored by the airlines. Jerome use

these free trips for his own personal vacations without formal
permission or negotiation with his employer.

B.   Due to his membership of certain frequent flyer programs,
Jerome always tries to schedule flights with United or TWA.
This results in choosing more expensive flights to some cities so
that he can get the benefit of frequent flyer miles. As a result
of this practice, organizations contracting for training sometimes
pay higher travel fees than would have been necessary.

C.   When Jerome drives to a training event in his home state, he is
paid $30 per day for meals if he leaves before 6:00 a.m. and
returns after 6:00 p.m. Jerome often leaves earlier than necessary
just to receive the benefit of the meal reimbursements.

*These are examples of how an employee can manipulate the work environment for
his or her own financial advantage. Benefits such as free trips obtained through
the expenditure of agency resources should accrue to the agency unless negotiated
as a specific perk for those who travel excessively. The manipulation of work
structures for financial gain unduly depletes agency resources, breaches the values
of honesty, loyalty and stewardship in the employee-employer relationship, and
can, as in the case of the above situation, breach the same values in the
relationship between an agency and its external clients.*

Self-disclosure

◇ ◇ **189** ◇ ◇

Betty, a recovering alcoholic who works for a substance abuse prevention
training institute, spends the majority of her time speaking to professional
audiences about various dimensions related to the assessment and
treatment of addiction.

Discussion Questions

Under what conditions would it be appropriate or inappropriate for
Betty to self-disclose her status as a recovering person?

What factors should be considered in this decision?

If Betty is an active member of a twelve step program such as Alcoholics Anonymous, how can she speak to professional groups about AA without inadvertently violating AA's tradition of anonymity?

What standards should guide the professional trainer (recovering and non-recovering) to avoid the appearance that they represent or speak for a Twelve Step Program?

There are direct parallels between the issue of counselor self-disclosure discussed in Chapter Six and the issue of trainer self-disclosure. The ethical question posed to a trainer working under a contractual obligation of service is simply this: whose needs are being met through the use of this self-disclosure—mine or those of the trainees? It is a question of whether the self-disclosure constitutes a technique of teaching or public confession—a learning tool for the trainee or a tool of catharsis for the trainer. The acknowledgement of a trainer's recovery status must be done carefully, if at all. Both recovering and non-recovering trainers need to explicitly define who they speak and not speak for. It is advisable for all persons in training roles to acknowledge that they speak about—NOT on behalf of—twelve step recovery programs and that they will be speaking from knowledge based on professional, rather than personal perspectives, on these programs. Acknowledging affiliation with a particular recovery program may or may not—depending on the training context—be a breach of compliance with the anonymity tradition governing the group life of most twelve step programs. Self-disclosure of self-help affiliation in a closed training context—outside the purview of press or other public media—might not be a violation of anonymity, but might still represent a violation of the trainer's pledge of service to the needs of the trainees. If the self-disclosure serves the trainer's needs rather than, and at the expense of, the trainees' needs, then it breaches the promise of service made to the trainees by the trainer. To the extent that self-disclosure is viewed by trainees as an exercise in narcissistic exhibitionism, the service relationship has been harmed by the act of self-disclosure, diminishing the trainer's capacity to serve.

Relationship Boundaries

◇ ◇ **188** ◇ ◇

Mark is a part-time counselor in a substance abuse treatment program who spends the remainder of his professional time working contractually as a substance abuse trainer. Most of his training activities involve 3-5 day residential training experiences that bring together trainees from throughout his state. Mark has developed over the past two years a fairly consistent pattern of sexual involvement with trainees during these training retreats.

Discussion Questions

Do the ethical boundaries that preclude counselor-client sexual involvement extend to the trainer-trainee relationship?

If a fundamental difference in the therapist-client and trainer-trainee relationship is the duration of power inequity and the duration of vulnerability, could a trainer get involved with a trainee *after* a training event without being suspected of a breach in ethical conduct?

Would a trainer who was attracted to a trainee be ethically prohibited from pursuing that relationship after the training event was over? Where the prohibition against a therapist-client sexual relationship might last forever, might any prohibition against a trainer-trainee sexual relationship be relatively time-limited?

Discuss ethical issues and standards related to this situation.

While the inequity of power and the vulnerabilities within the trainer-trainee relationship differ in intensity and duration from those found in the therapist-client relationship, there is still the potential for unethical and exploitive conduct within the milieu of training. This potential may differ according to training format and trainee group composition. One could posit that a trainer who presents for one hour to 300 people has less power to exploit this medium than a trainer involved in a five-day, highly experiential training process with 20 participants. The latter could, at least, for the time-span of the training, closely approximate the inequity of power and emotional vulnerability of the therapist-client relationship. Mark's behavior in the above vignette would raise ethical issues to the extent that the following conditions existed:

- *trainees were subjected to unwanted sexual advances by the trainer violating the trainee's physical and psychological safety*

- *the training content and process resulted in a significant imbalance of power in the trainer-trainee relationship that diminished the free choice and powers of assertion of the trainee*
- *the trainer manipulated the emotional vulnerability of the trainee for the sexual gratification of the trainer, e.g., sexually approaching the trainee at a time his or her defenses were weakened and/or*
- *the trainer utilized deceit or coercion in soliciting sexual favors, (e.g., framing the sexual relationship as part of the training experience, misrepresenting the nature of the relationship, or threatening removal of the trainee from the training group), if sexual favors were not granted.*

A pattern of predatory sexual behavior exhibited by a trainer within the training milieu breaches the fundamental contract of service which dictates that the trainer will structure the training process to meet the learning needs of trainees.

Marketing of Seminars

◇ ◇ **189** ◇ ◇

A brochure marketing a workshop on family counseling clearly outlines learning objectives and notes that the learning methodologies used in the workshop will include lecture and discussion of videotaped vignettes from family counseling sessions. During the workshop, the trainer alters the agenda and learning methodologies without negotiation with the trainees. Workshop participants find themselves suddenly "volunteered" to play key roles in psychodramatic recapitulations of their own families of origin.

Discussion Questions

What ethical issues are involved in this situation?

What guidelines should govern the use of highly experiential training methods?

A marketing brochure for a training event constitutes a promissory agreement between the trainer and his or her audience. Trainees chose to come to the workshop based on the learning objectives and teaching methods set forth in the brochure and reiterated at the beginning of the workshop. For a trainer to arbitrarily and significantly alter this content or the teaching methodologies without negotiation with the training audience is a breach of this promissory agreement. Principles of honesty and fidelity demand congruence between the workshop promoted and the workshop delivered.

Persons interested in ethical guidelines for conducting experiential groups will benefit from the work completed by the American Psychological Association in this area: *Guidelines for Psychologists Conducting Growth Groups,* (1973).

Professional Impairment

◇ ◇ **190** ◇ ◇

You are conducting a workshop with more than 35 participants representing health and human service workers from a variety of agencies in your state. The workshop involves a number of small and large group discussions. By mid-morning it is quite obvious that you have a participant who is highly impaired. The participant is experiencing flight of ideas, rambling incoherently, misinterpreting and personalizing other participant responses as highly threatening, and aggressively challenging comments by other participants and by you. By late morning, he retorts to the group, "well, if you aren't going to listen to my ideas, I'm just not going to share them; it's your loss" and remains silent. At the afternoon break, the participant leaves the workshop and doesn't return. The participant runs a private counseling practice that includes the assessment of DUI offenders.

Discussion Question

What duties and responsibilities do you have as the trainer in such a situation?

There are multiple interests that must be protected in the above vignette. The impaired participant must be managed to minimize his disruptiveness to the learning of the other participants. In short, the contractual agreement for learning must be kept with the participants. The trainer must also tend to the psychological safety of the impaired member who may be vulnerable to scapegoating by the group. Protection of the impaired trainee may involve supportive comments aimed at deactivating the trainee's defensiveness as well as actively diverting or dissipating group hostility targeted at the trainee. A more difficult issue is the potential threat to public safety resulting from the trainee's impairment within his professional practice. Given that this trainee works by himself in private practice, the trainer may be one of the few persons in a position to detect and intervene to address the impairment. If the trainer judges the trainee's impairment to pose a threat to his clients or to the public, the trainer is ethically bound to bring the potential of impairment to the attention of some investigative body. Potential agencies to be contacted would include the state counselor certification agency, the state agency that licenses and monitors DUI evaluation services, or the presiding circuit judge within whose courts the impaired professional's DUI evaluations are received.

◇ ◇ **191** ◇ ◇

You coordinate an addiction counselor training program that involves two years of formal classroom training and supervised field experience. One of your students, Leonard, a recovering alcoholic, who is 18 months into the training program and scheduled to begin his practicum experience next month, comes in today and confesses that he has relapsed.

Discussion Questions

How would you respond to this situation?

What potential ethical issues are involved in Leonard's continued participation in the program?

There are multiple issues involved in this situation. There is the threat to Leonard's health due to the relapse and some implied duties of the training program to support and protect Leonard's health. There is a potential threat to clients posed by an impaired intern or worker within the field. Depending on Leonard's drinking-related behaviors, there may also be potential threats to public safety, e.g., drinking and driving. There is also a threat to the reputation of the program if it is seen to have actively drinking alcoholics enrolled in training. An approach that would address all of the varied interests might involve the following steps:

1)   *Provide strong encouragement and support for Leonard to get into treatment or otherwise reactivate his recovery program,*

2)   *Assess any immediate threats to himself or others posed by Leonard's return to drinking, e.g., the intention to drive home from the office of the training program while intoxicated,*

3)   *Provide Leonard a health-related leave of absence from the training program, and*

4)   *Reassess the appropriateness of Leonard's career choice of addiction counseling after, and only when, he has re-established a stable program of sobriety.*

Consultation

Confidentiality

◇ ◇ **192** ◇ ◇

Sonya has served as an organizational consultant to a large number of substance abuse agencies and private businesses. She is also a prolific writer and is often called upon to make speeches at professional conferences. Sonya has routinely integrated stories drawn from her consultation experiences into her articles and speeches. Although she refers to her consultation clients by name and summarizes her consultation methodologies and their outcomes with particular agencies, she has been very careful not to disclose information she believes would hurt the agency in any manner. It has not occurred to Sonya that formal permission should be obtained from her organizational clients prior to such disclosure.

Discussion Questions

What rules of confidentiality should apply to this situation?

Do confidentiality expectations apply even where no discussion of confidentiality has occurred?

There is implied, and often contractually mandated, confidentiality governing the relationship between a consultant and his or her organizational clients. There are two basic ways that Sonya can ethically incorporate her consulting experiences into her articles and speeches. The first is to ask permission of her clients for such inclusion. The request should specify both the range of information to be disclosed and the precise audiences to which disclosure would be targeted. The second option is to delete the name and all information that would identify the organization from any story or anecdote. Where an organization or event is so unique as to defy masking of the organizational identity, then no disclosure can ethically occur without the permission of the organizational client.

Support of Toxic Organizational Conditions

◊ ◊ **193** ◊ ◊

Ricardo has a long and distinguished history as an organizational consultant to substance abuse agencies and other health and human service organizations. His name is always on the preferred consultant list for anyone seeking outside assistance to help with organizational problems. Over the past five years, a large service agency has developed the following pattern of interaction with Ricardo. At a time of internal crisis (three such crises in the five years), the agency contacts Ricardo to come in and provide assistance for a variety of presenting problems, most of which have severely impacted staff morale. For each of the three times, Ricardo utilized a process of problem identification and strategy development that involved all agency staff and resulted in a detailed plan of action. In each case, the agency failed to follow through on the plan; in each case, staff involvement and hope was elevated and then dashed.

Discussion Questions

How should Ricardo respond to the next request to come and work with the agency during a time of crisis?

Are there ethical issues involved in a consultant's complicity in being used to bail an organization out of crisis that has no apparent intention of resolving fundamental problems of leadership, structure or process?

Ricardo must ask himself whether he is being used to avoid change, rather than to facilitate change. There is concern that Ricardo's services are being used to sustain, rather than eliminate, toxic organizational conditions. There is a concurrent concern that the repeated use of Ricardo's services in this manner could damage his professional reputation as an organizational consultant. Organizational consultants who find themselves in such a dilemma may consider a number of the following options:

- *confront the contracting agency with what appears to be a historical breach of good faith in the intention of addressing problems identified within the consultation scope of work,*
- *refuse to do further work with the contracting agency, or*
- *structure any future contracts in definable stages, with each successive stage of work of the consultant being contingent upon clearly defined actions on the part of the contracting agency.*

Research

Sponsorship of Research

◇ ◇ **194** ◇ ◇

A substance abuse treatment program, after some years of pressure to report treatment outcome data to local and state funding sources, assigned a staff member to conduct a follow-up study of clients who had gone through treatment during the past five years. When the study was completed, the program widely circulated the results of the study but did not identify who had sponsored the research or who had conducted it. They merely reported that the program had been evaluated and what the findings were.

Discussion Questions

Does failure to disclose who sponsored a particular study constitute a breach of professional ethics?

If an outside agent had wanted to fund the research but wished their sponsorship to remain secret, what ethical issues would be raised by such agreement of secrecy?

The ethical principle of honesty demands a full disclosure of contextual elements of research so that its scientific integrity can be assessed and assured. In this case the researcher (staff member) may have a vested interest in the outcome of the research such that the conduct or interpretation of the research could be compromised. It is not the conduct of the research by internal staff that poses ethical problems, but maintaining the secrecy of the sponsor (in this case, self-sponsored) and the relationship between the sponsor and the research team (employer-employee). Such issues could be addressed by:

- *fully identifying the researchers and their credentials so others may make reasonable judgements about the qualifications of those conducting the research,*
- *fully disclosing the nature of the sponsor-research team relationship,*
- *providing a detailed presentation of the research methodology so that its integrity and rigor can be evaluated, and*
- *making raw data available to other researchers for independent evaluation.*

Research with Human Subjects

◇ ◇ **195** ◇ ◇

Bernard is a new outpatient therapist at a substance abuse treatment agency. Coming out of a primary mental health background, Bernard has been quite fascinated by various controversies surrounding the most appropriate substance abuse treatment interventions and the paucity of research available to answer such questions. Deciding that he can help answer some of his own questions with some informal research, Bernard decides to randomly assign his next forty clients to one of two very different counseling approaches and then follow the clients to see how the treatment outcomes differ for the two groups. Two months into this process, Bernard happens to mention to you (his supervisor) for the first time this informal research he is conducting.

Discussion Questions

How do you respond?

What ethical issues are raised by such informal research?

Bernard cannot escape the ethical mandates guiding research with human subjects simply by thinking of his research as "informal." To meet the normal protocol for research involving humans, Bernard would have to conduct such activities as:

- *developing a formal research plan which details the research design and an analysis of potential benefits and risks to participants involved in the research,*
- *seeking formal approval through an interdisciplinary research committee that exists or will need to be established within Bernard's agency, and*
- *assuring a process of informed consent for all persons participating in his study.*

(The standard text outlining procedures to assure ethical conduct in research with humans can be found in the National Research Act, Public Law 93-348, "Protection of Human Subjects" Code of Federal Regulations 45 CFR 46.)

Just a few of the ethical issues raised by Bernard's informal research would include the following:

- *The random assignment of clients to the two treatment approaches would violate the agreement that clients will be assigned treatment activities based on an objective assessment of their individual needs.*
- *Withholding information to the clients that they are in fact research subjects is a breach of honesty in the helping relationship.*
- *Failing to provide a process of informed consent through which the client is oriented to risks and benefits of the research and offered an opportunity to accept or refuse participation without coercion violates client autonomy.*

Confidentiality, Security and Disposition of Data

$$\diamond \ \diamond \ \mathbf{196} \ \diamond \ \diamond$$

A follow-up study is being conducted of clients in which interviews are being tape recorded, transcribed and then analyzed. The resulting report will include excerpts from the client interviews to illustrate key findings.

Discussion Question

What procedures would you recommend related to the confidentiality, security, and eventual disposition of the tapes and transcripts?

Research protocol for a study like the above should generally include a detailed description of the following:

- *the informed consent process that will be utilized with all clients participating in the study*
- *a specific client consent process for taping and transcribing of interviews that will include informing the client of the eventual disposition of the tapes, (e.g. "All tapes and transcripts will be erased following the completion of the final research report").*
- *an orientation on confidentiality that will be utilized with all transcriptionists working with client tapes*
- *a plan for controlled access and storage of tapes and transcripts and*
- *a plan for, and person designated in control of, destruction or long-term storage of tapes and transcripts.*

The purpose of such procedures is to assure the confidentiality of research participants and to assure that use of the data does not extend beyond the parameters of use that were agreed upon as conditions for participation.

Scientific Role Versus Clinical Role

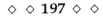

◇ ◇ **197** ◇ ◇

A follow-up study of adolescents and their families following substance abuse treatment was conducted using substance abuse counselors as trained interviewers for the study. You have been hired and oriented as one of the interviewers. Each interview consists of a one-hour structured interview in which data is solicited on post-treatment client and family functioning. In about 75% of the cases, you are able to conduct a straightforward interview and solicit all of the needed information. In the other 25% of the interviews, clients get into painful self-disclosure of the problems they have encountered since they left treatment. Some have intimated thoughts of suicide and others have referenced their need to get back in treatment. Your instincts are to respond to these disclosures as a counselor rather than as a researcher. The time constraints won't allow for a full clinical response to these clients needs and still allow you to collect all of the data you have been hired to collect.

Discussion Questions

How would you resolve the above conflict?

How does the researcher perform his or her scientific data collection function with clients who present problems of great immediacy and intensity that need assistance?

This vignette involves conflicts of loyalty between the researcher's contractual obligations to collect data and his or her human and professionally enhanced obligation to respond to persons in pain or crisis. The PRIMARY responsibility of the researcher in this situation is to collect scientific data and to conduct the interview in a manner that assures the most complete and objective presentation of information from the client. At the same time, the clinical researcher cannot simply ignore persons in imminent crisis. Resolution of these conflicting responsibilities can be enhanced by actions such as the following:

- *clearly define the purpose of the interview with the client and the role of the interviewer focusing on the distinction between information collection and problem resolution*
- *allow an adequate amount of time for the interview, recognizing that data collection involving very personal areas of life functioning is likely to be accompanied by strong emotion (Clients should have adequate time to both report information and emotionally re-center themselves prior to exiting the interview.) and*
- *arrange availability for direct and timely linkage for counseling services for those clients in crisis or who wish to seek additional help.*

Honesty in Reporting Findings

◇　◇　**198**　◇　◇

You are the principal investigator on the evaluation of a highly politicized service initiative within your state. The program was launched two years ago by the Attorney General to fuel his future candidacy for Governor. As a result of this political context, the program you are evaluating has received enormously positive press coverage. The state agency representatives that contracted for the evaluation research on the project have become quite concerned about the findings and tone of the evaluation report. As you complete the tabulation and analysis of the data, you are getting enormous pressure from multiple sources to frame the outcomes in the most positive of terms. There are numerous references to how much future contractual work may be available if this particular report is well-received.

Discussion Question

What ethical issues are raised by the interpretation of data and recommendations that are to be formulated in the above context?

The researcher has enormous control over the selection, presentation and interpretation of data. The primary ethical question in the above vignette is whether scientific integrity will be sacrificed for long-term financial gain. If the investigator capitulates to the political and financial pressure by positively framing interpretations and recommendations that are unsupported by the true findings of the research, a number of ethical breaches will have occurred and will further unfold from this action. These breaches include the following:

- *There will have been a breach in honesty through the misrepresentation of the effect and value of the project.*
- *There will have been a breach in professional fidelity to the principles of scientific research and to the promises inherent within the contract for the project.*
- *There will have been a breach in the principle of professional competence: errors resulting not from lack of knowledge and skill, but from exploitive self-interest.*
- *There will have been a potential breach in the principle of nonmaleficence if, as a result of the distorted findings in the research report, resources continue to be allocated to a project that may have no effect or potentially harmful effects.*
- *There will have been a potential breach in the principle of stewardship if continued and potentially expanded funding of the evaluated project*

will deny resources to other service projects of potentially greater need and effectiveness.

In addition to the above, scrutiny of the research report by the scientific community may lead to a recognition and public exposure of the extent of distortion resulting in damage to the reputation of the researcher and the research community as a whole.

Responsibility for Use of New Knowledge

◇ ◇ **199** ◇ ◇

One of the exciting areas of substance abuse research is the search for biological markers that could identify high risk for addiction prior to exposure to alcohol and other drugs. Futurists among the researchers predict a day in the not too distant future when an economical and reliable mass screening process could screen and identify those grade school children at high-risk for adult alcoholism and other addictive diseases.

Discussion Questions

If the discovery of such biological markers and mass screening devices were available today, what ethical issues might be raised related to their misuse?

Is it the responsibility of the researcher to explore the potential misuse or misapplication of his or her discoveries?

Potential ethical issues raised by such discoveries could include the following:

- *What concerns do you have about the released technology to identify high-risk persons for disease before there are breakthroughs in prevention and early treatment of the disease? How could the parent respond who is told his or her son or daughter is high-risk for adult alcoholism?*
- *Are there potential negative consequences that could be associated with the status of high-risk for addiction? Could the labeling of such risk have iatrogenic effects? Could it alter the developmental trajectory of*

those so identified?   Would labeling alter family and social relationships?

- *Could the identification as high-risk for adult addictive disease be used against someone in harmful ways, e.g., mandatory testing for risk and potential denial of health and life insurance or denial of occupational opportunities?*

The ethical mandate to think through and prepare for the potential implications of one's discoveries exists and is inescapable. The burden of consequence and its moral weight cannot be avoided.   Einstein always said in interviews that he deeply regretted the day he wrote a letter to President Roosevelt informing him of the German experiments to build nuclear weapons and encouraging a similar program of American research—research that when initiated would lead to the development of the hydrogen bomb, the devastation of Hiroshima and Nagasaki and the birth of nuclear proliferation.

Appendix

Resources for Codes of Ethical Standards

Organizational Code of Ethics

National Association of Addiction Treatment Providers
25201 Paselo-De-Alicia
Suite 100
Laguna Hills, CA 92653
714-837-3038

Ethical Codes Relevant to the Treatment Setting

National Association of Alcoholism & Drug Abuse Counselors
3717 Columbia Pike
Suite 300
Arlington, VA 22204
703-920-4644

Illinois Alcohol and Other Drug Abuse Professional Certification
Association, Incorporated
1305 Wabash Ave.
Suite L
Springfield, IL 62704
217-698-8110

American Psychiatric Association
1400 K Street NW
Washington, DC 20005
202-682-6000

American Psychological Association
1200 17th Street NW
Washington, DC 20036
202-955-7600

American Society of Addiction Medicine
5225 Wisconsin Avenue NW
Suite 409
Washington, DC 20015
202-244-8948

National Association of Social Workers
7981 Eastern Avenue
Silver Springs, MD 20910
301-565-0333

American Association for Marriage and Family Therapy
1100 17th Street NW
10th Floor
Washington, DC 20036
202-452-0109

American Association for Counseling and Development
5999 Stevenson Avenue
Alexandria, VA 22304
703-823-9800

National Board for Certified Counselors
5999 Stevenson Avenue
Suite 402
Alexandria, VA 22304
703-461-NBCC

Commission on Rehabilitation Counselor Certification
1835 Rohlwing Road
Suite E
Rolling Meadows, IL 60008
708-394-2104

American Nurses Association
600 Maryland Avenue SW
Suite 100 West
Washington, DC 20024-2571
202-554-4444

Ethical Codes for Employee Assistance Professions

Employee Assistance Program Association
4601 North Fairfax Drive, #1001
Arlington, VA 22203
703-522-6272

Prevention Specialist Codes of Ethics

Institute for Chemical Dependency Professionals of Minnesota, Inc.
596 Osceola Avenue South
St. Paul, MN 55102

Pennsylvania Chemical Abuse Certification Board
264 South Progress Avenue
Harrisburg, PA 17109

Ethical Standards for Cross-Cultural Counseling

See: Ibrahim, F. and Arredondo, P. Ethical Standards for Cross Cultural Counseling: Counselor Preparation, Practice, Assessment and Research *Journal of Counseling and Development*, Vol. 64, January, 1986, pp 349-352.

Ethical Standards for Research

American Evaluation Association (AEA)
9555 Persimmon Tree Road
Potomac, MD 20854
301-299-3989

Ethical Codes Relevant to Other Specialty Roles

American School Counselors Association
c/o American Association for Counseling and Development
5999 Stevenson Avenue
Alexandria, VA 22304
703-823-9800

Association for Volunteer Administration
P.O. Box 4584
Boulder, CO 80306
303-541-0238

American Library Association
50 E. Huron Street
Chicago, IL 60611
312-944-6780

Special Libraries Association
1700 18th Street Nw
Washington, DC 20009
202-234-4700

Bibliography

A.A. Guidelines for A.A. Members Employed in the Alcoholism Field New York, New York: General Service Office of Alcoholics Anonymous, N.D.

Advertising Code for Alcoholism Treatment Programs (1982). In *Principles and Practice.* Irvine, California: National Association of Addiction Treatment Programs, Inc.

Barry, V. 1983). *Moral Issues in Business.* Belmont, California: Wadsworth Publishing Company.

Bayles, M. (1989). *Professional Ethics,* Belmont, California: Wadsworth Publishing Company.

Biggs, D. and Blocker, D. (1987). *Foundations of Ethical Counseling,* New York: Springer Publishing Company.

Bissell, L. and Royce, J. (1987). *Ethics for Addiction Professionals,* Center City, Minnesota: Hazelden Foundation.

Bok, S. (1978). *Lying: Moral Choice in Public and Private Life,* New York: Pantheon Books.

Bowie. N. (1982). *Business Ethics* Englewood-Cliffs, N.J.: Prentice-Hall.

Casebook on Ethical Standards of Psychologists. (1967). Washington, D.C.: American Psychological Association.

Christopher, J. (1988). *How to Stay Sober: Recovery Without Religion,* Buffalo, New York: Prometheus Press.

Clinebell, H. (1956). *Understanding and Counseling the Alcoholic through Religion and Psychology,* New York: Abingdon Press.

Code of Ethics. (1979). Arlington, Virginia: National Association of Alcoholism and Drug Abuse Counselors.

Code of Ethics. (1985). Silver Springs, Maryland: National Association of Social Workers.

Conroe, R.M. and Schank, J.A. (1989). Sexual Intimacy in Clinical Supervision: Unmasking the Silence, in Schoener, G. et. al.

Ethical Principles of Psychologists. (1981). Washington, DC: American Psychological Association.

Grisso, T. and Vierling, L. (1978). Minors Consent to Treatment: A Developmental Perspective, *Professional Psychology, 9*, (1), 117.

Group for the Advancement of Psychiatry. (1990). *A Casebook in Psychiatric Ethics.* New York: Brunner /Mazel Publishers.

Guidelines for Psychologists Conducting Growth Groups. (1973). Washington D.C.: American Psychological Association.

Haas, L. and Malouf, J. (1989). *Keep Up the Good Work: A Practitioner's Guide To Mental Health Ethics.* Sarasota, Florida: Professional Resource Exchange, Inc.

Kasl, C. (1992). *Many Roads, One Journey.* New York: Harper Collins.

Kirkpatrick, J. (1986). *Goodbye Hangovers, Hello Life.* New York: Ballantine Books.

Kirkpatrick, J. (1986). *Turnabout.* New York: Bantam Books.

Levine, M. (1972). *Psychiatry and Ethics.* New York: George Braziller.

London, P. (1986). *The Modes and Morals of Psychotherapy.* Washington: Hemisphere Publishing Corporation.

Manning, G. and Curtis, K. (1988). *Ethics at Work: Fire in a Dark World.* Cincinnati, Ohio: South-Western Publishing Company.

Masson, Jeffrey Moussaieff. (1990). *Final Analysis: The Unmaking of a Psychoanalyst.* Reading, Massachusetts: Addison-Wesley Publishing Company, Inc.

Milgrom, Jeanette Hostee. (1992). *Boundaries in Professional Relationships: A training manual.* Minneapolis, Minnesota: Walk-In Counseling Center.

Peterson, Marilyn R. (1992). *At Personal Risk.* New York: W.W. Norton & Company.

Schoener, G. (1989). Sexual Involvement of Therapists with Clients After Therapy Ends: Some Observations, in Schoener et. al.

Schoener, G. , Milgrom, J., Gonstorek, J, Luepker, E. and Conroe, R. (1989). *Psychotherapists' Sexual Involvement With Clients.* Minneapolis, Minnesota: Walk-In Counseling Center.

Stein, R. (1990). *Ethical Issues in Counseling.* Buffalo, New York: Prometheus Books.

Szasz, T. (November, 1971). The Ethics of Addiction, *The American Journal of Psychiatry,* 128:5, pp33-37.

Temerlin, M. and Temerlin, J. (1982). Psychotherapy Cults: An Iatrogenic Perversion *Psychotherapy: Theory Research and Practice,* Volume 19: 2, Summer 1982, pp131-141.

Thibodeaux, M. and Powell, J. (1985). Exploitation: Ethical Problems of Organizational Power, *SAM Advanced Management Journal.* Spring, 1985, pp42-44.

Thompson, A. (1990). *Guide to Ethical Practice in Psychotherapy.* New York: John Wiley & Sons, Inc.

Trimpey, J. (1989). *The Small Book.* New York: Delacorte Press.

VandeCreek, L. and Knapp, S. (1989). *Tarasoff and Beyond: Legal and Clinical Considerations in the Treatment of Life-Endangering Patients.* Sarasota, Florida: Professional Resource Exchange, Inc.

Wagner, C. (1981). Confidentiality and the School Counselor, *Personnel and Guidance Journal,* 59(5).

White, W. (1986). *Incest in the Organizational Family.* Bloomington, Illinois: Lighthouse Training Institute.

White, W. (1990). *The Culture of Addiction, The Culture of Recovery.* Bloomington, Illinois: Lighthouse Training Institute.

White, W. (1990). The Ethics of Competition, Keynote Address, 21st Annual Chemical Dependency Fall Conference, October 25, 1990. Bloomington, Minnesota.

White, W. (1992). A Systems Perspective on Sexual Harassment and Sexual Exploitation, *Proceedings: Sex and Power Issues in the Workplace*, March 20-21, 1992. Bellevue, Washington.

Working as, for, or with Professionals. New York, New York: Al-Anon Family Groups.

Wrich, J. (1990). Ethics and EAP Practice, *EAP Digest*, July/August, 1990, pp. 36-40, 60-61.

Index